Through a
Nuclear Lens

RECENT TITLES

A complete listing of books in this series can be found online at www.sunypress.edu

Through a Nuclear Lens

France, Japan, and Cinema from Hiroshima to Fukushima

Hannah Holtzman

Cover: *Hiroshima mon amour* plays on a laptop with Saint-Laurent-des-Eaux Nuclear Power Plant in the background in *Le coeur du conflit / Kokoro no katto / The Heart of the Conflict* (2017, dir. Judith Cahen and Masayasu Eguchi). © 2017 Judith Cahen and Masayasu Eguchi

Published by State University of New York Press, Albany

For information, contact State University of New York Press, Albany, NY
www.sunypress.edu

Library of Congress Cataloging-in-Publication Data

Name: Holtzman, Hannah, author.
Title: Through a nuclear lens : France, Japan, and cinema from Hiroshima to
    Fukushima / Hannah Holtzman.
Description: Albany : State University of New York Press, [2024] | Series:
    SUNY series, Horizons of Cinema | Includes bibliographical references
    and index.
Identifiers: ISBN 9781438497846 (hardcover : alk. paper) | ISBN
    9781438497853 (ebook) | ISBN 9781438497839 (pbk. : alk. paper)
Further information is available at the Library of Congress.

10 9 8 7 6 5 4 3 2 1

For C.K.

Contents

Illustrations

Acknowledgments

This book is the product of many conversations, encounters, and sources of support. From the start, Alison Murray Levine has been a wise and grounded guide. I am immensely grateful for her continued support, thoughtful questions, and good humor. Aynne Kokas, an extraordinary mentor, has encouraged thinking across disciplines and beyond traditional frameworks. Ari Blatt and Janet Horne offered keen insight and helpful suggestions from the early stages of the project. Élise Domenach generously supported my work in France, and her own work helped me with much of the thinking here. Eric Smoodin's kindness and mentorship have been integral to the development of this book. My deeply valued friends and writing partners Lise Leet and Annie de Saussure read several drafts and provided thoughtful feedback.

Thank you to writers and filmmakers who make work that matters. I am especially grateful to Michaël Ferrier, Judith Cahen, Masayasu Eguchi, Keiko Courdy, Philippe Rouy, and Jun Yang for their inspiring work and correspondence.

Many people helped me navigate archives and institutions for this project. In France, Florence Dauman provided invaluable access to the Argos Films archive. Armelle Bourdoulous and Bruno Thévenon at the Institut Lumière's Bibliothèque Raymond Chirat offered helpful research assistance, as did staff in the Espace chercheurs and the Iconothèque at the Bibliothèque du Film in the Cinémathèque française, especially Bilel Bougamra, Karine Mauduit, and Régis Robert. At the Centre national du cinéma et de l'image animée, Laurent Bismuth and Daniel Brémaud provided guidance and access to material. Christine Watanabe at KAMI Productions, Anne Pernod at Comme des Cinémas, Véronique Fournier at Ardèche Images, and Franceline Fanton with Rhône-Alpes sans nucléaire kindly shared their time. Many thanks to numerous other staff members for their assistance at the Bibliothèque nationale de France, the Institut national de l'audiovisuel, the Bibliothèque Kandinsky at the Centre Pompidou, and the Maison de la culture du Japon à Paris. In Japan, material at the National Film Archive of Japan was indispensable for this project. I am grateful for conversation with Kawai Tomoyo at the legendary little bar in Shinjuku. In the United States, I thank the many librarians at the University of Virginia and the University of San Diego who facilitated access to materials far and wide. The Virginia Museum of Fine Arts and the Huntington Library are some of the loveliest places to work, and staff in both places provided ready assistance.

At the University of Virginia, the Department of French provided the structure, support, and freedom to develop an interdisciplinary project. Thanks in particular to Majida Bargach, Karen James, Cheryl Kreuger, John Lyons, Claire Lyu, Mary McKinley, Amy Ogden, Philippe Roger, and Jennifer Tsien for insightful feedback. My extended cohort Holly Runde, Tanya Déry-Obin, Bonnie Gill, Anna Keefe, Casey Shannon Morin, Liz Groff, Sage Morghan, Jessie Labadie, Antoine Guibal, Peter Chekin, and Whitney Bevill provided camaraderie and laughter over many a *pause café* and happy hour. Beyond the Department of French, Ann Beattie, Deborah Eisenberg, Jeb Livingood, and Chris Tilghman helped me develop as a writer and thinker. Rita Felski, Catarina Krizancic, Michael Levenson, Kath Weston, and Michiko Wilson pushed me to think across disciplines and frameworks. Emily Sandberg, Reed Johnson, Helen McLaughlin, Memory Peebles Risinger, Greg Seib, and Megan Fishmann saw seeds of this project in fiction and have been good readers and friends.

At the University of San Diego, Noelle Norton, Brian Clack, and Ron Kaufmann provided space, resources, and freedom to work across disciplines. Lindy Villa offered exceptional administrative and moral support. Roger Pace and Susie Babka have been kind and encouraging mentors. Several colleagues offered feedback and support during the research and writing process, especially Kristin Moran, Atreyee Phukan, Hiroko Takagi, Orly Lobel, Maritza Johnson, Eliza Smith, Marilynn Johnson, Tyler Hower, Angel Hinzo, and Sang-Keun Yoo. I am grateful to the bright undergraduate students in my Nuclear Cinema course for the curiosity and fresh perspectives they brought to the material. At Hampden-Sydney College, Loren Loving Marquez, Julia Palmer, Nelson Sanchez, and Renée Severin supported this work as well.

My colleagues in the Faculty of Liberal Arts at Sophia University offered feedback and support at a particularly important stage of this process. Thanks especially to Angela Yiu, Noriko Murai, Shion Kono, and Yen-yi Chan.

Many other colleagues, mentors, and friends in the field shared thoughts and gave formal and informal feedback at different stages of the project. I would especially like to thank Michael Gott, Leslie Kealhofer-Kemp, Ursula Heise, Daisuke Miyao, Yuko Shibata, Catherine Clark, Brian Jacobson, Livia Monnet, Pamela Genova, Laure Astourian, Isadora Nicholas, C. Wakaba Futamura, Vincent Michelot, Martine Boyer-Weinmann, Philippe Pelletier, Claire Dodane, Chris Walker, Jim Schwoch, Aswin Punthambekar, Brian Hu, Martin Sherwin, Leopoldo Nuti, Benôit Pelopidas, Leyatt Betre, Florian Galleri, Ben Wealer, Noriko Horiguchi, Dan Magilow, Troy Tower, and Melissa Croteau. A warm thanks to many others who enthusiastically attended talks, responded to emails, asked questions, and shared resources.

Early ideas for this book emerged during my time in Japan with the JET Programme. I am grateful to friends and former colleagues in Fukuoka and particularly to Hiroko Shimizu and Kimiko Suzawa for taking me under their wings. Since then, I have been fortunate to participate in exchanges with invitations to present this work at the École normale supérieure de Lyon, Chuo University, and at the UCLA Center for the Study of Women. Panels at the Society for Cinema and Media Studies Annual Conference, the Modern Language Association Convention, the American Comparative Literature Association Annual Meeting, the 20th and 21st Century French and Francophone Studies International Colloquium, the Contemporary French Civilizations Conference, and the World Cinema and Television in French Conference sharpened my thinking. The SCMS French and Francophone and Media and the Environment SIGs as well as the Nuclear Aesthetics Research Network and the (In)human Time Workshop at Vrije University in Amsterdam organized by Kyveli Mavrokordopoulou, Anna Volkmar, and Ruby de Vos have been especially productive forums for exchange.

Institutional support for research and exchange has come from a Chateaubriand Fellowship through the Embassy of France in the United States and the Institut d'Asie Orientale at the École normale supérieure de Lyon. The Carnegie Corporation of New York, the Wilson Center, University of Roma Tre, and the Nuclear Proliferation International History Project supported participation in the Nuclear

History Boot Camp. The University of Virginia supported much of the research, travel, and writing for this project through grants from the Center for Global Inquiry and Innovation and an Arts, Humanities, and Social Sciences Summer Research Award for work in France; a Dean's Dissertation Completion Fellowship; and travel grants from the Department of French. Work in Japan was made possible by a Buckner W. Clay Endowment for the Humanities Award from the Institute of the Humanities and Global Cultures. Additional research support was provided by Hampden-Sydney College, International Opportunity Grants and a Faculty Research Grant from the University of San Diego, and a Tillie Olsen Award from the UCLA Center for the Study of Women.

This book would not have been possible without support from James Peltz, Murray Pomerance, and the Editorial Board at SUNY Press. Additional thanks to those involved in the production and marketing of this book: John Britch, Michael Campochiaro, Julia Cosacchi, Susan Geraghty, Aimee Harrison, Amane Kaneko, Malerie Lovejoy, Céline Parent, and the rest of the team. I am especially grateful to the two readers whose prompt and perceptive feedback helped my revision of the manuscript.

Thank you to friends who have hosted, visited, fed, and nourished me culturally and intellectually while away from home. In particular, I am grateful to Hélène Couble, Katsumi Miyauchi, Ophélie Siméon, Cyril Houdayer, Déborah Dufour Vannier, Véro Beaugnier, Ariel Acosta, Maud Lecacheur, Kosuke Yoshida, Lara Giallo, Olivia Hessing Powell, Megan Lovett, Ashley Davidson, and Caroline Sandifer.

I am fortunate to have continued support from my family, especially my parents Peggy and Randy, who instilled a love of learning from an early age, my sister Rachel, a steady supporter, and my parents-in-law Vicki and Robert, who have graciously provided a home away from home. My grandmothers, both writers, have long been inspirations. My profound thanks to Caleb, who keeps me grounded and brings me joy at home and on the road.

Permissions

An earlier version of chapter 2 was originally published in *Contemporary French Civilization*, volume 43, issue 1 (2018) in an article entitled "A

Fifty-Two-Year Love Affair: Rewatching *Hiroshima mon amour* after Fukushima." Liverpool University Press has granted permission to reprint portions of the article here.

Judith Cahen and Masayasu Eguchi generously granted permission for the use of the cover image, which is analyzed in chapter six.

Names and Translations

Japanese names are given in the Japanese order of family name first followed by given name, except in cases where a Japanese artist or scholar often uses the Western convention of given name followed by family name. For the romanization of Japanese words in the text, macrons indicate long vowels but are not provided for words commonly used in English (e.g., Tokyo rather than Tōkyō).

Translations of text are the author's own unless otherwise indicated.

Introduction

Fission split the atom: the rupture of historical space-time was inseparable from the rupture of the components of matter itself.

—Gabrielle Hecht, "L'Empire nucléaire: les silences des 'Trente Glorieuses'"

Fine art and popular media alike can, at their best, be far more than symptoms of their age. They can voice its contradictions in ways few more self-conscious activities do, because both want to appeal directly to the senses, the emotions and the tastes of the hour, because both will sacrifice linear reason for rhetoric or affect, and because both have the option of abandoning the given world in favor of the image of something other than what, otherwise, we might feel we had no choice but to inhabit.

—Sean Cubitt, *Eco Media*[1]

෴

IN *TOKYO FIANCÉE*, THE 2015 filmic adaptation of Amélie Nothomb's novel *Ni d'Ève ni d'Adam* (2007), the real events of the March 2011 earthquake, tsunami, and nuclear disaster in Japan serve as a deus ex machina, bringing the narrative arc of the film to a swift if not entirely unexpected conclusion.[2] Director Stefan Liberski had been shooting in Japan during the triple disaster, which delayed filming for two years. Affected by these events, Liberski asked Nothomb's permission to integrate them into his film.[3] *Tokyo fiancée* is thus a film interrupted by the real-life triple disaster in Japan, an interruption that significantly diverges from the narrative of Nothomb's

1

novel: a woman who chose to leave Japan for personal reasons in the novel becomes in the film a woman compelled to leave because of an uncertain and ongoing nuclear disaster. The real-life nuclear disaster in a sense finished the adaptation that Liberski had begun and crossed an already uncertain boundary between fiction and what Sean Cubitt calls the "given world" we inhabit, or between diegetic and sociopolitical worlds.

Post-Fukushima filmic representations of Japan may be no less able to ignore the events of 3.11 than post-9/11 representations of New York were able to ignore those of September 11. As Gabrielle Hecht argues, the splitting of the atom had consequences well beyond the realms of technoscience and national defense; nuclear fission changed not only the rules of war and the course of history but also the cultural climate and everyday life within it. Since the first nuclear explosions—the Trinity test on July 16, 1945, and the atomic bombings of Hiroshima and Nagasaki a few weeks later on August 6 and 9—and the subsequent spate of cinematic nuclear narratives spanning genres from science fiction and monster movies to melodrama and noir, film has been a prime medium for the visualization of cultural and affective changes ignited by nuclear fission.[4] Serving as more than mere "symptoms of their age," as the epigraph from Cubitt proposes, these films also "voice its contradictions," "appeal directly to the senses, the emotions and the tastes of the hour," and allow for the imagination of other possible worlds.

While Hollywood has long dominated the production of nuclear movies and considerable scholarship has been devoted to American nuclear cinema, nuclear weapon states such as France and the United Kingdom and nuclear victims such as Japan have also produced a significant number of nuclear-themed films since the 1950s.[5] This book analyzes several French, Japanese, and Franco-Japanese films that engage with nuclear issues in a rather different way than Hollywood has; shifting the focus from monsters and mushroom clouds, these films explore the everyday effects of nuclear disaster on our lived experience of space and time. In this study, I articulate a different kind of nuclear cinema, a cinema of the nuclear mundane that emphasizes the specter or ongoing effects of atomic destruction and its reconfiguration of our experience of space and time.[6]

Nuclear films made outside of Hollywood share relative budgetary limitations but are often made with greater narrative and aesthetic freedom.[7] Nuclear films from France and Japan in particular stand out for a few reasons, not least of which are the strength of French and Japanese national cinemas and nuclear power industries. With the fourth largest nuclear weapon arsenal, France is currently the world's most nuclearized country in terms of energy, and before the nuclear disaster at Fukushima Daiichi in 2011, Japan was second. The Franco-Japanese nuclear lens in this study thus serves as a critical framework for cultural anxiety around nuclear power outside of the Cold War US-USSR dyad.

Despite a relatively horizontal geopolitical relationship between France and Japan, especially when compared with relationships between France and its former colonies in Africa and Asia and Japan's postcolonial relationships within East and Southeast Asia, Franco-Japanese exchange itself is neither symmetric nor perfectly balanced. Scholarship in the West has tended to focus on the French side of the exchange, as suggested by the term *Japonisme*, which is used to describe the appreciation for and inspiration provided by Japanese arts in the West during the second half of the nineteenth century. The Society for the Study of Japonisme, which launched in 1980 in Japan, and the more recent emergence of the international and multi-disciplinary *Journal of Japonisme* in 2016 attest to a resurgence of scholarly interest in the aesthetic tradition of Japonisme and in the entanglements of Japanese and Western cultures with increasing attention to its historical blind spots such as contributions of women and the Japanese side of exchange.[8]

The historical context of Franco-Japanese cultural exchange is central to this story about Franco-Japanese cinema. This book argues that Franco-Japanese exchanges and collaborations in cinema continue a longer tradition of mutual cultural fascination, from the nineteenth-century tradition of Japonisme and even earlier, while shifting from primarily aesthetic preoccupations to nuclear concerns and their broader environmental entanglements. As one of the first feature-length Franco-Japanese cinematic coproductions and as a provocative new kind of nuclear film, *Hiroshima mon amour* is the heart of this book and a through line serving as a key reference for several of the other films under study. This book shows how *Hiroshima mon amour* launched a transnational film cycle about atomic aftermath and reflecting the politics of the nuclear era.

The interdisciplinary approach in this book drawing on film studies and the environmental humanities is also informed by my background in French studies. Accordingly, I focus first on images of Japan in French cinema. And yet, to move beyond a one-sided Orientalist study, I pay attention not only to how nuclear concerns have shaped French visions of Japan but also to how Japanese film-makers have worked with and responded to these French visions in film and how French and Japanese creators have collaborated on such work. One of the implicit arguments I make is for the reciprocity of Franco-Japanese cultural exchange around nuclear concerns. For Japanese filmmakers, spectators, and readers, the distant views found in French films (and from an American scholar) may lack the nuance and authenticity of views of Japan from within but offer indirect and broader angles of approach to the history and global memory of nuclear catastrophe in Japan.

The Nuclear Era, from Hiroshima to Fukushima

The temporal boundaries of this study span the atomic bombings of Hiroshima and Nagasaki to the nuclear disaster at Fukushima Daii-chi in 2011 and its ongoing aftermath. In many ways, the disruption of *Fukushima*—which has come to stand for the triple disaster of earthquake, tsunami, and nuclear disaster that began in the Tōhoku region of Japan on March 11, 2011—recalls that of *Hiroshima*, a name that is often understood outside of Japan as a metonym for the US atomic bomb attack on Hiroshima (and in many cases Nagasaki). The aftermaths of both events show certain similarities, most notably the discrimination faced by survivors and the fight for recognition by officials and institutions prone to opacity if not censorship.[9] And yet, while the place name Fukushima "is accompanied by the sinister privilege that makes it rhyme with Hiroshima,"[10] Jean-Luc Nancy warns against conflating the two events, distinguishing the enemy bombing of Hiroshima from the techno-political and natural disasters behind the Fukushima Daiichi meltdowns. Still, he argues "this rhyme gathers together—reluctantly and against all poetry—the ferment of something shared. It is a question—and since March 11, 2011, we have not stopped chewing on this bitter pill—of nuclear energy itself."[11]

Reducing a disaster to a proper name narrows its geospatial reach and ignores the human agency that created it. The names *Hiroshima* and *Fukushima* used in the title of this book are thus not in reference to the places themselves but rather to French visions—and, more broadly, Western imaginaries—of these places. Barbara Geilhorn and Kristina Iwata-Weickgenannt point out the problematic use of these same terms in Japan: "In order to differentiate between the geographical place and the event, the nuclear catastrophe soon became frequently referred to as 'Fukushima' written in *katakana* instead of *kanji* (similar differentiations are used for the atomic bombings at Hiroshima and Nagasaki, and the Minamata disease.)"[12] Kanji, derived from Chinese characters, are used for most Japanese words, while katakana is the simplified syllabary used for foreign borrowings, suggesting a cultural distancing from mediations of disaster in these places.

Michaël Ferrier, a French writer who lives in Japan and has written extensively about the 2011 triple disaster, acknowledges the imprecision and exoticism inherent in the use of the term *Fukushima* in reference to what is more commonly called *3.11* in Japan, while admitting that in the West, the terminological damage is to a certain extent already done. As such, he argues, the choice to use *Fukushima* should be an informed one that resists the inclination to allow the foreignness of the name to hold the ongoing disaster at a distance.[13] For director Suwa Nobuhiro, who was born in Hiroshima after the war, the culturally distant view of the city in *Hiroshima mon amour* provided an entry point into the subject, and he used this French vision of Japan to inspire his own film *H Story*, ostensibly a remake of *Hiroshima mon amour*.

More broadly, *from Hiroshima to Fukushima* evokes the *nuclear era*, which is commonly understood to have begun with an explosion: the Trinity test or the atomic bombing of Hiroshima. Tracing the wider boundaries of the nuclear era would involve a return to Wilhelm Conrad Röntgen's discovery of the X-ray in 1895 and Henri Becquerel's discovery of radioactivity in 1896. However, it was not until nearly a century later in 1984 that the nuclear era became the subject of critical cultural reflection when philosophers and scholars gathered for a colloquium at Cornell University to create a field of study called Nuclear Criticism. The chief aims of Nuclear Criticism were to read "critical and canonical texts for the purpose of uncovering the unknown shapes of our unconscious nuclear fears" and "to show how the terms of the current nuclear discussion are shaped by literary or critical assumptions whose implications are often, perhaps systematically ignored."[14] Nuclear Criticism was to be applied not only to apocalyptic writing but also to discourses across a variety of fields, from psychology of the arms race to nuclear ideologies and interests promoted in journalistic and artistic media.

Jacques Derrida, the only French philosopher at the colloquium, contributed a piece that was published a few months later as "No Apocalypse, Not Now (Full Speed Ahead, Seven Missiles, Seven Missives)" in an issue of *Diacritics* entitled Nuclear Criticism. Derrida opens with an argument for the importance of Nuclear Criticism for the humanities, "given that the stakes of the nuclear question are those of humanity, of the humanities," and calls for a critical slowdown in response to the acceleration of the nuclear age.[15] For Derrida, nuclear war is "a speculation, an invention in the sense of a fable or an invention to be invented in order to make place for it or to prevent it from taking place."[16] If nuclear apocalypse is only a textual event, then for Derrida the textual anticipation of imagined nuclear war triggers the "reality" of the nuclear era, or the stockpiling and capitalization of nuclear weapons.[17]

For this study of nuclear cinema, I draw on Derrida's conception of nuclear time in "No Apocalypse, Not Now." In place of "era," Derrida uses the Greek term *épochè*, drawing on the etymology of "epoch," a stoppage or fixed point of time, to underscore the sense of suspension in time in the nuclear age.[18] I develop this notion of suspension in time in reflecting on the mundane nuclear present, which seems to be at once infinite, impossible, and inescapable. While Derrida's *épochè* serves as a model for the cinematic nuclear present developed in this study, I also join scholars across the humanities in contesting Derrida's idea that nuclear war is merely a textual event. Jessica Hurley argues from an ecocritical and materialist perspective that nuclear infrastructures and fallout from testing are real events that resemble "existing forms of historical and structural violence" in their disproportionate effects on subaltern subjects.[19] Drew Milne and John Kinsella draw attention to Derrida's exclusive focus on nuclear war to the exclusion of nonmilitary uses of nuclear materials. "The risk of idealizing, romancing or reifying some aspect of 'the nuclear' as a paradigm, tentacular object or ideology . . . suggests the need to see the nuclear as a many-headed hydra, a nuclear leviathan or behemoth, perhaps even a root system whose extended mycelium finds its teleological explosion of spores in the mushroom cloud."[20] These scholars build on the work of others who have proposed new modes of nuclear criticism that focus on materialities, subjectivities, decolonizing pedagogies, and on the nuclear uncanny and the nuclear mundane in place of the nuclear sublime.[21]

Risk Criticism, an approach that came out of Nuclear Criticism and ecocriticism, follows Ulrich Beck's contention that risk is virtual and imperceptible until it is represented.[22] For Molly Wallace, the risk approach is necessary as it extends criticism to science and scientists, who have created problems they cannot undo and whose consequences they cannot predict. More broadly in the environmental humanities, Rob Nixon's call for attention to slow violence in the unimagined or forgotten communities of disaster sheds light on the particular consequences of radioactive contamination on places beyond the megalopolis. I draw on these frameworks in turning attention to risk in places like the Tōhoku region in Japan or rural reactor sites in France and the slow violence committed against these areas and their residents by gradual destruction that takes various forms as it is dispersed across space and time.[23]

The films in the following chapters show an interest in the slow material and cultural violence of nuclear disaster and its impact on everyday life, which is often overshadowed by the nuclear spectacle. At the same time, the concept of slow violence is increasingly under pressure today given the fast-moving nature of climate-related crises such as rising temperatures, carbon dioxide accumulation, wildfires, floods, and extinction events. This tension between the slow violence of nuclear fallout and waste and the much faster violence of climate change has led some—and particularly those with connections to the nuclear industry—to call for nuclear power as an expedient if imperfect fix. The risks of disaster and terrorism and the problems of pollution and waste are at best afterthoughts explained away with solutions that include new technologies that have yet to be developed or proven to work at scale.

While the nuclear era supposedly concluded in 1991 with the breakup of the Soviet Union and the end of the Cold War, it is the hope for a nuclear-free world that remains a textual fantasy. The past decade has seen a resurgence of aggressive nuclear posturing and a new war initiated by the world's largest nuclear power. Despite efforts such as the Treaty on the Prohibition of Nuclear Weapons (TPNW) entered into force on January 22, 2021, proliferation continues. The

United States and Russia continue to modernize their arsenals. China is on track to double its stockpile by 2030, and North Korea's has roughly doubled in the last few years.[24] The New START Treaty, the final remaining nonproliferation agreement between the United States and Russia, was extended through February 4, 2026.

Less spectacularly, the hazards of uranium mining have become increasingly recognized as an environmental justice concern. The global nuclear energy industry also faces real challenges from cheaper and cleaner sources of renewable energy. The nuclear anxiety that was pervasive in the Cold War era has shifted to widespread concern for climate change. Continued investment in nuclear reactors, which have historically cost much more and taken much longer to build than promised, as well as in the holy grail of nuclear fusion, comes at the expense of developing cheaper, cleaner, and safer renewables in a race against irreversible impacts of climate change.[25] Even if a transition away from nuclear energy were imaginable, the continued possibilities of accidents, terrorism, and war along with the asymptotic nature of radioactive decay point to a nuclear era that will never truly end. Accordingly, the nuclear question weighs not only on the psyches of those in military laboratories and research and testing sites but also on the minds of those who witnessed the blinding flashes and experienced the fallout from nuclear explosions, of those who remember the 1950s campaign to "duck and cover" in a nuclear attack, and of those potentially most vulnerable to attack today in areas of ongoing political instability and war. As Gabriele Schwab writes, "Whether or not we are aware of it, we are constituted as nuclear subjects, endowed with a nuclear unconscious that profoundly shapes our being in the world."[26] Increasingly, this nuclear unconscious has shaped the work of cultural creators around the world who, themselves, contribute to a reshaping of the nuclear world order.

The global dimensions of nuclear power can be seen quite clearly in the 2011 disaster at Fukushima Daiichi. As many towns in the immediate area around the power plant in the Tōhoku region were devastated, projections at the time suggested that a change in the wind direction could have led to dangerous levels of contamination as far south as Tokyo, which would have affected the prefecture's 13.2 million residents.[27] In the days following the accident, high levels of radioactivity were detected even farther south at the US naval base at Yokosuka.[28] Japan waited until after the delayed 2021 Tokyo Olympic

Games to release more than one million tons of radioactive waste-water from the destroyed reactors into the sea, a release that began on August 24, 2023, and will ultimately take decades to complete, but contaminated water had been leaking into the Pacific Ocean for years.[29] In 2015, the Woods Hole Oceanographic Institute reported the arrival of a small level of Fukushima-derived cesium on the North American west coast.[30] As radioactive contamination respects no boundaries, the 2011 nuclear disaster at Fukushima Daiichi is not only Japan's concern but also the world's problem.

The Nuclear Lens, the Chronotope of the Nuclear, and Multisensory Perception

The nuclear lens as a critical concept in this book reveals the historical entanglements of visual and nuclear technologies.[31] If the lens, an organ and technology of perception, magnifies or brings into focus that which may be difficult to perceive, my conception of the nuclear lens magnifies and brings into focus less visible nuclear concerns embedded in everyday life and in the experience of space and time as represented in cinema.[32] Nuclear power occupies the extreme registers of visibility: the hypervisibility of explosions and the invisibility or concealed visibility of mining, technology development, weapons stockpiles, pollution, and waste storage. Spectacular nuclear films embrace the hypervisibility of nuclear explosions and graphic depictions of contamination. These films require no such magnifying lens to better perceive nuclear danger. The films in this study, on the other hand, conceal, blur, or question their nuclear status. They focus on the invisibility of nuclear risks and the anxiety around dangers that cannot be detected by the bodily senses alone. In engaging with this tension between invisibility and hypervisibility, these nuclear films form a subset of a broader category of disaster and apocalypse films. Unlike Eva Horn's "catastrophic imaginary" that develops from a sense of "the looming catastrophe without event," the nuclear lens in this study is trained on the concrete and specific if mostly invisible aftermaths of catastrophic nuclear events.[33] In revealing and magnifying less visible nuclear concerns, the nuclear lens brings to light the destabilization of understandings of space and time and the fragmentation of narrative by nuclear fission. The same narrative fragmentation and spatiotemporal instability seen in postwar nuclear films continue in films responding to the 2011 disaster in an ongoing crisis of representation.

After the spectacle of explosion, a more insidious danger sets in with radioactivity that is invisible, odorless, and silent, seemingly detectable only by a dosimeter with readings that change step by step. Ele Carpenter identifies a shift in recent scholarship in nuclear aesthetics "from the distant sublime atomic spectacle to a lived experience of the uncanny nature of radiation."[34] In *The Nuclear Culture Source Book*, Carpenter includes a 1958 letter to the International Conference for the Detection of Nuclear Explosions from French artist Yves Klein, who satirically proposes to color future explosions his signature Klein Blue for easier visual detection. Color as a means of visual detection is also explored in the "Mount Fuji in Red" vignette in Kurosawa Akira's film *Dreams* (1990). "Mount Fuji in Red" shows the spectacular explosions of six nuclear reactors around the iconic Japanese volcano and its subsequent eruption, releasing radioactive elements that are rendered visible in Technicolor clouds: red for plutonium-239, yellow for strontium-90, and violet for cesium-137. Klein Blue and Technicolor radioactive elements are at once spectacular and pragmatic proposals to make visible atomic explosions, suggesting that the "lived experience of the uncanny nature of radiation" is embedded and awaiting detection in many nuclear cultural productions.

If the nuclear spectacle was made in the USA and inaugurated with documentary footage of the Trinity and Castle Bravo tests, the continued reproduction of terrifying and awe-inspiring mushroom clouds continues today. Most notably, Peter Greenaway's short film *Atomic Bombs on Planet Earth* (2011) shows the mushroom clouds of 2201 atomic bomb explosions to date. In French and Japanese cinemas, on the other hand, film has more often been used to explore the nuclear mundane or what Joseph Masco calls the *nuclear uncanny*, the sense of dislocation and anxiety produced by partial knowledge of risks introduced by the international nuclear complex. This includes the possibility of nuclear annihilation at any moment and the certitude of widespread nuclear contamination at present.[35] Just as Hollywood nuclear movies such as *Dr. Strangelove* (1964) and *WarGames* (1983) reflect a Cold War nuclear imaginary in the United States, Japanese and French nuclear cinemas tend to convey more intimate and on-the-ground knowledge of the horrors caused by nuclear technologies.

The historically marginal status of nuclear cinema in France reflects widespread suppression of criticism of the French nuclear industry. As Spencer Weart writes, "French filmmakers created no visions of radioactive monsters," and "when the French thought of atoms they thought of Marie Curie, a national glory."[36] In a catalog of 212 global nuclear films from 1935–1985, Hélène Puiseux reports a tendency of science fiction and monster movies mostly coming from the United States and Japan, with the exception of the post-apocalyptic French film *Malevil* (1981). Puiseux's list of primarily American and Japanese nuclear films does include thirty-two French films and coproductions.[37] The list is of course incomplete; with digitized catalogs searchable by keyword today, the number of films would be much higher, especially if every short film and television documentary were included. Until recently, however, few big-budget nuclear movies were made in France.[38] French nuclear films tend to be experimental, avant-garde, or documentary in style, and as I show in this study, many reference or engage with Japan and specifically with the atomic bombings of Hiroshima and Nagasaki and the disaster at Fukushima Daiichi.[39]

The Franco-Japanese nuclear lens is thus a critical lens on cultural anxiety outside of the Cold War US-USSR dyad and beyond the traditional opposition of East v. West, an ever-shifting geopolitical model. The relationship between Japan and France, geographically East and West, is complicated by the fact that Japan has always occupied a rather ambiguous place in East-West discourse. While geographically the Far East, Japan is often considered part of the geopolitical West due to its Western-style democracy and capitalist economy. Given the colonial and imperial pasts of both France and Japan, the lack of a long-standing colonial relationship with one another, and the similar challenges both face in dealing with colonial legacies that have been subject to institutionalized forgetting if not denial, France and Japan have a relatively horizontal if not always symmetrical relationship.[40] Accordingly, this relationship might serve as a model for both France and Japan in their postcolonial entanglements for more lateral exchange and solidarity built around shared concerns.

In particular, the Franco-Japanese nuclear lens brings into focus ways in which films represent or engage with nuclear spatiotemporality, and what emerges is a different kind of nuclear film. I use the chronotope of the nuclear to distinguish nuclear films with unstable spatiotemporality and fragmented narratives from more spectacular nuclear movies. I borrow the concept of the chronotope from M. M. Bakhtin, who himself borrowed the term from Albert Einstein, who introduced it in his theory of relativity.[41] Bakhtin uses the chronotope to conceptualize literary narrative types or genres according to their specific, textual spatiotemporalities. In Bakhtin's literary chronotope, time and space are fused and interdependent categories for analysis in a text. The chronotope is then "an optic for reading texts as x-rays of the forces at work in the culture system from which they spring" without privileging only time or space in the analysis.[42] Mary Louise Pratt, who coins the Anthropocenic chronotope, alludes to the emergence of a chronotope of the nuclear in 1945 with "the human mastery of nuclear fission in the 1940s mark[ing] one new time-space configuration."[43]

In my conception of the chronotope of the nuclear, nuclear spaces are vast, dynamic, and unbounded but often falsely delimited by spatial markers such as place names (e.g., *Fukushima*), graphic representations (e.g., concentric circles intended to approximate contamination levels), and national borders, all of which suggest containment of radioactivity. Nuclear time can be understood as ongoing disaster in an inescapable present. This notion of time challenges temporal boundaries such as the one suggested in the designation *3.11*, which would limit the disaster to a single date in history. As Christian Doumet and Michaël Ferrier argue about the meltdowns at Fukushima Daiichi and ensuing nuclear contamination, there is no *after* or *post* in an ongoing catastrophe.[44]

Robert Stam has argued that the Bakhtinian chronotope, traditionally used in literary analyses, "seems in some ways even more appropriate to film than to literature," and suggests that "more important than searching for cinematic equivalents to Bakhtin's literary chronotopes, perhaps is the construction of specifically filmic chronotopes."[45] Michael V. Montgomery uses the chronotope as a way to "reinvigorate older studies of film based on genre,"[46] and Vivian Sobchack, who coins the chronotope of film noir, sees the chronotope as a more specific classification tool than genre, such as the western.[47] For Sobchack, the chronotope is also used to understand the phenomenological relationship between text and context, the boundary between which is not absolute.[48] The chronotope of the nuclear is useful in this sense to articulate the specifically nuclear spatiotem-

porality explored within the film as well as the viewer's experience
of the film in the context of ongoing nuclear disaster in the world.

Given the instability of nuclear space and time, I use the
chronotope of the nuclear in an attempt to envision if not definite
boundaries then indefinite zones for nuclear spatiotemporality. This is
different from Sobchack's rather precise delineation of the chronotope
of 1940s lounge time. However, Bakhtin also uses the chronotope in
less clearly delimited ways. The chronotope of the adventure found in
Greek romance is situated in "adventure-time," which lacks everyday
cyclicity and indications of historical time and occurs in "an *abstract*
expanse of space."[49] Spatiotemporal abstraction and flexibility is essential to the chronotope of the adventure, as Bakhtin explains, "for any
concretization—geographic, economic, sociopolitical, quotidian—would
fetter the freedom and flexibility of the adventures and limit the
absolute power of chance."[50] Following this more open conception
of spatiotemporality in the chronotope, I underscore the fluidity and
flexibility of the chronotope of the nuclear. Nuclear spatial borders
are porous, shifting, and uncertain. As Karen Barad remarks about
nuclear terrain, elements such as wind "trouble any static notion of
landscape."[51]

Nuclear temporality, too, exists on an unimaginably long scale, as
"[r]adioactive decay elongates, disperses, and exponentially frays time's
coherence. Time is unstable, continually leaking away from itself."[52]
The chronotope of the nuclear is thus a way of connecting Timothy
Morton's hyperobjects, which are "things massively distributed in time
and space relative to humans,"[53] to specific types of nuclear narratives.
Not all nuclear movies engage with nuclear spatiotemporality, but
those that do tend to have a few other things in common: a troubled
or oppositional relationship to nuclear spectacle, and formal hybridity
or fragmentation.

The chronotope of the nuclear also brings together reflection on
nuclear weapons and energy through the common disruptions, threats,
risks, and anxieties they provoke. In many fields, civil and military
nuclear technologies are largely kept separate despite their connections
in concepts such as *nuclearity*. For Hecht, this term expands common
understandings of what it means to be *nuclear* beyond nuclear weapon
state status or use of nuclear energy to include places where uranium
or where other materials are mined and where radiation levels are not

always detected or even measured.[54] The chronotope of the nuclear is expansive enough to apply to creative work in a variety of modes and mediums in which the everyday experience of nuclear disaster and its concomitant spatiotemporal instability are explored. It also allows for a more expansive understanding of nuclear disaster to include undetected and unacknowledged or underacknowledged sites with harmful levels of radioactivity due to industrial accidents, pollution from mining, and fallout from weapons testing.

As the atomic scale defies the senses and radioactivity evades sensory detection, I propose a form of multisensory perception in my analyses of nuclear undercurrents in certain films, and most notably in those of Chris Marker. Multisensory perception emphasizes interactions and interdependencies between the senses and invites a broader definition of the senses to include complex forms of perception such as chronoception, or the subjective experience of time. My use of multisensory perception draws on Gilles Deleuze's time-image and the idea that pure optical situations put the liberated senses into a direct relationship with time and with thought. For Deleuze, one extension of the opsign is "to make time and thought perceptible, to make them visible and of sound." The films under study here show this direct relationship to time and thought with the disappearance of the action-image and the movement-image "in favour of pure optical situations"[55] such as the Polaris missile in Marker's *Sans soleil* (1982) and the meditating filmmakers in front of nuclear reactors in *Le cœur du conflit / Kokoro no katto / The Heart of the Conflict* (2017).

The multisensory perception called for in this book develops more broadly from cognitive and phenomenological approaches in film philosophy with an interest in the viewer's experience both cognitively, in terms of hardwired mechanisms of perception, and phenomenologically, in terms of subjective perception as constructed by the viewer.[56] A multisensory approach facilitates perception of the effects of radioactivity, which is largely undetectable by the five senses individually, and allows for a Deleuzian direct relationship with nuclear time.

Outline of Chapters

In the chapters that follow, I consider how nuclear disasters have shaped French visions of Japan and Franco-Japanese cultural exchange in cinema. In doing so, I show the emergence of new forms of transnational solidarity through cinematic exchange, and I elaborate a different kind of nuclear cinema. The book begins with a historical overview of Franco-Japanese cultural exchange since the mid-nineteenth century followed by analysis of films and digital media that show formal fragmentation and spatiotemporal instability. The work under study is thematically and formally diverse including some commercial but mostly art and experimental (*art et essai*) films as well as fiction, documentary, and hybrid modes. The filmmakers tend to be avant-garde and interstitial thinkers, but they demonstrate a common interest in margins, peripheries, and environments rather than dominant subjects, centers, and spectacles. The films span over fifty years, from the first Franco-Japanese coproductions *Typhon sur Nagasaki / Typhoon over Nagasaki* (1957) and *Hiroshima mon amour* (1959) to work responding to the 2011 nuclear disaster at Fukushima Daiichi. The films from France can been seen as gestures of solidarity with victims and survivors of nuclear disaster in Japan, and some of their creators might be understood as filmmaker-activists in Rob Nixon's expansive sense of the term.[57] As an art form of the continual present—or the illusion of continual present with the steady progression of twenty-four frames per second—cinema provides particularly fertile ground for the eternal or impossible present of the chronotope of the nuclear. And despite the fact that France and Japan have been leaders in the development and promotion of the seventh art at home and abroad, cinema is a newer area of focus in Japonisme studies.

To lay the cross-cultural foundation for this book, the first chapter, "From Japonisme to the Nuclear Era," provides a historical overview of Franco-Japanese exchange. Some scholars argue that *Japonisme* refers to the Western fascination with Japanese aesthetics that ended in the early twentieth century. For many of them, revivals of the term in *néo-Japonisme* and *post-Japonisme* seem Western-centric, oversimplifications, and inaccurate descriptors of Franco-Japanese exchange today. Chapter one contextualizes this exchange from the inception of the term *Japonisme* to its reappearance in revised forms today. Understanding the aesthetic orientations of France's historical fascination with Japan and Japan's with France allows for a fuller appreciation of the interruption of that tradition by the Second World War and the American use of the atomic bomb on Hiroshima and Nagasaki. Alongside the history of Franco-Japanese cultural exchange, I outline parallel developments in cinema and nuclear technologies and their impact on this cross-cultural exchange, beginning with the discoveries by Becquerel and the Lumière brothers. These histories are brought together to show how the atomic bombings interrupted the primarily aesthetically oriented visions and refracted them through a nuclear lens, magnifying certain shared sociopolitical and environmental concerns.

Chapter two, "Learning to See with Japan in *Hiroshima mon amour*," introduces French visions of a nuclear Japan in the first Franco-Japanese cinematic coproductions, Yves Ciampi's *Typhoon over Nagaski* (1957) and Alain Resnais's and Marguerite Duras's *Hiroshima mon amour* (1959). Archival material in this chapter reveals that *Hiroshima mon amour* was in part a response to Ciampi's nearly forgotten film. Both films evoke the atomic bombings in their titles but engage little with them in their narratives. In its vision of Japan through a nuclear lens, *Hiroshima mon amour* breaks with the linear narrative, cultural stereotypes, and visual clichés seen in *Typhoon over Nagasaki* by inverting stereotypical gender dynamics and introducing narrative fragmentation and spatiotemporal instability, key characteristics of the chronotope of the nuclear. As one of the most important films for the *nouvelle vague* and for global art cinema, *Hiroshima mon amour* also played a pivotal role in the postwar era in initiating Franco-Japanese collaboration in cinema and in providing a new and updated vision of Japan to Western viewers.

Hiroshima mon amour was less well received by popular Japanese audiences than by those in the West; however, it had a significant impact on Japanese New Wave and independent filmmakers Ōshima Nagisa and Suwa Nobuhiro. Chapter three, "Tu n'as rien vu: Japanese Responses to *Hiroshima mon amour*" looks at the legacy of this film in Japanese films that reference and respond to it: Ōshima's *Max mon amour* (1986) and Suwa's *H Story* (2001) and *A Letter from Hiroshima* (2002). In their responses to the nuclear vision of Japan in *Hiroshima mon amour*, Ōshima and Suwa create work in which the traditional narrative arc breaks down even further and in which generic boundaries are increasingly blurred as the filmmakers turn to the absurd and the meta. With increasing temporal distance, these Japanese films acknowledge the tradition of cultural exchange in which they participate, and through aesthetic experimentation the films implicitly illustrate the limitations of a single cultural perspective. Like *Hiroshima mon amour*, these films ultimately refuse completion or conclusion, exhibiting the unbounded time of the chronotope of the nuclear. With its focus on Japanese responses to French visions of Japan through a nuclear lens, this chapter shows the increasingly reciprocal and dialogic nature of Franco-Japanese cinematic exchange.

If *Hiroshima mon amour* was a transformative film for Resnais as a director, it was also his only film made in Japan. Chris Marker, a contemporary and friend of Resnais, had a more sustained interest in Japan and found the place a source of inspiration over the course of his career. Chapter four, "Things That Quicken the Heart: Sensing the Nuclear in Chris Marker's Japan," focuses on a nuclear undercurrent in several of Marker's films dealing with Japan. The portrait of postwar Japan in *Le mystère Koumiko / The Koumiko Mystery* (1965) includes a reference to nuclear concerns, which resurface in the travelogue essay film *Sans soleil / Sunless* (1982) and in *Level Five* (1996), which shifts focus to the Battle of Okinawa. Drawing on material from the Chris Marker archive at the Cinémathèque française, I use the nuclear lens and chronotope of the nuclear to argue for a multisensory approach to these works in order to perceive the nuclear, which cannot always be seen. Examining these films and the circumstances of their production through a nuclear lens magnifies Marker's attention to the Battle of Okinawa in particular, as the event was overshadowed in the visual and historical archive by the atomic bombings of Hiroshima and Nagasaki. Marker's sustained engagement with Japan and nuclear concerns serves as an example of how the nuclear was increasingly woven into the background of French visions of Japan during the intervening period between disasters.

As French and Japanese filmmakers continued to make films about nuclear issues in the 2000s, the 2011 triple disaster in Japan served as a call to several French filmmakers to express solidarity through their work with those suffering in the aftermath. Chapter five, "Interaction and Solidarity through a Digital Nuclear Lens" turns attention to digital films and a web-documentary about the nuclear disaster at Fukushima Daiichi. I argue that the digital age offers filmmakers increased opportunities for collaboration and expression of solidarity through their work. This chapter uses the nuclear lens and the chronotope of the nuclear to analyze work by the French filmmaker Philippe Rouy, who both embraces and critiques the abundance of images of the nuclear disaster as he uses them to construct his trilogy of films *4 bâtiments, face à la mer / 4 Buildings, Facing the Sea* (2012),

Machine to Machine (2013), and *Fovea centralis* (2014). Rouy made these films while in France using footage from the Tokyo Electric Power Company's (TEPCO) live-stream webcams at the Fukushima Daiichi reactors. The representation of the webcam that never stops in these films illustrates the seemingly eternal present temporal aspect of chronotope of the nuclear. By contrast, Keiko Courdy's web-documentary *Au-delà du nuage °Yonaoshi 3.11 / Beyond the Cloud* (2013) was made in Japan as a Franco-Japanese coproduction. The web-documentary was remediated and released as a traditional, linear documentary, followed by the short film *A Safe Place* (2017) and *L'île invisible / The Invisible Island* (2021), Courdy's second feature-length documentary about Fukushima. The more recent works in this chapter are smaller productions than those of Resnais and Marker, and it is too soon to say whether they will endure in the same way—if, indeed, anything in the digital age will. They are included alongside more well-known work from recognized auteurs as they show a similar spirit of formal innovation and directorial independence but also represent a shift from commissioned work supported by states and institutions to crowd-funded and publicly sourced digital work that is more immediately accessible for global audiences.

The sixth chapter, "Reframing *Hiroshima mon amour* after Fukushima," examines recent films that reference *Hiroshima mon amour* in the context of the 2011 nuclear disaster at Fukushima Daiichi. This chapter shows the continued relevance of *Hiroshima mon amour* today for transnational filmmakers such as Jun Yang and his film *The Age of Guilt and Forgiveness* (2016) and for transnational filmmaking teams such as Judith Cahen and Masayasu Eguchi and their film *Le cœur du conflit / Kokoro no katto / The Heart of the Conflict* (2017). Through comparative analysis of these films and *Hiroshima mon amour*, I show how the chronotope of the nuclear has evolved from its initial manifestation as the eternal present against a nuclear background to a form that accommodates the idea of a deep radiological future. The nuclear lens also reveals the development of the alternative nuclear iconography initiated by *Hiroshima mon amour*. More broadly, I argue that these coproductions engage with the Franco-Japanese cinematic tradition while opening a wider transnational lens on nuclear concerns and implicitly call for global solutions.

The nuclear lens brings into focus a different kind of nuclear film. Rather than defeatist or celebratory apocalyptic nuclear visions or mere updated French visions of Japan, the visions presented in these Franco-Japanese films show anxiety, concern, dialogue, and transnational solidarity around the nuclear risks that remain in everyday life across vast and uncertain expanses of space and time. As such, these films force us to rethink nuclear disaster as an ongoing reality rather than a spectacular possibility. They serve as gestures of solidarity in a cooperative and politically engaged cross-cultural encounter.

Given France's status as a nuclear weapon state and the sustained level of French investment in nuclear energy, it is perhaps unsurprising that French artists have taken up nuclear concerns in their work. Considering Japan's history with nuclear disaster, it may be just as unsurprising that Japan would serve as the object of so many of these French nuclear visions, fantasies, and fears. If French responses to the nuclear disaster at Chernobyl were shaped through the lens of Cold War geopolitics, the disaster at Fukushima Daiichi undermined any essentialist expectations of Japanese technoscientific control. And if French visions of a nuclear Japan interrupted earlier aestheticentric visions of Japonisme, interest in the 2011 disaster is still rooted in many ways in the tradition of Japonisme, as will be seen in the chapters that follow. This may explain why French responses to Fukushima far outnumber those found in Spanish, German, and even English.[58]

1

From Japonisme to the Nuclear Era

I N 1958, THE WORLD'S tallest freestanding tower was added to the
Tokyo skyline. If traditional Japan was associated with Mount Fuji,
rebuilt postwar Tokyo would signal revitalization and modernization. The Tokyo Tower, much like the Eiffel Tower after which it was
modeled, was a symbol of internationalism and technological prowess.
"If we're going to make it, let's make it surpass the height of the
Eiffel Tower," the website for the Tokyo Tower imagines its founder
Hisakichi Maeda thinking. At 333 meters, the Tokyo Tower surpasses
its model by nine meters.[1] The Franco-Japanese connection around
this symbol of modernization continues in Paris, where the Maison
de la culture du Japon (completed in 1997) sits next to the Eiffel
Tower in a spatial rapprochement of high culture and national icons.

In 1959, the year *Hiroshima mon amour* was released, the Tokyo
Tower attracted a record 5.2 million visitors. A Japanese poster for
Hiroshima mon amour (entitled *Nijūyo jikan no jōji* in Japanese, or *A
Twenty-Four-Hour Love Affair*) included an image of the Eiffel Tower,
a seemingly inexplicable choice for a film that does not take place in
Paris and in which the iconic tower never appears. However, in 1959
the Eiffel Tower would evoke the latest instance of Franco-Japanese
cultural exchange, a marketing strategy to reach Japanese audiences
keener on symbols of internationalism and technological progress
than on images of mass technological destruction.

21

The end of the Second World War signaled a turning point in the tradition of mutual cultural fascination between France and Japan. Postwar era developments in technology—and particularly in nuclear technology—played an important role in the transformation of this transnational relationship. To better highlight the significance of the postwar era as a turning point in the history of Franco-Japanese exchange, this chapter provides an overview of Franco-Japanese cultural encounters with particular attention to those in and around cinema. Alongside this chronology, I outline developments in nuclear history and in Japonisme studies in the context of Edward Said's *Orientalism* and its legacy. Said's *Orientalism* largely overlooks East Asia but provides a useful framework for Japonisme studies and for the contention of this book that Orientalism as a Western creation reveals more about the West (France) than it does about the Orient (Japan).

While Japonisme studies offers a compelling framework for matters of aesthetics and form, I join many scholars in questioning whether *Japonisme* remains a useful term for describing cultural exchange between Japan and the West today. The term is particularly problematic in its lack of implied reciprocity. *Japonisme* provides a historical frame and context for the Western side of the exchange and remains the subject of important ongoing interdisciplinary scholarly conversations, but I am ambivalent about employing the term or its more recent iterations such as néo-Japonisme, post-Japonisme, second Japonisme, new waves of Japonisme, and the never-ending story of Japonisme.[2] Such terms can easily become shorthand for a complex and ongoing relationship in an increasingly interconnected world in which binary divisions such as East and West have lost purchase. Especially given its history and grounding in the visual arts, the term *Japonisme* still conveys a certain aestheticentrism without leaving much room for geopolitics.[3] This chapter seeks a balance of the two and thus will focus on the entwinement of aesthetics and geopolitics, particularly in the nuclear era in which the atomic bomb initiates a global epistemic turn.[4]

From Marco Polo to Japonisme

One of the earliest written accounts of European travel through East Asia that mentions Japan can be found in Marco Polo's thirteenth-century Old French travelogue *Le livre des merveilles du monde / The Travels of Marco Polo*. Marco Polo's understanding of Japan ("Chipangu") as a civilized, isolated island of great wealth came to him through oral reports from China. It was not until 1542 that the first Portuguese sailors are said to have entered Japan for trade, adventure, and missionary work. However, in Tokugawa Japan, Jesuit missionaries came to be seen as agents of European expansionism, and by 1635 the borders of Japan were closed to foreigners. Following the 1637–38 Shimbara Rebellion of Catholics in Nagasaki (dramatized in Martin Scorsese's 2016 film *Silence*), the shogun expelled remaining Westerners from the country, and trade was restricted to a single port in Nagasaki that was only accessible to the Dutch.

During the Tokugawa period starting in 1600 and extending for over two and a half centuries, a time when Japan was mostly isolated from the West, accounts of Japan still reached France. Enlightenment writers Montesquieu and Voltaire derived their conceptions of Japanese laws and customs in part from Englebert Kaempfer's *History of Japan*, which was translated from German to French in 1729. Montesquieu's *De l'esprit des lois / The Spirit of Laws* (1749) includes a chapter on the "Impuissance des loix Japonoises" (Impotency of Laws in Japan) that critiques the use of the death penalty as a punishment to avenge wrongdoing to the emperor rather than to correct offenders' behavior. In 1749, the third volume of Buffon's *Histoire naturelle / Natural History* on "Variétés dans l'espèce humaine" (Varieties in the Human Race) was also published, a volume in which Japanese people are described as having essentially the same physical attributes and customs as the Chinese.[5] During that period and likely drawing on many of the same sources as his contemporaries, the Chevalier de Jaucourt wrote a series of entries on Japanese geography, arts, religion, and government for the *Encyclopédie*, first published in 1751. Voltaire devotes a chapter to Japan in *Essai sur les mœurs et l'esprit des nations / An Essay on Universal History, the Manners, and Spirit of Nations* (1756), noting similarities between French and Japanese civilizations in terms of shared morals and similar customs.[6]

In the mid-nineteenth century, the end of Japan's isolationist foreign policy allowed for more extensive Franco-Japanese exchange. After the forced opening of Tokugawa Japan by American Commodore Matthew C. Perry in 1853–54, the 1858 *Traité d'amitié et de commerce entre la France et le Japon* (Treaty of Amity and Commerce between

France and Japan) was signed. The agreement allowed for diplomatic exchange between France and Japan and for the opening of several Japanese ports for travel and trade. The overthrow of the shogun in 1867 marked the end of the Tokugawa period and the start of the Meiji era in 1868, which ushered in a Westernization of Japan and a general spirit of internationalization.

While the earliest instances of Franco-Japanese exchange may be difficult to pinpoint, exchange clearly began decades before the 1858 treaty. Dutch presence in Japan had allowed for French language instruction there as early as 1808, and a substantial French-Japanese dictionary had already appeared in Japan as early as 1854.[7] Japanese woodcut prints arrived in France in 1812 with the sale of a Dutchman's collection in Paris, but their "discovery" in 1856 makes for a better story, as Félix Braquemond reportedly came across Japanese prints used as wrapping for ceramics at Auguste Delâtre's shop in Paris.[8]

The Paris World Expositions that took place in 1867, 1878, 1889, and 1900 were key to the broader introduction and dissemination of a variety of Japanese arts in France. The 1867 exposition coincided with the end of the Tokugawa period and featured Japanese decorative objects such as bronzes, porcelains, and lacquered goods, and more ukiyo-e (floating world) woodcut prints, which were by then out of fashion in Japan but in France were a "revelation."[9] While artists, writers, and collectors expressed an aesthetic appreciation of the prints, Japanese decorative objects were also commercialized for a wider public who valued the *japonaiseries* as accessories and status symbols. And as Elizabeth Emery shows in *Reframing Japonisme: Women and the Asian Art Market in Nineteenth-Century France, 1853–1914,* the origin narrative of Japonisme has minimized or erased the contributions of French women, who were active collectors and dealers of Japanese art as well as artists and writers themselves.[10]

In 1872, this French interest in Japanese art was given a name. In a series of articles for *La renaissance littéraire et artistique* (The Literary and Artistic Renaissance) entitled "Japonisme," the collector and critic Philippe Burty details his encounters with Japanese arts, beginning with a description of death and cremation in Japan and of an album of Japanese paintings "d'une sensibilité, d'une noblesse d'allure et d'une poésie qui n'ont jamais atteintes nos danses macabres européennes, impies et prétentieuses"[11] (of a sensibility, of a noble appearance and poetry that our impious and pretentious European danses macabres never reach). Burty's "Japonisme" articles remarked on poetry, drawing, religion, and language, among other subjects. They came to be understood as having "designate[d] a new field of study in Japanese arts and aesthetics" and identified "a full-fledged movement that helped Western artists in all media achieve new heights of creative liberation."[12] The term would be applied to work by French Impressionist painters for whom "the new Japanese aesthetic arrived at a moment of crisis in Western painting" as well as to writing by poets and novelists such as Charles Baudelaire and Émile Zola whose work has also been shown to reflect Japanese influence.[13]

While French interest in Japanese art may have been centered in Paris, it also spread beyond the capital. In 1876, the industrialist and art collector from Lyon Émile Guimet traveled with the artist Félix Régamey to Japan and returned with relatively nuanced accounts in contrast to those of many of their predecessors.[14] In Lyon, Guimet opened a natural history museum where he displayed his Asian art collection until 1889, when it was moved to the Musée Guimet in Paris. In 1883, the Impressionist painter Claude Monet moved to Giverny, where he installed a Japanese garden, hung prints from his extensive ukiyo-e collection on his walls, and entertained Japanese guests.[15] As the Claude Monet Foundation now describes the site, "Passant du jardin à son intérieur, Monet 'vivait au Japon' en Normandie!" (Whether in his garden or inside his home, Monet was 'living in Japan' in Normandy!). However, as Japanese goods flooded the market, their exotic novelty wore off for French consumers.[16] The 1889 World Exposition in Paris, which coincided with the centennial of the French Revolution, featured the Siegfried Bing collection of Japanese prints but is best remembered for its introduction of the Eiffel Tower.

In the literary realm, Louis Marie Julien Viaud (who wrote under the pen name Pierre Loti) became one of the first notable French writers to visit Japan. In 1888, Loti published the influential *Madame Chrysanthème*, a novel based on his time as a naval officer in Nagasaki and his life with a Japanese woman he paid to be his wife. Loti's novel inspired works from Giacomo Puccini's opera *Madame Butterfly*, premiering in 1904, to paintings by Van Gogh and writing by Paul Claudel and Marguerite Duras, whose parents were reportedly seduced by Loti's vision of Japan and decided to move to Asia.[17] In the opening essay of *L'empire des signes / Empire of Signs* (1970), Roland

Barthes cites Loti's Orient as a model for his vision of the system of signs he calls *Japan*.[18] Literary scholar Kawamoto Kōji remarks on the influence of Loti in Japan seen, for example, in the Loti bust erected in Nagasaki in 1980, a monument that is "one of the most popular sightseeing spots in today's Nagasaki."[19] Since 2007, the Prix Pierre Loti is awarded each year to a French work of travel literature.

The story of Japonisme and the artists, writers, and collectors who participated in and promoted this tradition in the second half of the nineteenth century is well documented by art historians and literary scholars.[20] In addition to Monet, a number of French painters are associated with the tradition, as is the French Impressionism movement as a whole. More recently, art historians such as Elizabeth Emery and Christopher Reed have approached Japonisme through the lens of gender and queer theory to reveal the contributions of women and to show how Japanese aesthetics contributed to understandings of masculinity in the West.[21] Jan Hokenson provides the most comprehensive English-language study to date of Japonisme in French literature, a study complemented by Pamela Genova's analysis of aesthetic translation in the work of nineteenth-century writers Edmond de Goncourt, Joris-Karl Huysmans, Émile Zola, and Stéphane Mallarmé.[22] Akane Kawakami has focused on writers such as Pierre Loti, Henri Michaux, Paul Claudel, Roland Barthes, and Michaël Ferrier, who traveled to or have lived in Japan since the nineteenth century and their ways of seeing as Orientalists, journalists, ethnographers, photographers, and flâneurs.[23] Edited collections from Ferrier and Philippe Forest offer other recent French perspectives on Franco-Japanese literary exchange.[24] The 2016 emergence of the *Journal of Japonisme* with Gabriel Weisberg at the helm attests to a resurgence of scholarly interest in the influence and inspiration of Japanese culture in the West and in an aesthetic style often considered to have ended in the nineteenth or early twentieth century.

On the other side of the exchange in the visual arts and less studied in Francophone and Anglophone scholarship was a small movement referred to as "The Impressionist School in Japan." Kuroda Seiki, who had traveled to France in 1884 and studied plein air painting in Paris, returned in 1893 to Japan where he started the Impressionist School with a group of Western-style Japanese painters.[25] Art historian Kawakita Michiaki writes, "the Japanese 'impressionist' school was not a revolt against academism. Instead, it became a type of academism in its own right. And before it had developed a really strong backbone, it gave way to the next wave of fashion."[26] In many ways, this small movement in Japan followed the aesthetics of French Impressionism while mostly ignoring its politics, echoing the spirit of Japonisme in France.

Hayashi Tadamasa, a collector and "the single most important supplier of Japanese art to the French market" at the end of the nineteenth century, sold ukiyo-e prints, manga, and Japanese paintings to clients including Bing, Monet, Degas, and Van Gogh. He also brought French painting to Japan, with an exhibition of Barbizon painters in 1890 and one of Impressionist paintings in 1893.[27] And Foujita Tsuguharu, who studied art in Tokyo and was inspired by a Monet painting his father showed him, had his first work shown in France at the 1900 World Exposition. After studying French and art in Tokyo, Foujita arrived in Paris in 1913 where he went on to mix Eastern and Western styles in his work and become an international sensation.[28]

In a volume on postwar Franco-Japanese exchanges, Doug Slaymaker seeks to remedy the imbalance of work focused on French receptions of Japanese culture, proposing that "the influence of French painting, literature, and thought on Japan, from even before the Meiji Revolution, is hard to overstate. . . . Practically all artistic movements in Japan have drawn in significant amounts from the French fountain."[29] Japanese visions of France, which also stem from particular national needs and self-image, are distorted as well. For Slaymaker, both sides of the exchange stem from similar impulses: an "image of the other . . . predicated on the particular image each holds of itself"; "pride in a long cultural heritage"; and a sense of national identity that "proceeds from self-identification with that heritage," particularly linguistic and literary heritage.[30]

Also worth noting is a certain institutional promotion of linguistic purity in both cultures. Since 1635, the Académie française has sought to protect the French language from inelegant intrusions including a 1996 decree encouraging French neologisms "afin d'éviter l'emploi en trop grand nombre de termes étrangers, le plus souvent anglo-saxons" (in order to avoid the use of too many foreign terms, most often Anglo-Saxon ones).[31] In Japanese, foreign words are relegated to a different syllabary—katakana—the simplified forms of which come from fragments of kanji, which themselves come from Chinese ideograms and are used for words of Japanese origin.

Technological Developments
through the Twentieth Century

As the wave of Japonisme was cresting at the end of the nineteenth century in France, new developments in science and technology would begin to shape Franco-Japanese exchange for the twentieth century. The field of nuclear physics emerged with Wilhelm Conrad Röntgen's 1895 discovery of the X-ray and Henri Becquerel's discovery of radioactivity in 1896. Becquerel's discovery used photo plates from the Lumière brothers' factory, where cinema had been invented the year before with the Cinématographe, a motion picture apparatus that served as both a camera and a projector.

The early years of cinema saw an important instance of Franco-Japanese exchange with trips by Lumière camera operators Constant Girel and Gabriel Veyre to Japan where they filmed what they imagined to be everyday life. In 1897–98, Girel and Veyre made thirty-three films of Japanese actors, dancers, singers, and diners, among other subjects, to add to the Lumière catalog. These thirty-three films shot in Japan—more films than were shot in any other part of Asia except French Indochina—"captured a dialogic moment where French cinematographers and Japanese people communicated with each other."[32] As Daisuke Miyao has argued, these short films show the influence of Japanese aesthetics in negotiation with French Orientalism on early cinema. Unlike earlier visions of Japan from the West, the Japanese people Girel and Veyre filmed were no longer simply passive objects of the Orientalist gaze as the "monologic Orientalist fantasy turned into a fully dialogic work."[33] While these films in many ways maintained the Orientalist fantasy, Miyao has shown that they also reveal "a much more complicated image of Orientalism" that maintains a monologic Orientalist fantasy while also entering into the mutual dialogue of Japonisme.

Miyao attributes the Lumière brothers' interest in Japan both to the fashion of the time and to their personal connection with Inabata Katsutarō, a former Japanese classmate at La Martinière Institute in Lyon. The Japan films in the Lumière catalog are also quite different from others shot abroad, which tend to document formal events such as coronations and official ceremonies. "But curiously," Miyao writes, "in Japan neither Girel nor Veyre photographed political events, governmental officials, modernized urban areas, or anything similar. . . . The focus appeared to be on the everyday life of ordinary Japanese people and daily scenes in Japan." For example, one of the films entitled *Repas en famille* (1897) features Inabata and his family but reveals its French orientation as "nobody in this film eats anything at all," "two infants are forced to drink some tea," "the dish placed in front of Inabata is not a food dish but a brazier," and "no Japanese filmmaker would title this film 'A family meal.'"[34] Film scholar Komatsu Hiroshi also highlights the imbalance of this early era of exchange arguing that few Japanese people used the Cinématographe to shoot moving pictures and that the films shot in Japan by Girel and Veyre were rarely screened there and primarily made for French audiences.[35]

In both French and Japanese early cinemas, interest in cinematographic technologies and the cinematic illusion often surpassed that in narrative. Noël Burch suggests that while Thomas Edison with his Vitascope in the United States sought the "total reproduction of life," the Lumière brothers were more interested in the technical challenge of capturing movement and approached their competing technology the Cinématographe "as if it were a scientific toy."[36] Donald Richie argues that early Japanese cinemagoers were also more interested in the cinematographic technology than in the filmed narrative. Accordingly, projectors were placed inside the screening room for audiences to view as part of the projection spectacle. From its origins until the early 1920s, Japanese cinema was more akin to theater than to photography. There was little expectation of narrative realism but instead of the theatrical staple of the *benshi*, an authoritative narrator who brought unity to an otherwise fragmented spectacle including an introduction, a film, advertisements, and music.[37] Early twentieth-century trick films in France also appealed to an interest in the cinematic illusion. In one such 1904 Pathé film entitled *Japonaiserie*, a magician arranges rows of blocks in a sort of projection screen and conjures images of a young girl's face and a rooster.[38]

French cinema itself has always been more interested in the question, What is cinema? than in the ideal of narrative continuity that would so preoccupy Hollywood. As T. Jefferson Kline writes, "when the Hollywood directors plan a film they do so on a 'storyboard' which enables them to establish a fluid sense of the continuity (in both space and time) between scenes. When French directors begin their work, they make a 'découpage'—a 'cutting board.'"[39] Richie finds a similar tendency in Japanese cinema for looser narratives in which "various scenes suggest not so much a story as a relationship, of one character to another, or of one character to his or her environment."[40] He also observes a parallel between Japanese cinematic aesthetics and the essay form, both of which need not rely on narrative logic. "In Japanese writing, for example, particularly in essay writing, it is not only acceptable but even elegant to jump about from one subject to another. Likewise, in films, variety is often preferred to logic."[41] This writing style recalls the French *essai* form as developed by Michel de Montaigne in the sixteenth century. In the French *essai*, writing that "jumps about from one subject to another" is also appreciated for its elegance. With a common embrace of this looser structure, French and Japanese cinemas align in their modernist formal responses to the hegemonic Hollywood pleasure palace.

The 1930s, a time of rising nationalism in Europe and Japan, were a golden age for French cinema with the arrival of sound in 1929 and the emergence of poetic realism.[42] It was a golden age of sorts for Japanese cinema as well with the transition to synchronous sound and "the lingering survival of the *benshi*."[43] This period saw the emergence of realism and the influence of Expressionism on directors such as Kurosawa Akira. New film genres emerged that focused on the lives of ordinary people (*gendaigeki*) and of the lower middle class (*shomingeki*). Film became a medium for social criticism of an increasingly oppressive Japanese government until the militarist totalitarian government prohibited films that questioned loyalty to Japan.[44]

The 1930s also saw the return of the Japanese actor Sessue Hayakawa to France. Hayakawa, a Hollywood star who had impressed international audiences with his role in Cecil B. DeMille's *The Cheat* (1915), had acted in a few French films during the silent era as well. He returned to Japan to work for several years until nationalistic censorship drove him in 1936 back to France, where he stayed throughout the war and became even more popular with French audiences.[45] In Max Ophuls's *Yoshiwara* (1937), Hayakawa appeared as a Japanese spy who falls in love with a geisha, herself involved with a French lieutenant. As Miyao points out, the film draws on the Orientalist *Madame Butterfly* narrative and racist stereotype of the deceitful Japanese spy.[46] And although the exotic novelty of Japonisme had long since worn off, Colleen Kennedy-Karpat argues that Hayakawa's continued popularity in France was due to this "enduring taste for the exotic in French popular narrative cinema."[47]

At the outset of the Second World War after the 1940 Tripartite Pact initiated the alliance between Japan and Nazi Germany, Adolf Hitler toured an occupied Paris and secured the support of Philippe Pétain, allowing for the occupation of France under the Vichy government. Japan quickly negotiated with the Vichy government the shared occupation of French Indochina. Meanwhile, wartime cultural policies in Japan banned American and British films, while French films were allowed "but to preserve the martial atmosphere, the love scenes were cut."[48] There was a return to the "national" styles, which had become "so completely an amalgam of international influences that any attempt to regain a purely 'Japanese' vision or to proscribe stylistic imports could not be successful."[49] In France, the German invasion suspended much of the film industry's activity, but a ban on Anglo-American films may have actually encouraged French filmmaking in a context free from foreign competition.[50] Film was also a medium for propaganda, and antisemitic policies were put in place along with the prohibition and destruction of films seen to threaten the new social order.

When the United States dropped the atomic bombs on Hiroshima and Nagasaki in August 1945, the explosions marked the beginning of the nuclear era and initiated a new way of seeing and understanding the world. Rey Chow calls this era the "age of the world target." The dropping of the bomb initiated a global epistemic turn "in which everything has become (or is mediated by) visual representation and virtual reality."[51] In the West, common knowledge of the bombings of Hiroshima and Nagasaki came from above with the iconic image of the mushroom cloud, a picture that became a sign of terror. Reframing Heidegger's contention that the world becomes a picture in the modern age, Chow argues that in the age of the atomic bomb, the world as picture becomes a target for destruction, a formulation that exemplifies the deep entwinement of aesthetics and geopolitics in the nuclear era.[52]

In the United States, Ruth Benedict provided Americans with a wartime vision of Japan in her anthropological study *The Chrysanthemum and the Sword: Patterns of Japanese Culture* (1946). Benedict's work also insisted on the intersection of aesthetics and politics, or what she saw as fundamental contradictions in Japanese culture, as expressed in the title of the book. The book was commissioned by the United States Office of War Information to better understand and predict Japanese behavior. As it was not possible to do fieldwork in Japan during the war, the study was conducted from afar; Benedict relied on Japanese films and other materials to determine patterns of behavior that suggested what scholars today have called a "homogenous and ahistorical group identity."[53] Her work was influential in shaping American ideas about Japanese culture during the occupation of Japan until 1952 and in establishing certain stereotypes for years to follow. Notably absent from Benedict's study is any mention of the atomic bombings of Hiroshima and Nagasaki. The final chapter of the book begins, "Americans have good reason to be proud of their part in the administration of Japan since VJ-Day."[54] That same year, however, Americans were given reason to question that administration when John Hersey's on-the-ground account of the aftermath of the bombing of Hiroshima based on interviews with survivors was published in the *New Yorker* magazine, which devoted its entire August 31, 1946, issue to the story.

Hersey's account is all the more remarkable given the strict censorship code implemented during the American postwar occupation of Japan under which representations of devastation from the bombings were banned. The ban extended to any mention of crimes committed by American soldiers and of the Battle of Okinawa, an event referenced decades later in Chris Marker's *Sans soleil* (1982) and more fully explored in his film *Level Five* (1996). The censorship process involved checks by both civilian and military censors for violations of the pictorial code and extended not only to foreigners who wanted to document the aftermath of the bombings but also to any critical, theoretical, and promotional writing about films.[55] Kyoko Hirano, who has written extensively on Japanese cinema during the American occupation, argues that American censors afraid of moral questions around the bombings of Hiroshima and Nagasaki sought with this code to restrict and manage information around it and to minimize its visual impact.[56]

Matt Matsuda shows how postwar views from France were in many ways dominated by the American narrative that occupied Japan was "modernizing." But French visions were also "framed by a particular imagery, one largely drawn from contacts since the nineteenth century" and "the artistic currents to be known as *Japonisme*."[57] While Japonisme had inspired a modern way of looking for the Impressionists, Matsuda sees postwar Japan as offering an "'alternate' model of a modern society," one that is both modernizing and traditional, in opposition to the market capitalism and individualism of the United States, and without the same threat of cultural imperialism.[58]

During the postwar period, both France and Japan confronted the traumas and devastations of war, an experience brought together in the film *Hiroshima mon amour*. Both also faced physical rebuilding of the country and reconstruction of the abstract sense of nation. And technological modernization was key to the efforts in both places. France saw a return to research in radioactivity, a national tradition pioneered by Becquerel and Marie and Pierre Curie and continued by their daughter and son-in-law Irène and Frédéric Joliot-Curie. In 1945, Charles de Gaulle, head of the provisional government in postwar France, created the Commissariat à l'énergie atomique (CEA) (Atomic Energy Commission) and put Frédéric Joliot-Curie at its head. In 1946, Électricité de France (EDF) (Electricity of France) was established as the nationalized electric utility that would collaborate in the construction of nuclear power reactors. Two years later, the French experimental reactor Zoé was activated, and shortly after the first milligrams of French-produced plutonium were extracted from reprocessed irradiated fuel at the site. As Daniel P. Aldrich has argued, "[t]he French state built its early nuclear plants under a veil of secrecy because of their dual military/civilian use: they produced meager amounts of electricity alongside refined weapons-grade nuclear materials such as plutonium."[59] Brian R. Jacobson has documented how nuclear proponents such as the CEA also battled for public opinion through the use of newsreel images of the aftermath of the atomic bombings of Hiroshima and Nagasaki, images that would "sear the visual memory of the event into the French cultural imaginary."[60]

The end of the war brought new prosperity to the French film industry, which succeeded in its return to the *tradition de qualité* filmmaking of the 1930s and the development of film noir. The Blum-Byrnes agreements signed in 1946 allowed more American imports—including films—as a form of repayment for war debts. After a flood of American films on the market, the French government modified the agreement and imposed a quota on US imports. In 1949, the French industry turned to coproductions as a way to pay for expensive

new filmmaking technologies such as color and widescreen.[61] The
majority of coproductions over the course of the next decade were
with Italy, but in 1957 Yves Ciampi's big-budget *Typhon sur Nagasaki
/ Typhoon over Nagasaki* featuring major stars from France and Japan
was released as the first feature-length Franco-Japanese coproduction.
It was followed two years later by Alain Resnais's *Hiroshima mon amour*,
a Franco-Japanese art film with a relatively smaller budget.

Enthusiasm for Japanese cinema had been building in France in
the preceding years. Kurosawa Akira's Golden Lion award at the 1951
Venice Film Festival for *Rashomon* launched the internationalization of
Japanese cinema and dazzled the critics at the new film journal *Cahiers
du cinéma*. These young critics, who would go on to make their own
films later that decade, were impressed by the work of Kurosawa and
to an even greater extent by that of Mizoguchi Kenji. For the *Cahiers*
critics, however, Japanese cinema may have been more important for
the visions it provided of themselves as critics than as a window on
Japan. Isadora Kriegel-Nicholas argues that critical discourse found
in the pages of the *Cahiers* echoes nineteenth-century Japonisme with
the same "abiding imprint of both desire and anxiety at the heart of
the twentieth-century French filmgoer's gaze."[62]

The European festivals were seen as commercially valuable for
Japan in opening the national film market to the world. Nagata Masaichi, president of Daiei Studios in the 1950s and 1960s, recognized
the opportunity for new export markets, which film scholar Tezuka
Yoshiharu argues "became part of the national project of rebuilding
Japan's image abroad along with its national economy, self-confidence
and self-identity."[63] Nagata had traveled abroad and knew his market;
he supported self-Orientalizing films and visions of an exotic or traditional Japan that would satisfy the expectations of Western audiences.[64]

Kawakita Nagamasa, founder of the Towa company dedicated
to importing foreign films in Japan and exporting Japanese films to
Europe, also promoted international coproductions as a way to generate
greater cross-cultural understanding. Kawakita had been disappointed
by a culturally inaccurate German production of *Madame Butterfly*
and vowed to remake it with a Japanese actress and costumes. As a
producer at Tōhō, he worked on a Japanese-Italian coproduction of
Madame Butterfly (1954), directed by Carmine Gallone.[65] His wife
Kashiko, or Madame Kawakita as she became known, played an
important role as his partner and a shrewd critic in her own right.[66]

As an ambassador of cinema, she met with Henri Langlois at the Cinémathèque française in 1953, which led to an exchange of 150 French films to Tokyo for 150 Japanese films in Paris and events such as a 1963 retrospective of Japanese cinema marking the opening of the Cinémathèque française at the Palais de Chaillot.[67]

The late 1950s saw record admissions at movie theaters in France (1957) and in Japan (1958).[68] The transition in 1958 to the French Fifth Republic under Charles de Gaulle in the midst of the Algerian War of Independence coincided with the emergence of the *nouvelle vague* in cinema, a marketing term used to describe a group of young critics-turned-directors who sought to overturn traditional methods and modes of filmmaking in France. The *nouvelle vague* filmmakers trained their cameras on a young and lively Paris with the Eiffel Tower still "exud[ing] an enigmatic fascination" as an iconic if ambiguous film star.[69] While Claude Chabrol, François Truffaut, and Jean-Luc Godard were making films in the streets of Paris, the Left Bank Group including Alain Resnais, Chris Marker, and Agnès Varda would turn their cameras outward for films that were more explicitly concerned with social and political problems.[70]

As Alain Resnais completed work on *Hiroshima mon amour* in 1958, de Gaulle announced that France would build a nuclear arsenal. And in fact, the process was already well underway.[71] The emergence of France as the fourth nuclear power at this moment in history is deeply imbricated with the changing status of France on the global stage. As Gabrielle Hecht has argued, the development of nuclear technologies in France came from a desire to "define Frenchness in the postwar world," starting with a unique French reactor design and extending to a distinctively French workplace culture and French communities built around nuclear plants.[72] Nuclear power not only served the goals of energy independence and nation rebuilding but also promised to "add to the radiance of France," echoing the former glory of the Sun King Louis XIV and the *mission civilisatrice* of the colonial empire emanating from metropolitan France. As decolonization of the Francophone world proceeded in the 1960s, nuclear power in France became a substitute for colonialism and "a means of preventing their own colonization by the superpowers."[73]

On February 13, 1960, France conducted its first of four atmospheric nuclear weapon tests, code-named *Gerboise bleue*, in the Algerian Sahara during the Algerian War. As a condition of the Évian

Accords, the independence treaty signed by President de Gaulle in 1962, nuclear testing continued underground in Algeria until 1966, when it moved overseas to French Polynesia, which would be subject to 193 nuclear explosions over the course of three decades. While noting a "historiographic tendency to segregate" the French nuclear tests and the Algerian War, Roxanne Panchasi argues that "[t]he French bomb was always a weapon in and of empire."[74] Panchasi shows how the tests were acts of French nuclear imperialism and "yet another incarnation of the European/Western/white exploitation of Africa."[75] In French Polynesia, the impact of this testing on local populations and culture has been addressed by Sebastien Philippe and Tomas Statius in their groundbreaking study *Toxique. Enquête sur les essais nucléaires français en Polynésie*, which found that more than 90 percent of the Polynesian population was likely exposed to fallout from atmospheric testing above the threshold necessary for compensation. In a study of Pacific francophone literature, Anaïs Maurer finds that "about 80 per cent of novels and autobiographies published since the 1960s feature characters dying of cancer, and/or suffering from the loss of a foetus or a child."[76]

In Japan, rebuilt postwar Tokyo became an increasingly cinematic city as well with the addition of the Tokyo Tower to the skyline. The clash of old and new is underscored in Teshigahara Hiroshi's collective short film *Tokyo 1958*, an experimental city symphony recalling in its ludic tone and bird's-eye view street shots city symphonies such as Jean Vigo's *À propos de Nice* (1930). *Tokyo 1958* is also a self-Orientalizing film made for export, with French and English voiceover narrations offering an anthropological look at Japan and its modernization due in large part to products from the West.[77] The film acknowledges Western fascination with Japanese culture with its opening series of low angle shots of Donald Richie looking down in wonder and delight at ukiyo-e in a shop window.

As Teshigahara filmed Tokyo for Western audiences, *Hiroshima mon amour* was being envisioned for international audiences. The film was proposed by Anatole Dauman at Argos Films to Nagata Masa-ichi at Daiei Studios. Nagata and his company had come under fire after insulting the French and agreed to the coproduction in part to restore his image and also in an attempt to win more European festival prizes.[78] *Hiroshima mon amour* was finally excluded from competition at Cannes out of fear of insulting the Americans, but it more than fulfilled the promise of renown that Nagata sought, though perhaps not in the way he had hoped for the film. *Hiroshima mon amour* also brought together the shared French and Japanese experiences of wartime trauma and postwar national rebuilding, laying the foundation for a more dialogic, lateral exchange. The narrative of the film revolves around its absent center: the atomic bomb and the beginning of the nuclear era. As the nuclear came to connote not only power and force but also modernity and technological prowess, it offered a way forward in rebuilding both French and Japanese notions of national identity and pride.

By the end of the 1950s, Japan had launched its own cinematic New Wave, a term that, Richie explains, had been "coined in imitation of the French Nouvelle vague, itself another commercial invention."[79] David Desser includes in this movement overtly political and formally disjunctive films made in the wake of Ōshima Nagisa's *Ai to kibō no machi / A Town of Love and Hope* (1959). Desser points out that comparisons between the Japanese and French New Waves "typically to imply greater integrity to the latter" are also problematic in that they "have served the cultural cliché that the Japanese are merely great imitators" and ignored the unique Japanese context out of which the simultaneous movement arose.[80] In Japanese film scholarship, directors such as Ōshima, Imamura Shōhei, and Shinoda Masahiro are more often understood as rebelling against French favorites Ozu, Mizoguchi, and Kurosawa. With common interests in theater, literature, and youth culture, Ōshima, Shinoda, and Yoshida Yoshishige (Kijū), who majored in French literature, all worked at Shōchiku Studio, where the Japanese New Wave essentially originated. Scott Nygren challenges the idea of Japanese imitation and argues that the French New Wave could have begun in Japan, citing French borrowings from Japanese cinema such as Godard's "trademark" use of directorial voiceover, the switching on of traffic sounds mid-scene as a character crosses the street, and the layering of flashback used after a character's death in the middle of a film, all strategies used years earlier in Kurosawa's *Ikiru / To Live* (1952).[81]

Nygren argues that two foundational French visions of Japan in the twentieth century, *Hiroshima mon amour* and Roland Barthes's *L'empire des signes / Empire of Signs* (1970), "occupy a transitional terrain between the late modern and the postmodern. They reconfigure the Western representation of Asia from an Orientalist objectification to a modernist limit, but they do not yet enter into a postmodern hybridity that recognizes Asian voices, discourses, and texts as bound up with Europe."[82] Roland Barthes's essays on Japanese culture in *Empire of Signs* also signal an anthropological turn in 1970s French visions of Japan. The first essay "Là-bas" / "Faraway" begins with a preemptive defense against charges of Orientalism. Barthes's insistence that he was not trying to represent a true Japan, his delight in not being able to understand the language, and his return to the idea of emptiness or absence introduced by the second image in the book of the kanji *mu*, nevertheless shows a more deeply engrained Orientalism shaping the work. These essays have been called Barthes's "happy mythologies" in that they continue, albeit with a less critical perspective, the demystifying project begun in his analyses of French culture in *Mythologies* (1957).[83] Such a comparison suggests that Barthes tried to see Japan through a similar lens as that which he turned on France and, perhaps due to his inability to comprehend the language, found emptiness.[84]

Chris Marker, whose first film made in Japan was supposed to be a documentary of the 1964 Tokyo Olympics, also ended up taking an anthropological view in *Le mystère Koumiko* / *The Koumiko Mystery* (1965), a film that documented not so much the Olympic Games as Marker's days spent with the woman who served as his interpreter. The film opens with a citation from Jean Cocteau about "the true Japan" from a popular French comic book from the late nineteenth century, an acknowledgment of the film's own French vision. While the film exoticizes Koumiko in many ways and attempts to define her Japaneseness, Koumiko also inverts the gaze with a remark on the unusualness of the filmmaker's blue eyes. When Marker returned to Japan in the 1980s and made the epistolary travelogue *Sans soleil* (1982) and its photo-textual companion *Le dépays* (1982), his anthropological interest merged with a deeply personal one. As I have written elsewhere, *Sans soleil*, a film that draws attention to the overlooked street corners of Tokyo, also continued Marker's earlier preoccupations with social movements and the environment and is shot through with references to nuclear technologies and to the Battle of Okinawa.[85] This event, overshadowed in the historical archive by the atomic bombings, becomes the subject of Marker's later film *Level Five* (1996).

At the same time in metropolitan France, nuclear nationalism had been gaining traction for the twin promises of energy independence and economic prosperity. The nuclear project was a key component, for example, of *Les Trente Glorieuses* (The Glorious Thirty), the term coined by economist Jean Fourastié in 1979 to describe the period of economic expansion in France from 1946 to 1975.[86] The 1973 OPEC embargo and oil shock marked the end of the *Trente Glorieuses* (and of the concurrent Japanese Economic Miracle) as oil prices quadrupled. Acutely aware of the vulnerability of dependence on foreign oil, both France and Japan shifted resources to the development of their respective nuclear industries. The 1974 Messmer Plan, named after Prime Minister Pierre Messmer, called for the acceleration of nuclear energy production in France with as many as 170 reactors envisioned by the year 2000 and a total move to nuclear energy.[87] The Messmer Plan "did not come up for formal discussion by the Assemblée Nationale until May 1975, more than a year after it was launched" and reactor building was already well under way.[88] The stealthy implementation of the Messmer Plan echoed the belated announcement from de Gaulle of the French weapons program in 1958, reflecting the highly centralized and secretive decision-making in France and the legal, administrative, and coercive force employed by the state in decisions regarding the nuclear industry.[89] In 1970, the international Treaty on the Non-Proliferation of Nuclear Weapons (NPT) was entered into force to prevent the spread of weapons and weapon technology and to protect peaceful uses of nuclear power. France was the last of the five original nuclear weapon states to accede to the treaty in 1992.

While in some respects Japan followed a similar path as France, Japan was much more constrained in its nuclear ambitions. Emperor Hirohito's speech on August 15, 1945, framed the nation as the victim of the atomic bombs, but a speech the next day by Prime Minister Higashikuni Naruhiko blamed Japan's war loss on shortcomings in science and technology.[90] Prohibited by Article IX of the 1947 Japanese constitution from developing nuclear weapons and subjected during the American occupation to a strict censorship code that limited cinematic exports, Japan, too, turned to nuclear energy as a way to rebuild the nation.[91] In 1950, future Prime Minister Nakasone Yasuhiro claimed that it was Japan's right and duty to conduct atomic energy research in order to restore Japan's place on the global stage. If nuclear power allowed France to display national technological prowess, in Japan the turn to this source of energy also offered a chance to invert the horrific use of nuclear weapons on Hiroshima and Nagasaki. Nakasone's claim was supported by American President Dwight D. Eisenhower's move after the atomic bombings of Hiroshima and Nagasaki to rebrand nuclear technologies by promoting nuclear fission as a force for good in his 1953 Atoms for Peace speech. In this speech, Eisenhower proposed a future in which "experts would be mobilized to apply atomic energy to the needs of agriculture, medicine, and other peaceful activities . . . to provide abundant electrical energy in the power-starved areas of the world. Thus the contributing powers would be dedicating some of their strength to serve the needs rather than the fears of mankind."[92]

Matthew Penney details the "technological nationalism at the heart of Japan's conservative political culture." The government drew on discourse of "eliminating poison with poison" in developing the nuclear power industry to counter anti-nuclear sentiment in Japan after the atomic bombings and even more so after the Lucky Dragon Number Five incident on March 1, 1954, when Japanese workers on the Lucky Dragon Number Five fishing boat were contaminated by fallout from the American test of a hydrogen bomb on the Bikini Atoll.[93] The test, code-named Castle Bravo, was one thousand times as powerful as the bombs dropped on Hiroshima and Nagasaki and more than twice as powerful as predicted, making it the largest nuclear explosion ever initiated by the United States.[94] The incident mobilized widespread fear of radiation, and the radioactive monster Gojira (Godzilla) emerged on the screens in Japanese cinemas just a few months later.

After the Lucky Dragon incident, the Japanese Ministry of International Trade and Industry (MITI) drew on the "Atoms for Peace" framework and in 1955 set up a nuclear energy division, petitioned for funds to support nuclear energy research, and passed the Basic Atomic Energy Law.[95] Public support for nuclear energy was galvanized through social control strategies such as the 1956 American Atoms for Peace exhibition following Eisenhower's 1953 speech. The exhibition opened at the Hiroshima Peace Memorial Museum, a site better known for its exhibits on the horrors of the atomic bombs.[96] Ran Zwigenberg describes the exhibit as "instrumental in solidifying the dominant Japanese view that atomic energy was a legitimate, indeed essential, source of energy in a Japan that relied heavily on imported oil and natural gas."[97] Hiroshima was a particularly significant location for the exhibition, which provided an opportunity to showcase the modern rebuilt city as capable of embracing peaceful applications of nuclear technologies.

Despite protest from the nascent anti-nuclear movement, the central government formed the Atomic Energy Commission (*Genshiryoku Iinkai*) in 1956 to manage nuclear power policy. Consensus formed around the new program with help from popular culture propaganda such as Disney's 1958 *Our Friend the Atom*, nuclear-friendly manga characters such as *Tetsuwan Atomu* (Astro Boy) and Doraemon, and an increasingly benign Godzilla.[98] The Japanese government also organized an annual Nuclear Power Day, the first of which was held on October 26, 1964, and included essay contests on the safety of nuclear power, free concerts, and pro-nuclear propaganda in the form of commercials, pamphlets, and posters.[99] The first Japanese commercial nuclear reactor went online in 1966, and Japan's mobilization of nuclear power contributed to its own economic miracle. In 1973, the global oil shocks "changed the political landscape for nuclear power in Japan" as the government took over the siting of plants.[100] By the 1980s, Japan was seen as a "leader in atomic energy,"[101] and by 2011, there were fifty-four active reactors across Japan, making it the second most nuclearized country after France.[102]

While the French and Japanese states embraced nuclear technologies for nationalistic purposes, civilians were not uniformly supportive. Anti-nuclear sentiment in France started long before the 1974 Messmer Plan with general opposition on the left to the atomic bomb; however, it was not until the 1970s that militant *soixante-huitards* (participants in the May 1968 demonstrations and strikes across France) and local communities mobilized against nuclear energy and the construction of power plants in their regions. Demonstrations in 1969 and 1970 at the proposed sites of Fessenheim in Alsace and Bugey near Lyon were the first to draw large groups of protestors and attention from local and independent media outlets, which were more likely to critique the national nuclear program than mainstream national media and scientific journals were.[103]

In France, documentary film became an important media form for bringing visibility to the protests and asking critical questions about nuclear power, from Guy Seligmann's site-specific *La bataille de Fessenheim / The Battle of Fessenheim* (1971) and censored films such as Claude Otzenberger's *Les atomes nous veulent-ils du bien? / Do Atoms Wish Us Well?* (1975) and Serge Poljinsky's *Nucléaire, danger immédiat / Nuclear Energy, an Immediate Danger* (1977) to the militant ISKRA collective films *Mets pas tes doigts dans ton nez, ils sont radioactifs / Don't*

Put Your Fingers in Your Nose, They Are Radioactive (1975), *Condamnés à réussir / Condemned to Succeed* (1976), and *Dossier Plogoff / The Plogoff Case* (1980). Recognizing the power of audiovisual media, the French government and its nuclear industry exerted pressure to censor films and other sources of information that could spread alarm among the general public.[104]

In 1981, President François Mitterrand, who had risen to power on the left with a host of anti-nuclear promises, deceived supporters and demoralized anti-nuclear activists by dropping all but his pledge to cancel the planned Plogoff reactor in Brittany. Mitterrand, who ordered the largest number of nuclear tests of all French presidents, was also supported by a parliament that voted overwhelmingly in favor of the national energy program.[105] Anti-nuclear French activists were further provoked in 1985 when government operatives under Mitterrand's defense minister Charles Hernu bombed the Greenpeace ship *Rainbow Warrior*, which had been moored in New Zealand in protest of ongoing nuclear tests in French Polynesia. The former colony was never granted independence during the period of decolonization "mainly in order to provide France with a location for nuclear weapons testing."[106] The bombing, which has been called "the only documented case of state-sponsored terrorism by a Western, supposedly democratic government,"[107] had been meant to intimidate activists, but instead it "served as a turning point in the history of Greenpeace as an organization" by bringing global attention and new financial support to its campaigns.[108] The Chernobyl disaster the next year induced further anxiety among the French population, a feeling that only increased with the distortion and downplaying of the accident by pro-nuclear media and governmental officials.[109]

In 1995, President Jacques Chirac, a known Japanophile, decided to restart nuclear testing in the Pacific after a brief moratorium earlier that decade, a decision that strained the Franco-Japanese relationship. The filmmaker René Vautier, a contemporary of Resnais and Marker who had been involved with Marker's work with the Groupes Medvedkine, documented the fiftieth anniversary of the bombing of Hiroshima and the impact of Chirac's decision to resume testing in the Pacific in the polemical *Hirochirac 1995* (1995).[110]

Aesthetic and political worlds collided again when the Japanese writer and Francophile Ōe Kenzaburō denounced Chirac's decision and refused to attend the Festival of Japanese Literature in Aix-en-Provence where he was to be the guest of honor. In what became a highly publicized literary feud, the French novelist Claude Simon condemned Ōe's refusal in a letter addressed to him published in *Le Monde*. In his letter, Simon defended Chirac and admonished Ōe, his fellow Nobel laureate, for hostility toward France, reminding him that Japan had also committed wartime crimes. In response, Ōe published a letter in *Le Monde* acknowledging Simon's criticism of the hypocrisy of the Japanese government and pointing out that Simon's patriotism blinded him to the great French tradition of humanism and, more generally, to concern for the planet. Ōe's letter concludes: "Au lieu d'interpréter [cette] action comme anti-française, je souhaite que la majorité des Français la ressentent comme l'expression d'un espoir en l'avenir"[111] (Rather than interpret [this] action as anti-French, I hope that the majority of the French experience it as the expression of hope in the future).

Despite a history of challenges and disappointments, nuclear protest is ongoing in France by political and independent organizations such as *Les Verts* (the Green Party, in 2022 *Europe Écologie Les Verts*), Greenpeace, and *Réseau Sortir du nucléaire* (Nuclear Phase-out Network). Work by activists and nuclear counter-expertise organizations such as the *Groupement des scientifiques pour l'information sur l'énergie nucléaire* (GSIEN) (Association of Scientists for Information on Nuclear Energy) and the *Commission de recherche d'information indépendante sur la radioactivité* (CRIIRAD) (Commission for Independent Research and Information on Radioactivity) alert the public to occasional causes for concern such as leaks and contamination, but "[b]eyond the moment of 'alert,' . . . [they] have had trouble getting traction."[112] The nuclear industry for its part maintains its strength and participates in greenwashing in promoting nuclear energy as key to combatting global climate change.[113]

In 1970s Japan, anti-nuclear activism increased and led to public-awareness campaigns, lawsuits against the construction of new reactors, and a campaign to recall a pro-nuclear mayor.[114] Opponents of nuclear power were countered with propaganda and often bought off with cash and development initiatives, if not outright threatened. The bureaucratic priority was managing public relations over safety, which became clear with the Tokaimura nuclear accident in 1999 that caused two deaths and exposed hundreds to unsafe levels of radioactivity and with the 2007 radiation leak after a 6.6 magnitude earthquake in Niigata prefecture.[115] While the meltdown of three nuclear reactors at Fukushima Daiichi in March 2011 led to a pause on nuclear energy use in Japan and reignited national and global conversation about its safety, for many citizens and scholars the priority of the Japanese government appears to be the management of public anxiety over the protection of public health.[116]

Aldrich connects anti-nuclear activism in France and Japan through their corresponding "site fights," arguing that a similar state strategy of targeting areas with high unemployment, low population growth, and weak civil society as sites for nuclear reactors has been employed in both places and that "unitary governing systems and elite professional bureaucracies" have been used to increase nuclear power in the national energy mix.[117] The French and Japanese nuclear programs "are sufficiently alike that private nuclear authorities from both countries meet annually as the 'nuclear twenty' (N20)—comprising ten delegates from Japan and ten from France—to discuss issues of nuclear power plant siting and public acceptance."[118] Where France and Japan diverge, however, is in the strength and success of their anti-nuclear movements. While French activists have faced stronger and more violent forms of state coercion as well as marginalization as "leftist radicals and criminals," Japanese anti-nuclear efforts have been more successful, stopping almost half of all planned nuclear sites.[119] Despite these efforts, nuclear nationalism has become the norm across the political spectrum in Japan, from the Liberal Democratic Party to the Democratic Socialist Party. In France, only the Green Party still mounts consistent opposition to nuclear energy.[120]

While nuclear energy has been considered by some a peaceful use of the atom since Eisenhower's speech in 1953, it has been the source of significant social and environmental violence around the world. Accidents such as the little publicized 1957 Kyshtym nuclear disaster at Mayak in the former Soviet Union, the 1979 disaster at Three Mile Island, the 1986 Chernobyl disaster, and the series of meltdowns and explosions at Fukushima Daiichi in 2011 have contaminated large and ill-defined areas of land, water, and air and resulted in immense social, economic, and environmental consequences, while the institutions that manage these sites work to avoid taking responsibility. More insidiously and extensively, fallout from global nuclear testing, waste from production sites of nuclear technologies, and the occupational exposure of uranium miners worldwide have inflicted the slow violence of radioactive contamination on even less visible communities.[121] Ultimately, the rebranding of the nuclear from a horrific weapon to a tool for peace and economic prosperity serves as a reminder that military and civil uses of nuclear energy are two sides of the same coin. For the purposes of this study, it also underscores the connection between the nuclear disasters at Hiroshima and Fukushima as events unfolding within integrated nuclear infrastructures in an enduring nuclear era.

Franco-Japanese Exchange into the Twenty-First Century

By the end of the twentieth century and into the twenty-first, French fascination with Japan expanded to many cultural theaters with a significant legacy in literature. In *Le Japon depuis la France: un rêve à l'encre / Japan from France: A Dream in Ink* (1995), Michel Butor responds to French figures such as Loti, Claudel, and Barthes and their visions of Japan. Jacques Roubaud draws on high art and popular Japanese culture as a point of departure for his own poetry in *Tokyo infra-ordinaire / Infra-ordinary Tokyo* (2005), as he did in his earlier collection *Mono no aware (le sentiment des choses) / Mono no aware (the feeling of things)* (1970). Writers in the twenty-first century engage both fleetingly and profoundly with Japan in works such as Stéphane Audeguy's *La théorie des nuages / The Theory of Clouds* (2005); Éric Faye's *Nagasaki* (2010), *Malgré Fukushima: journal japonais / Despite Fukushima: Japanese Journal* (2014), and *Éclipses japonaises / Japanese Eclipses* (2016); Maxence Fermine's *Neige / Snow* (1999) and *Zen* (2015); Laurent Mauvignier's *Autour du monde / Around the World* (2014); and Olivia Rosenthal's *Un singe à ma fenêtre / A Monkey at My Window* (2022). Muriel Barbery's *L'élégance du hérisson / The Elegance of the Hedgehog* (2006) is another notable example featuring the fictional Japanese character Kakuro Ozu, a distant relative of filmmaker Ozu Yasujirō.

Franco-Japanese exchange extends beyond the borders of France to Francophone Belgian writers such as Jean-Philippe Toussaint with the Marie novel cycle; Amélie Nothomb, who has written several novellas on Japan; and the late member of the Académie française

François Weyergan's *Je suis écrivain / I Am a Writer* (1989). Fellow *académicien*, the Haitian-Canadian writer Dany Laferrière wrote *Je suis un écrivain japonais / I Am a Japanese Writer* (2008) showing "un usage ludique et stratégique du Japon" (a playful and strategic use of Japan), according to Michaël Ferrier.[122] In Japan, Akira Mizubayashi writes of his relationship to the French language as his *langue paternelle* (father tongue) in *Une langue venue d'ailleurs / A Language from Another Place* (2011). Ryōko Sekiguchi, who writes in both French and Japanese and was living in Paris in 2011, analyzes her response to the triple disaster in Japan both from France and from Japan in the book *Ce n'est pas un hasard: chronique japonaise / This Is No Accident: Japanese Chronicle* (2011). Scholarly conversations have developed around Franco-Japanese exchange in literature and the arts with critical work presented at colloquiums and in several editions published by Éditions Cécile Defaut and Éditions Philippe Picquier.[123]

Contemporary French cinema has also continued the tradition of fascination with Japanese culture. Many films focus on Tokyo, such as Olivier Assayas's films *Laissé inachevé à Tokyo / Left Unfinished in Tokyo* (1982) and *Demonlover* (2002). Assayas admits that because of his lack of deep connection to Japan, he sticks to the surface with his interests in graphic and visual arts.[124] The admission is surprising for a director who has many connections to East Asia and suggests a willful distancing from a more profound engagement with Japan and perhaps a desire to see the place that conforms to familiar French visions of it.[125] Other Tokyo-centric films include Gérard Krawczyk and Luc Besson's *Wasabi* (2001), an action-comedy set between France and Japan, Gaspar Noé's *Enter the Void* (2009), and contributions from Michel Gondry and Leos Carax (along with Bong Joon-ho) to the transnational triptych *Tokyo!* (2008), a production of the Paris-based Franco-Japanese company Comme des Cinémas that departs from the known world and clichés of the city into visions of Tokyo tinged by science fiction.

Contemporary Japanese filmmakers have shown reciprocal interest in France and French culture. Ōshima Nagisa's *Ai no korida / L'empire des sens / In the Realm of the Senses* (1976) and *Max mon amour* (1986) allude in their titles to French works about Japan by Barthes, Duras, and Resnais. In the "Crows" segment of Kurosawa's *Dreams* (1990), a Japanese art student who speaks French meets Vincent van Gogh (played by Martin Scorsese) in an impressionist landscape painting. "The Peach Orchard," another segment in the film, pays homage to

François Truffaut's *Les quatre cents coups / The 400 Blows* (1959) with its freeze-frame ending on a boy's face. Catherine Cadou's role in Franco-Japanese exchange in cinema also deserves greater attention, particularly her work with Kurosawa (including a brief appearance in *Dreams*), her documentary *Kurosawa: la voie / Kurosawa's Way* (2011), and her work as an interpreter and translator for Franco-Japanese films. Cadou is also acknowledged in the credits of Suwa Nobuhiro's *H Story* (2001). After *H Story*, Suwa directed the short "Place des Victoires" featuring Juliette Binoche in the collective film *Paris, je t'aime* (2006); *Yuki et Nina* (2009), a coproduction with the French filmmaker Hippolyte Girardot about a Japanese girl and her French friend; and *Le lion est mort ce soir / The Lion Sleeps Tonight* (2017), a film set in the south of France and starring Jean-Pierre Léaud, immortalized by Truffaut's freeze-frame.

Other contemporary Japanese directors contributing to the exchange include Fukada Kōji, who cites Eric Rohmer and Marcel Carné's *Les enfants du paradis / Children of Paradise* (1945) as influences.[126] Fukada engages with French culture in his animated short film *La grenadière* (2006), an adaptation of a short story of the same name by Honoré de Balzac, and in *Au revoir l'été* (2013), in which characters travel to France and talk about seeing the *Mona Lisa* at the Louvre. Fukada's film *Sayonara* (2015) about an evacuation after nuclear disaster features the Franco-Japanese actress Nakai Noémie, the French actor Jérôme Kircher, and the Franco-Swiss actress Irène Jacob. In an acceptance speech at Cannes for his film *Harmonium* (2016), which was awarded the Jury Prize in the Un Certain Regard section, Fukada said, "I want to work to strengthen ties between Japanese and French movies."[127] Kore-eda Hirokazu, who won the Palme d'Or at Cannes and an Academy Award nomination for his film *Shoplifters* (2018), chose France for his first film made outside of Japan, *La vérité / The Truth* (2019), starring the iconic French actresses Catherine Deneuve and Juliette Binoche. Peter Pugsley and Ben McCann's insightful survey *The Cinematic Influence: Interaction and Exchange between the Cinemas of France and Japan* explores the longer history of mutual influence and reverence between French and Japanese filmmakers such as Kurosawa Akira, Kore-eda Hirokazu, Kawase Naomi, Jean-Luc Godard, and Claire Denis.[128]

I propose that this rich and reciprocal transnational relationship in cinema can be seen more specifically as one of *affinitive transnation-*

alism. Mette Hjort conceives of the term as centering on a "tendency to communicate with those similar to us," and an "ethnic, linguistic, and cultural affinity," but that "need not . . . be based uniquely on cultural similarities that have long been recognized as such and are viewed as quite substantial, but can also arise in connection with shared problems or commitments in a punctual now."[129] The significant if limited history of Franco-Japanese cinematic encounters suggests the depth of this affinity with encounters beginning in the late nineteenth century with the arrival of the Lumière cameras in Japan and reinforced in the twentieth century most notably by Argos Films, which produced *Hiroshima mon amour, Sans soleil,* and *Level Five.* The support Argos Films showed for Franco-Japanese collaborations in cinema demonstrates its important role in this story of cultural exchange. Argos Films also found success in producing and distributing Ōshima's sexually explicit *In the Realm of the Senses* (1976) and *Ai no bōrei / L'empire de la passion / Empire of Passion* (1978), for which he won Best Director at Cannes.

Today, Franco-Japanese production companies in Paris continue affinitive transnationalism with films around shared nuclear concerns and environmental commitments. Based in Paris, the Franco-Japanese company KAMI Productions has produced several documentaries for French television such as *Le monde après Fukushima / The World after Fukushima* (2012); *Fukushima, des particules et des hommes / Fukushima, Particles and Men* (2014); *Notre ami, l'atome: Un siècle de radioactivité / Our Friend the Atom: A Century of Radioactivity* (2020); and *Indochine, une guerre japonaise / Indochina, a Japanese War* (2021). Comme des Cinémas, another Franco-Japanese production company based in Paris, has supported films such as *Tokyo!* and *Yuki et Nina* as well as several of Kawase Naomi's films, which have premiered at the Cannes Film Festival. Kawase's *Voyage à Yoshino / Vision* (2018) stars Juliette Binoche as a traveler in Japan. Les Productions Balthazar, which produced *Le lion est mort ce soir,* also produced Jacques Deschamps's Franco-Japanese film *Tsunami* (2015) evoking the triple disaster in 2011 and Kurosawa Kiyoshi's *Le secret de la chambre noir / Dagereotaipu no onna / Daguerreotype* (2017), which was shot in France with a French cast and crew. The Eurospace mini-theaters in Japan founded by Horikoshi Kenzō, who also supported European filmmakers such as Leos Carax, suggest further support for Franco-Japanese exchange in cinema. In 2005, Horikoshi started the Graduate School of Film and New Media at the Tokyo University of the Arts and created a partnership with the top French film school La Fémis to encourage Franco-Japanese student coproductions.[130]

Many of the filmmakers involved in Franco-Japanese productions do not speak the other language, an important condition for deeper cross-cultural engagement. However, documentaries such as Jill Coulon's *Tu seras sumo / A Normal Life. Chronicle of a Sumo Wrestler* (2013) and Idrissa Guiro and Mélanie Pavy's *Cendres / Ashes* (2015) were made by filmmakers whose lack of Japanese may have paradoxically allowed them greater access to their Japanese subjects. Coulon was able to film in the intimate quarters of a Japanese sumo stable where someone who could understand what was said might not have been allowed. Still, when Coulon's translator was not at her side, Coulon could not follow the conversations she was filming and often turned the camera off at consequential moments or continued to film when nothing much was being said.[131] For *Cendres*, Guiro and Pavy had met the family of the deceased actress Kyōko Kosaka Gaisseau, who had appeared in Godard's 1966 *Made in U.S.A.* and shared her apartment in Paris with Koumiko Muraoka, the subject of Marker's *The Koumiko Mystery*.[132] Guiro and Pavy were invited to participate in Kosaka Gaisseau's funeral and relied on nonverbal communication during their interviews in Japan.

Many French films about Japan made after 2011 focus on the nuclear disaster at Fukushima Daiichi. Documentaries such as Alain de Halleux's *Welcome to Fukushima* (2013), Claude-Julie Parisot and Gil Rabier's *Fukushima, des particules et des hommes / Fukushima, Particles and Men* (2014), Marc Petitjean's *De Hiroshima à Fukushima / From Hiroshima to Fukushima* (2015), and Jean-Paul Jaud's *Tous cobayes? / All of Us Guinea-Pigs Now?* (2012) and *Libres! / Free!* (2015), as well as formally and conceptually experimental work such Keiko Courdy's web-documentary and film *Au-delà du nuage °Yonaoshi 3.11 / Beyond the Cloud* (2013), Pierre Huyghe's *Sans titre (masque humain) / Untitled (Human Mask)* (2014), and Philippe Rouy's trilogy of films about the Fukushima nuclear disaster show concern for and solidarity with human and non-human victims of the 2011 triple disaster. Implicitly and explicitly these films turn the nuclear question back on France and its own nuclear commitments, challenging the claim of a nuclear renaissance.[133] Olivier Peyron's *Tokyo Shaking* (2021) is the first big-budget French fictional account of the 3.11 triple disaster and centers a French woman working at a bank in Japan who must decide whether to stay or leave. The nuclear disaster at Fukushima Daiichi destabilizes the foundation of postwar national identity rebuilt on notions of scientific development and technological prowess.

Solidarity around this disaster can be seen in organizations such as the Nos Voisins Lointains 3.11 (Our Faraway Neighbors 3.11) association created in 2013 by Sugita Kurumia, a retired Japanese researcher at the CNRS (National Center for Scientific Research) in France to encourage Franco-Japanese collaboration and solidarity in the face of nuclear risks. The association organizes conferences, film screenings, and fundraising events for victims of the 3.11 disaster. It also maintains an active website with videos featuring Japanese victims of nuclear technologies telling their stories. These videos are subtitled in French and English to reach broader global audiences.

Since 2011, the terms of Franco-Japanese cultural exchange have changed. What was once a mutual cultural fascination based on aesthetic appreciations, stereotypes, and cultural clichés has been inflected by a changing geopolitical landscape and humanitarian and environmental concerns introduced by nuclear weapons and "atoms for peace." Writers such as Michaël Ferrier and Philippe Forest propose a move away from the term *Japonisme* to describe ongoing encounters today.[134] And as Franco-Japanese exchange continues in visual arts such as manga, *bandes dessinées* (graphic novels), and animation, recent work such as Géraud Bournet's *FRANCKUSHIMA: Essai graphique sur la catastrophe de Fukushima et le risque nucléaire en France* (2016) also turns toward the nuclear. Using a form he calls the "graphic essay," Bournet, a self-taught illustrator with a background in environmental engineering, offers a comprehensive yet accessible approach to the Fukushima disaster and the nuclear industry in France through collaboration with French and Japanese filmmakers such as Keiko Courdy and Alain de Halleux, as well as photographers, scholars, expatriates, activists, and Fukushima residents.[135]

Institutionally supported Franco-Japanese cultural exchange beyond the realm of cinema continues as well. In Japan, for example, the Program of Overseas Study for Upcoming Artists run by the Agency for Cultural Affairs since 1967 has sent Japanese visual artists abroad to support their development and to promote Japanese culture worldwide. From 1967–2020, the program sent 181 Japanese artists to France, more than were sent to any other European country and second only to the United States.[136] The Villa Kujoyama in Kyoto supports French artists working in Japan in a variety of mediums. This cultural center, supported by the Ministry of Europe and Foreign Affairs, the Institut français du Japon, and the Fondation Bettencourt Schueller, has hosted artists in residence since 1992, including film-makers Philippe Rouy and Judith Cahen.

Contemporary cultural flows extend to the commercial and aesthetic domain of fashion: Louis Vuitton's collaborations with Japanese artists Murakami Takeshi and Kusama Yayoi; and notable Japanese fashion designers in Paris such as Takada Kenzo, Miyake Issei, Yamamoto Yōji, and Kawakubo Rei of Comme des Garçons, which devoted its entire 2021 catalog to photography from Chris Marker. In the 1990s and early 2000s, French brands such as Chanel, Hermès, and Louis Vuitton, already popular in Japan, began to open shops there. The Japanese language has also integrated French terms such as *mannequin*, *haute couture*, and *prêt-à porter*.[137]

Gastronomy has been another important theater of Franco-Japanese exchange. While the Meiji era Japanese imperial court served French cuisine at official functions such as the emperor's birthday and court dinners with diplomats, Japanese visitors to France in the 1860s reported discontent with French cuisine, which was too fried and contained too much butter and meat for their tastes. Rodolphe Lindan, a French tourist in Japan at the same time, reported back on the variety in and refinement of Japanese cuisine and the central role of rice and tea.[138] Over a century later in 1972, Paul Bocuse traveled to Japan to give cooking courses, and Kurihara Taïra went to Paris to work in the Michelin-starred Tour d'Argent restaurant in the Eiffel Tower before opening his own Franco-Japanese restaurant in the city.[139] Today, Sadaharu Aoki's upscale Franco-Japanese patisserie has multiple locations in Paris and in Tokyo, and the French tea boutique Mariage Frères has numerous locations across Japan. In popular food culture, rue Sainte-Anne in the heart of Paris is a Little Tokyo where diners wait hours for a bowl of the best udon. In Japan, crepes have become a specialty of the Harajuku teen mecca district in Tokyo.

Cultural works "made in France" and "made in Japan" continue to serve as status symbols around the world, as do quotidian borrowings like udon and crepes, which inevitably undergo transformation for reception in markets abroad. In both France and Japan, haute cuisine is not only an art but also now an Intangible Cultural Heritage of

Humanity, as identified by UNESCO. And yet the vast majority of exports between France and Japan are of the more mundane variety: computer equipment, medicaments, vehicles, and nuclear machinery.[140] Data suggest that the exchange of small *c* culture may in fact be much more pervasive than that of *Culture* and that the sharing of technology can create and enrich the contexts of Culture's reception.

Discussions of *Japonisme* after 1978 must also contend with the term in a post-Said context. Said's *Orientalism* launched postcolonial studies with its contention that the "Orient" is a Western invention and as such an object of domination in an implied hierarchy of West over East. Of the many critiques Said's work has received for its oversimplification of East and West, the one most pertinent to Japonisme studies is the absence of the Far East in Said's study of European domination of the Middle and Near East. Marie-Paule Ha problematizes *Orientalism* from the perspective of a non-European postcolonial woman in the West, arguing that in the context of France and Japan, French writers assimilate Orientalist ideas and references but also supplement, reaccentuate, and fill them in with other thoughts and discourses.[141] Hokenson pushes back against *Orientalism*'s monologic view of the West, a perspective that notably ignores women's travel writing that subverts paternalistic colonial discourse.[142] Iwabuchi Kōichi criticizes Said's own Orientalism of Japan in *Culture and Imperialism* (1994), which ignores Japan's imperialist history. In Said's formulation, Iwabuchi writes, "Japan is treated predominantly as a non-Western, quasi-Third world nation which has been a victim of Western (American) cultural domination," when in his own view Japan plays a mediating role between East and West.[143]

In the 2003 preface to the 25th anniversary edition of *Orientalism*, Said responds to general criticism of the work by arguing "I emphasize in [*Orientalism*] that neither the term Orient nor the concept of the West has any ontological stability."[144] Said even seems to support the argument that a more horizontal exchange, such as that between France and Japan, might emerge as a model for East-West studies: "Rather than the manufactured clash of civilizations, we need to concentrate on the slow working together of cultures that overlap, borrow from each other, and live together in far more interesting ways than any abridged or inauthentic mode of understanding can allow."[145]

For Joshua Paul Dale, this kind of lateral exchange might describe the gaze in Barthes's *Empire of Signs*, a gesture in which difference is neither neutralized nor parallel but coming from the side, "two gazes that pass each other by unseeing . . . two subjects orbiting the lateral gaze of the Other."[146] However, for Kojin Karatani and Sabu Kohso, the gaze of Japonisme remains one of aestheticentrism, a form of orientalism in which the Japanophiliac Frenchman (and throughout the twentieth century, it usually was a man) who "loves the aesthetic Japan and the Japan that is represented in the French mind" turns away from Japan as an economic power that threatens France and brackets "the concerns of pedestrian Japanese, who live real lives and struggle with intellectual and ethical problems inherent in modernity." For Karatani and Kohso, the mutual gazes come together in a problematic way: "looking down on the other as an object of scientific analysis and looking up to the other as an aesthetic idol are less contradictory than complicit" in objectifying the Other.[147]

For the purposes of the exchanges described in this study, the term *Japonisme* is insufficient as it lacks reciprocity, and in referencing the nineteenth-century tradition in the visual arts and literature, it describes an old phenomenon. Continuing to use *Japonisme* and its derivations seems to create more confusion than clarity. While the tradition of Japonisme and visual images in particular have played an important role in developing French imaginaries of Japan, I seek to situate the work in the chapters that follow in the context of visions and exchange. Visions suggest distance, subjectivity, and the influence of fantasy. Exchange is reciprocal and may be at once balanced and asymmetrical, shallow and deep.[148]

In this study, it would also be injudicious to argue for both a never-ending Japonisme and a never-ending nuclear era. One is a thought-provoking debate among scholars and the other, a regrettable certainty. The chapters that follow shift analysis away from discourses of Japonisme and the East-West binary to focus on the intersecting and disintegrating borders between aesthetics and politics, between Culture and cultures. In doing so, I aim to show how global questions posed and intercultural responses offered in the films under study serve as instances of transnational Franco-Japanese solidarity in the nuclear era.

Learning to See with Japan in *Hiroshima mon amour*

La magie de ce film est celle du regard extérieur. La tragédie ne
peut être vue et comprise qu'à travers un regard étranger.

(The magic of this film is that of the view from the outside.
Tragedy cannot be seen and comprehended other than by an
outside view.)

—Suwa Nobuhiro[1]

❧

THE FLASH OF LIGHT IS often the first sensory experience of the
atomic bomb attacks on Hiroshima and Nagasaki mentioned
in accounts from survivors. In his diary of the days and weeks
in Hiroshima after the bombing, Doctor Hachiya Michihiko writes,
"Those who experienced the bombing from the outskirts of the city
characterized it by the word: 'pikadon,' or 'flash-boom.' Those in the
city, on the other hand, had heard no sound at the moment of explosion and referred to it only as 'pika.'"[2] Distance from the epicenter
provided not only protection from the most immediate effects of the
bombing but also a different sensory experience of it.

Over a decade later and halfway around the world, *Hiroshima
mon amour* was commissioned as a documentary (tentatively titled

"Pikadon") about the atomic bomb. Alain Resnais was recruited on the strength of his previous documentary *Nuit et brouillard / Night and Fog* (1955) about the Nazi concentration camps during the Second World War. The vision for the film that would become *Hiroshima mon amour* evolved as Pathé Overseas and Argos Films producers corresponded with their counterparts at Daiei Studios in Japan. Daiei approached the project with caution and only agreed to coproducer status after seeing the scenario from Marguerite Duras and receiving reassurance that it would be a "quality film" and not a risky financial venture, as had been *Typhon sur Nagasaki / Typhoon over Nagasaki* (1957), the first official Franco-Japanese feature-length coproduction.[3]

Still, there were risks. Resnais was a documentary filmmaker who had yet to make a feature-length fiction film. He had no particular connection to Japan, nor did he speak Japanese. Duras, a novelist with no experience in cinema at that point in time, had been invited to write the screenplay, which read nothing like a traditional screenplay. And no one was quite sure what to call the film. The evocative title "Pikadon" became "Tu n'as rien vu," a repeated line of dialogue in the film, before it was released as *Hiroshima mon amour*, a title that would inspire numerous imitations but that was thought to be off-putting to audiences in Japan, where the film was released without reference to the site of the atomic bombing as *Nijūyo jikan no jōji* (A Twenty-Four-Hour Love Affair). Ultimately the risk paid off, at least for France, where the film was met with critical acclaim and is still seen as one of the most important films ever made. The original title remains largely untranslated in the film's international distribution with this notable exception in Japan.

As much as it was a response to the escalation of nuclear testing at the end of the 1950s, *Hiroshima mon amour* was also a response to *Typhoon over Nagasaki*, released two years earlier.[4] For non-Japanese audiences, both films evoked nuclear concerns with their titles referencing the atomic bombings while also showing reluctance to fully engage with the attacks. *Typhoon over Nagasaki* includes a brief visit to a commemorative monument but otherwise avoids the subject. *Hiroshima mon amour* devotes more time to the bombing with the incorporation of documentary footage and dramatic representations of the aftermath; however, the iconic mushroom cloud explosion was avoided, and the bomb was ultimately deemed the backdrop for the film.

This chapter uses a nuclear lens to perceive what I refer to as the nuclear background of *Hiroshima mon amour* with a focus on the relationship between space, time, and nuclear concerns. *Hiroshima mon amour* is one the most discussed films in world cinema, and yet engagement with its nuclear subject matter has been minimal.[5] In considering how nuclear subject matter impacted formal aspects of the film, I propose looking beyond the atomic bomb as a metaphor for the explosion of form, as others have done, to a more uncertain and invisible kind of narrative volatility.[6] In this view, *Hiroshima mon amour* is not simply a film of exploded fragments but one of mutated, unstable narrative form and uncertain spatiotemporality.

Resnais describes the atomic bomb as the "backdrop" for the film, and surface-level engagement with nuclear concerns can be seen in its mise-en-scène: the setting in Hiroshima, the photographs and objects destroyed by the bomb on display at the museum, the peace film within the film, and the anti-nuclear demonstration in the streets of Hiroshima. Beyond the surface, however, nuclear concerns permeate other aspects of film form—cinematography, editing, and sound—through emphasis on instability and uncertainty. This broader engagement with nuclear concerns suggests that the atomic bomb is not simply the *backdrop* for the film, a word that evokes theater and mise-en-scène, but its *background*, a word suggesting a framework or foundation and also radiation present in the environment.

The nuclear manifests specifically in the film's treatment of time. Nuclear time in *Hiroshima mon amour* can be understood as an eternal present, which is repeated in later art and experimental films dealing with nuclear concerns. From Bakhtin's concept of the chronotope, the interdependent time-space in a text, I develop a chronotope of the nuclear at work in *Hiroshima mon amour* and these later films that engage with nuclear spatiotemporality. In *Hiroshima mon amour*, the chronotope of the nuclear reveals a film suspended in an inescapable present, which is the perpetual present of cinema and of nuclear disaster.

In a broader global and environmental context, *Hiroshima mon amour* can be seen as a response not only to the atomic bombing of Hiroshima but also to thermonuclear testing in the South Pacific in the 1950s. The Castle Bravo test at Bikini Atoll in the Marshall Islands on March 1, 1954, a turning point in nuclear history, was the largest bomb ever exploded by the United States, the worst radiological disaster in US history, and an event that led to broad public backlash against atmospheric testing.[7] The explosion produced radioactive fallout over the Japanese Lucky Dragon Number Five fishing boat, leading to the acute radiation poisoning of all those aboard, of Marshallese inhabitants of nearby islands, and of US servicemen.

Japanese films such as Honda Ishirō's *Gojira / Godzilla* (1954) and Kurosawa Akira's *Ikimono no kiroku / I Live in Fear* (1955) responded to this incident and broader fears stoked by nuclear weapons and by the hydrogen bomb in particular. As a French-initiated Franco-Japanese coproduction dealing with nuclear concerns and made shortly after these films, *Hiroshima mon amour* might be seen as a gesture of solidarity with global victims of nuclear weapons and testing and particularly with those in Japan. In early correspondence regarding the film, French producers appealed to a shared Franco-Japanese conscience regarding nuclear concerns: "In Japan especially, your Government and your people terrified at the mere idea of new experiments in the South Pacific are frantically trying to stop the dreadful tests announced by the British and the qualm of consciousness felt in Japan is now spreading in many countries including France, a nation which would be helpless in case of a nuclear war."[8]

While the French state responded to nuclear anxiety by inaugurating its own testing program in 1960 with the *Gerboise bleue* plutonium bomb test in the Algerian Sahara near the town of Reggane, French New Wave cinema offered a different kind of response in grappling with what nuclear warfare meant for narrative and film form. *Hiroshima mon amour* was the only New Wave film to directly address the atomic bombing of Hiroshima with its incorporation of documentary images of the aftermath. The film also serves as a gesture of solidarity in its dramatization of the shared trauma of war, in its reflection on the incommensurability of personal trauma and national catastrophe, and in its formal treatment of nuclear anxiety.

Hiroshima mon amour marked a turning point for Franco-Japanese cultural exchange, a move into the realm of cinema at a key moment for the artform, which was itself surging through a succession of new waves around the globe.[9] As one of the first Franco-Japanese filmic coproductions and the first to present a radically new French vision of Japan, *Hiroshima mon amour* marks a cultural reopening of Japan in the postwar period a century after the country's forced opening to the West in 1854. The film's focus on nuclear issues disrupted not only narrative continuity but also the Western narrative of Japonisme. *Hiroshima mon amour* was thus as much a response to *Typhoon over Nagasaki* and its exoticizing view of Japan as it was to the tradition of Japonisme itself.

In contrast to visual art and literature, the primary artforms associated with Japonisme, cinema and its cultural institutions offered opportunities for significant collaboration and exchange between French and Japanese practitioners. While Western artists associated with Japonisme tended to take a unidirectional gaze toward Japan, the French producers of *Hiroshima mon amour* sought significant if not equal participation from their Japanese counterparts. The film was shot over the course of four weeks in France and four weeks in Japan. Japanese contributions to the project included the "best actor in Japanese cinema," a Japanese production team, and translators, local guides, and equipment in Japan. The collaboration was supported at an institutional level with Jacques Flaud, director of the Centre national de cinématographie in France, deeming the coproduction "un nouveau témoignage de l'amicale et féconde coopération cinémato-graphique franco-japonaise"[10] (a new gesture of friendly and fertile Franco-Japanese cooperation in cinema).

In her postcolonial analysis of the film, Yuko Shibata posits that the trauma of the Japanese protagonist "concerns not the destruction of Hiroshima, but rather the defeat of Japan and the loss of its colonies."[11] From this perspective, the shared Franco-Japanese trauma would be in the failure of the imperial project in French Indochina following French and Japanese cooperation in ruling the colony between 1940 and 1945. "When considering this historical reference," Shibata asks, "is it not possible to speculate that the French woman and the Japanese man might have already met in French Indochina in an allegorical sense, just as she and the German man encountered each other in the occupied Nevers?"[12] Shibata's interpretation does not preclude but rather suggests the possibility of a complex shared trauma of war that accounts for both the loss of empire and of national status.

This chapter argues that *Hiroshima mon amour* laid a founda-tion for a new French way of seeing Japan by subverting what Kojin Karatani and Sabu Kohso have called the aestheticentric framework of Japonisme and by reconfiguring film form and spatiotemporality.[13] This new French vision of Japan is a powerful one that has continued to play out in world cinema for decades, establishing *Hiroshima mon amour* as a key reference for several other films to be explored in the following chapters of this book. Central to this study is the new vision of Japan through a nuclear lens presented in *Hiroshima mon amour* and what that vision means in the context of the historical mutual cultural fascination between France and Japan.

In an interview, Resnais described his walks around Hiroshima before shooting the film: "Il ne s'agissait pas tellement de voir comment était Hiroshima, mais de savoir si Hiroshima correspondait à ce qu'on en avait écrit."[14] (It wasn't so much about seeing Hiroshima, but knowing if Hiroshima corresponded to what had been written about it.) Lui poses Elle a similar question the morning after they meet: "Qu'est-ce que c'était pour toi, Hiroshima en France?" (What was it for you, Hiroshima in France?). This interest in how others see, remember, and understand historical trauma—at a distance—is a first step in reflection on shared trauma and concerns closer to home and in the possible expression of transnational solidarity around such issues.

The Forgotten First Franco-Japanese Coproduction

If *Hiroshima mon amour* hardly needs introduction, *Typhoon over Nagasaki* is less familiar, having been more or less forgotten by critics and scholars. *Typhoon over Nagasaki* was an immediate commercial if not critical success in both Japan and France with high-profile actors from both countries. The story follows Pierre Marsac (played by Jean Marais), a Frenchman in Nagasaki who has fallen in love with the place and with Noriko (played by Kishi Keiko), a young woman who works in her family's kimono shop. When Françoise Fabre (played by Danielle Darrieux), a journalist who has a romantic history with Pierre, arrives in Japan, Pierre finds himself at the center of a love triangle. A destructive typhoon forces him to choose between Noriko and Françoise and between staying in Japan or returning to France. Pierre chooses Noriko, but she ultimately perishes in the storm. In the French version of the film Pierre stays in Japan despite her death, while in the Japanese version the final scene showing Pierre in Japan after the typhoon was cut for a more ambiguous ending.[15]

Despite the film's success at the box office in both France and Japan, François Truffaut did not hold back disappointment in his review of it: "Partant à l'aventure au Japon, Yves Ciampi revient avec le très conventionnel Typhon sur Nagasaki . . . plus les films sont chers, plus ils sont bêtes dans notre système de production, plus aussi ils sont impersonnels et anonymes."[16] (Seeking adventure in Japan, Yves Ciampi returns with the very conventional Typhoon over Nagasaki . . . in our production system the more expensive the film, the stupider it is, and also the more impersonal and anonymous it is.) Donald Richie's more tempered evaluation decades later nevertheless echoes Truffaut's: "[G]iven the opportunity to say something meaningful about East-West love affairs, [Ciampi] chose instead to have his heroine perish in a gale. . . . In this same film, the destruction of Nagasaki is only briefly touched upon. . . . A conventional story-line was allowed to triumph over all else."[17]

The well-known narrative of *Hiroshima mon amour*, on the other hand, was anything but conventional. A French actress (played by Emmanuelle Riva), referred to in the scenario as Elle (She), is in Hiroshima for work on a peace film. She has an affair with a Japanese man (played by Okada Eiji), referred to in the scenario as Lui (He), and their encounter triggers memories of her wartime relationship with an occupying German soldier. Experimental techniques are employed throughout the film such as the opening sequence of dissolves of the lovers in bed with their skin covered alternately in ashes and sweat, the use of excerpts from other documentary and narrative films about the atomic bombing of Hiroshima, and nontraditional use of flashback, which serves not to explain the narrative present but rather to be explained by it.[18] As Donald Richie points out, the flashback in early Japanese cinema was used in a similar way, "not employed to elucidate the present by reference to the past but rather, as in Japanese poetry, to suggest a parallel."[19]

The reception of *Hiroshima mon amour* was markedly different from that of *Typhoon over Nagasaki*, particularly in Japan. As Shibata and Seki Mirei have argued, *Hiroshima mon amour* was unlikely to have been seen by moviegoers in Japan where it was a box-office failure and pulled from nearly empty theaters in Tokyo after less than a week.[20] In addition to its brief theatrical release, the film's title in Japanese, *Nijūyo jikan no jōji* (A Twenty-Four-Hour Love Affair), suggested a very different story than the one promoted in France. A Japanese movie poster for the film reinforced the centrality of the love affair by featuring images of the couple and the iconic Eiffel Tower, which never actually appears in the film. For a Japanese general audience, it was thought, a film about a transnational love affair would have greater appeal, as a relationship between a French woman and a Japanese man would be more surprising than another film—and a Western one at that—about the bombing of Hiroshima.[21] Early critiques in Japan were eclipsed by the worldwide success of the film and its acclaim on the festival circuit. Still, *Hiroshima mon amour* was overshadowed in Japan by other French releases in 1959 such as Claude Chabrol's *Les cousins / The Cousins* and Louis Malle's *Les amants / The Lovers*.[22] Neither is *Hiroshima mon amour* mentioned on the National Diet Library "Modern Japan and France" webpage on encounter and exchange in cinema. A section on the French New Wave mentions only Godard's *À bout de souffle / Breathless* (1960) and stars popular in Japan such as Brigitte Bardot and Alain Delon.[23]

In France, by contrast, *Hiroshima mon amour* was celebrated by critics at the *Cahiers du cinéma* as an entirely new kind of film and possibly the most important one since the Second World War.[24] As a collaboration between novelist and playwright Marguerite Duras, who was associated with the avant-garde nouveau roman, and then-documentary filmmaker Alain Resnais, who was associated with the Left Bank group and more broadly with the *nouvelle vague*, *Hiroshima mon amour* was seen as an aesthetic achievement for its experimental, literary, and thoroughly modern qualities. It also dealt with Japan, a place French writers and artists had long looked to for inspiration and for new ways of seeing the world. As Roland Barthes would later write, this Japan was an abstract system, a fantasy.[25] The Japan envisioned in *Hiroshima mon amour*, however, ruptured the French fantasy and was all the more modern for doing so. The film was briefly in competition for the Palme d'Or at the 1959 Cannes Film Festival alongside François Truffaut's *Les quatre cents coups / The 400 Blows* and Marcel Camus's *Orfeu negro / Black Orpheus* before being withdrawn out of concern for insulting Americans.[26] In France, however, its reputation was set: *Hiroshima mon amour* was a striking film with a memorable title that would be referenced and reworked for decades to come.

Why didn't *Typhoon over Nagasaki* have the same cultural impact? In many ways, the film was better positioned to offer a new French vision of Japan, especially as the first Franco-Japanese feature-length coproduction. Scenarist Jean-Charles Tacchella had been invited for a seven-month stay in Japan to tour the country and write a scenario before the arrival of director Yves Ciampi. The film was an expensive production involving high-profile actors and the creation and destruction of an entire neighborhood during a lengthy typhoon scene.[27] And Yves Ciampi, who later married the Japanese lead Kishi Keiko, would seem to have had greater access if not insight into Japanese culture.

Typhoon over Nagasaki shows signs of savvy marketing from both French and Japanese contributors. The film promoted a Japan that foreign audiences expected to see, in line with tropes of Japonisme and with what Daisuke Miyao has called nativized Orientalism.[28] The filmmakers reworked the familiar Pierre Loti narrative of a Frenchman (also named Pierre) in Nagasaki for work who becomes temporarily involved with a local Japanese woman. Loti's *Madame Chrysanthème* may have also provided a model of sorts for Ciampi, who traveled to Nagasaki to make the film and then married Kishi. The film was shot in Technicolor, which enhanced the lush settings and exotic décor, affirming a Western fantasy of a Japan of gardens, temples, kimonos, and dolls. This vision of Japan was a dutiful, mostly uncomplicated one that had been marketed to the West since the early days of Japonisme.

Making a film in Japan presented greater challenges for Alain Resnais, who did not have a particular connection to the place, did not speak Japanese, and exchanged ideas for the film by mail with Duras in France. The Japanese lead Okada, chosen for his background in theater and his westernized features, did not speak French and thus learned the script phonetically.[29] Resnais directed a Japanese technical crew using filmic allusions, such as to Jean Cocteau's *Orphée / Orpheus* (1950), drawing on a universal visual language. Donald Richie recognizes yet another kind of universality found in *Hiroshima mon amour* in *mono no aware*:

> What the film does have, and this Resnais would probably be surprised to learn, is the elegiac *mono no aware* attitude which also happens to be the predominant Japanese attitude toward bombed cities. Like most Japanese Hiroshima films, it opens with an evocation of horror . . . and then goes into an official memoriam. . . . This is followed by a full statement of a basic *mono no aware* tenet: one forgets, it is too bad, but one forgets pain as one forgets pleasure, one cannot hold this smooth and moving life. The very fact that Alain Resnais' film is so imbued with it [*mono no aware*] more than suggests its universality.[30]

Echoing many of the film's contemporary Japanese critics, Rey Chow suggests that Resnais's vision of Hiroshima, which draws in part on documentary footage of the city after the bombing, seems prosaic in contrast to the poetic character of the scenes shot in Nevers. Yet, as Seki points out, this evaluation is contradictory as many of the same critics thought Hiroshima ought to be shown as a somber city in contrast to Nevers.[31]

Resnais seemed to balance authenticity and accuracy on the one hand with lyricism and poetry on the other. Okada's interpreter in Paris Iwasaki Tsutomu recalls Resnais asking about a more poetic pronunciation of the name of the river in Hiroshima: "Ne pourrait-on pas prononcer Ora (Aura?), au lieu de Ota?"[32] (Couldn't we pronounce it Ora (Aura?) instead of Ota?). Iwasaki told him they could not. In the film, Lui's remark about the name of the French town—"C'est un joli mot français, Nevers," (It's a pretty French word, Nevers)—is dismissed by Elle: "C'est un mot comme un autre. Comme la ville." (It's a word like any other, like the town.) In an interview soon after the release of the film, Resnais explained, "Nous avons choisi Nevers comme lieu de l'action passée parce que c'était un beau nom."[33] (We chose Nevers as the place for the past action because of its beautiful name.)

The language barrier is addressed at a couple of points in the film as well. During an early scene of the pair in the shower, Elle remarks, "Tu parles bien le français," (You speak French well) and Lui responds, "Je suis content que tu remarques enfin comme je parle bien le français." (I'm glad you finally noticed that I speak French well.) He adds, "Moi, je n'avais pas remarqué que tu ne parlais pas le japonais . . ." (I never pointed out that you do not speak Japanese . . .) In noting that Elle took it for granted that he could speak French and that he did not expect her to speak Japanese, Lui exposes her Eurocentric view. They return to the question of language when Lui reveals that he is an architect and involved in politics. "Ah, c'est pour ça que tu parles si bien le français," (Ah, so that's why you speak French so well) Elle says. They both laugh, and Lui responds ambiguously, "C'est pour ça. Pour lire la Révolution française." (That's it. To read about the French Revolution.)

Toward the end of the film, the scene at the train station again addresses the linguistic barrier and raises the question of cultural and linguistic translation. Elle walks into the station where announcements are made in Japanese, announcements that she cannot understand and seems to not even hear. For Elle, memories of Nevers return and dominate the screen. These images are accompanied by the extradiegetic Nevers musical theme. Elle remembers her late German lover, and the camera cuts from a medium close-up of her to a shot of Lui and an elderly Japanese woman sitting between them (fig. 2.1). Elle disappears from the frame, and Lui and the Japanese woman converse in Japanese. In this moment, Lui becomes a translator between two women, two generations, and two cultures unable to engage directly through verbal communication. This is the first significant Japanese dialogue in the film and the first instance during which Elle becomes the Other. In this scene Lui's multilingualism establishes his culturally elevated position, his ability to move between languages, cultures, and generations. Incidentally, this conversation in the film was not initially translated in subtitles for French audiences. Peter Cowie suggests that the subtitles were missing "as though to emphasize the impenetrable nature of the Japanese culture."[34]

Figure 2.1. Lui as translator in the train station in *Hiroshima mon amour*. Resnais, Alain, dir. *Hiroshima mon amour*. 1959; Criterion Channel.

While *Typhoon over Nagasaki* begins with the Rudyard Kipling epigraph "East is East / West is West," accepting the apparent impenetrability of the other culture and the opposition of East and West, *Hiroshima mon amour* confronts the problem of language and linguistic incomprehension that was for so long accepted and even integral to French visions of Japan in the tradition of Japonisme. Duras summarizes her approach to the subject matter—a place she had never seen and a historical trauma she had not experienced—in the introduction to the scenario: "Impossible de parler de HIROSHIMA. Tout ce qu'on peut faire c'est de parler de l'impossibilité de parler de HIROSHIMA." (Impossible to speak about HIROSHIMA. All one can do is speak about the impossibility of speaking about HIROSHIMA.)[35] In *Hiroshima mon amour*, the linguistic barrier evokes the larger obstacle of cross-cultural understanding. As Emma Wilson argues, the film shows a negotiated acceptance of what might be termed a "new ignorance," or "a refusal of resolution or meaning."[36]

This refusal of resolution or meaning can be seen in the film's demonstrated suspicion of French attempts to understand and represent Japan. The international peace movie that is being made in the film serves as a critique of its own naïve approach and objectives. When talking about her work, Elle says, "Il y a bien des films publicitaires sur le savon. Alors, à force peut-être." (There are lots of commercials for soap. Maybe by pressing the point.) Lui responds, "Oui, à force. Ici, à Hiroshima, on ne se moque pas des films sur la paix." (Yes, maybe. Here, in Hiroshima, we don't make fun of films about peace.) Elle is also certain that she has seen and understood everything about the bombing of Hiroshima after visiting a hospital and the Hiroshima Peace Memorial Museum. As she insists repeatedly, "J'ai tout vu" (I saw everything), she is challenged by Lui with the response "Tu n'as rien vu" (You saw nothing). The film's suspicion of French attempts to understand and represent Japan is suggested in Elle's multiple attempts to understand Hiroshima, which for her represents first and foremost the end of the war. The film as a whole acknowledges the limitations of understanding from archival documents and recreations as well as the broader uncertainty of nuclear knowledge.

Typhoon over Nagasaki, on the other hand, admits the superficiality of its engagement with Japanese history without appearing to challenge it. Françoise asks Pierre to accompany her to the commemorative monument in Nagasaki and explains, "Il fallait que je voie Nagasaki pour mon reportage, le côté bombe atomique, tu comprends." (I had to see Nagasaki for my report, the atomic bomb aspect, you understand.) Pierre appears indifferent to historical and cultural context but agrees to join Françoise as part of her tour around Nagasaki. Like Elle, Françoise also insists on a kind of cross-cultural mastery. She explains that she has already been to China and seen everything there: "J'ai fait toute la Chine avant de venir au Japon. *Toute* la Chine." (I did all of China before coming to Japan. *All* of China.)

If *Typhoon over Nagasaki* is another Pierre Loti story that seems to reluctantly acknowledge the atomic bombings, *Hiroshima mon amour* both reverses expected gender roles by showing a Western woman involved with a Japanese man, and directly engages with nuclear issues throughout the narrative and form of the film. Whereas Pierre in Nagasaki finds himself at a personal crossroads by the end of the film, Elle is left in Hiroshima contending with personal and political issues connected to the nuclear history of the city. The collaboration by Duras and Resnais thus tells a new kind of story, that of a French woman whose cross-cultural engagement in Japan is uncertain and challenged and whose grappling with the atomic bomb destabilizes her sense of space and time.

Hiroshima through a Nuclear Lens

Resnais said that the atomic bomb was only a backdrop for *Hiroshima mon amour*, but the vision of Hiroshima presented throughout the film reveals sustained and profound attention to nuclear issues. Representing the bomb, however, posed a problem. The image of the iconic mushroom cloud would have been too demonstrative.[37] Hiroshima, rebuilt since the bombing in 1945 and starting to offer Atomic Tours, as shown in the film, looked like a modern Japanese city (fig. 2.2). To represent a nuclear Hiroshima then, Resnais relied on reconstructions: uncredited excerpts from Japanese documentaries and feature films about the bombing, photography and drawings at the Peace Memorial Museum, shots of a peace parade, and the peace film within the film. After the opening act of the film, the narrative of *Hiroshima mon amour* turns to the couple and Elle's personal trauma in Nevers. The nuclear vision of Japan presented in *Hiroshima mon amour* is thus a cautious yet suggestive one, a nuclear vision of Japan without the nuclear, an acknowledged incompleteness.

The Japanese concept of *ma*, or the value of space between or subtraction, offers one way of understanding the centrality of the nuclear despite its limited presence in *Hiroshima mon amour*. As seen in Japanese arts such as ikebana, scroll paintings, and Japanese gardens, *ma* seems to have shaped Resnais's vision of a nuclear Hiroshima just as space, line, and perspective in ukiyo-e prints did for the French Impressionists. The aesthetic influence of *ma* differs from Barthes's interest in the concept of *mu*, or emptiness, with this kanji preceding his essay "The Unknown Language" on his relationship to Japanese in *Empire of Signs*. Melissa Croteau distinguishes the two concepts as applied to cinema by noting that while *mu* has been "represented by the static image of frozen time," *ma* "refers to structuring absences; that is, it denotes a type of interval *between* elements" and "assumes

Figure 2.2. Atomic Tours bus in *Hiroshima mon amour*. *Source*: Resnais, Alain, dir. *Hiroshima mon amour*. 1959; Criterion Channel.

movement rather than stasis, as the pause or interval is considered interstitial space to be traversed as part of a process or journey."[38]

Viewing *Hiroshima mon amour* through a nuclear lens brings into focus the film's nuclear background as well as its unstable, hybrid form. The vision of Hiroshima presented in the film—that of a city imagined on the page and reconciled with lived experience as it was filmed for the screen—is at times a poetically documentary one. And yet, the film often calls into question the authority of what might be called its documentary elements as Resnais upends conventions of both documentary and fictional modes in cinema. *Hiroshima mon amour* becomes both a narrative of destruction and an illustration of the destruction of narrative.

Although he was commissioned to make a documentary, Resnais used fiction to stimulate the spectator's imagination about the bombing of Hiroshima. However, from the start, documentary elements encroached on the film. The opening act incorporates footage from Sekigawa Hideo's *Hiroshima* (1953), Kamei Fumio's *Ikiteite yokatta / It Is Good to Live* (1956) and *Sekai wa kyofu suru / The World Is Terrified* (1957) as well as footage from Itō Sueo's *The Effects of the Atomic Bomb on Hiroshima and Nagasaki* (1946), the first documentary about the bombings and a film that "gives voice to the atomic bomb itself."[39] Echoes of Resnais's previous documentaries also resound throughout *Hiroshima mon amour*. As Emma Wilson remarks, "Resnais appears to commemorate the documentary he might have made about Hiroshima in the first fifteen minutes of *Hiroshima mon amour*. The film even sounds in places like his earlier film *Nuit et brouillard*."[40] Jean-Luc Godard saw the documentary resemblance most clearly in the subject of memory and forgetting in Resnais's documentary about the Bibliothèque nationale de France *Toute la mémoire du monde / All the Memory in the World* (1956).[41] The Hiroshima Peace Memorial Museum, like the Musée de l'homme in Paris featured in *Les statues meurent aussi / Statues also Die* (1953), is another public institution charged with creating and keeping national memory. The institution of the museum leaves visitors with the impression that in seeing artifacts they have more authentic knowledge or a greater understanding of history without necessarily considering the motivations behind the creation and framing of such displays.

Aesthetically and generically, *Hiroshima mon amour* marks a transition for Resnais from short-form documentarist to feature-length fictional filmmaker. When asked about the difficulties of moving from short to long format, Resnais remarked that *Hiroshima mon amour* is more of a long *court métrage* (short film) than a true *long métrage* (feature-length film).[42] Resnais's formal transition as a filmmaker coincided with and even encouraged a turn in the way French filmmakers would envision Japan. Resnais's model was stylistically experimental but also transnational and collaborative, representing development from French visions of Japan in the tradition of Japonisme. Additionally, the hybrid, unstable form of *Hiroshima mon amour* ushered in a new way of evoking nuclear subject matter.

The argument by some critics that Resnais's vision of Hiroshima was documentary and prosaic, especially when compared with the poetic, lyrical shots of Nevers, overlooks the poetic documentary mode, which for Bill Nichols "stress[es] the visual and acoustic rhythms, patterns, and the overall form of the film."[43] Resnais's interest in visual and acoustic rhythms is evident in the opening dissolves of the actors' body parts, in parallel tracking shots in Nevers and Hiroshima, and in the musical themes associated with each place. Sound was intimately related to form for Resnais: "Par la musique, j'ai voulu retrouver le côté opéra de manière à créer une espèce de continuité par rapport aux dialogues de Marguerite Duras."[44] (With the music, I wanted to rediscover the operatic side in order to create a sort of continuity in relation to Marguerite Duras's dialogue.)

The documentary elements that shape the film affirm Resnais's background as a documentarist while shattering conventions of traditional fiction film and creating formal instability. The documentary fragments that persist in *Hiroshima mon amour* might be said to lend the film a documentary half-life. The further in time viewers find themselves from the film as formal, theoretical, and historical analyses of the work accumulate, the better equipped they become to perceive the film's documentary elements from a critical distance, to unpack their apparent archival authority, and to understand how these elements destabilize the film and subvert its generic categorization.

The term *documentary* also poses a problem with the attendant expectations of authenticity and truth, even if access to truth comes via recreations and representations. In an early critique of the film, Bernard Pingaud writes, "Entre ces deux événements, ces deux situations, existe une différence capitale: ni l'héroïne, ni son amant japonais n'ont vécu le bombardement. Ils ne peuvent en avoir qu'une connaissance dérivée, par les traces qu'il a laissées dans la mémoire des autres."[45] (Between these two events, these two situations, exists a crucial difference: neither the heroine nor her Japanese lover experienced the bombing. They can only understand it as derived from the traces it left in others' memories.) In the film, the past of Hiroshima is shown in the form of a documentary, necessarily derived from archival material and recreations, and inevitably complete. For Pingaud, the documentary is the most fragile form of memory, showing us images as we might have seen them but did not:

> C'est en quelque sorte une vision dérivée, un substitut. Si, par surcroît, le documentaire . . . veut évoquer un événement ancien par les traces matérielles qu'il a laissées dans la mémoire publique qui constituent les monuments, les musées, les documents officiels, il ne fait que plus tragiquement ressortir l'insuffisance de cette mémoire dérivée, de cette mémoire apprise.[46]

> (In a way, it is a derived vision, a substitute. If, moreover, the documentary . . . seeks to evoke a past event by the material traces that it left in the public memory formed by monuments, museums, official documents, it only more tragically emphasizes the inadequacy of this derived memory, of this learned memory.)

How might one interpret a film that explicitly acknowledges its derived memory, as does *Hiroshima mon amour*? Elle recognizes that the traces she has seen at the museum are recreations. These traces point to their own insufficiency and to the insufficiency of the documentary mode, outlining the need for a more hybrid way of telling.

The mushroom cloud presented another challenge. As the most iconic documentary image of Hiroshima, the cloud is no longer simply a mimetic picture; as Chow argues, it becomes in the global imaginary a sign of terror.[47] Resnais decided against using the image or one if its variants, such as the much larger mushroom cloud from the Castle Bravo test (and the image Duras called for in the script), and in doing so made clear a preference for the evocative over the demonstrative. "L'événement lui-même d'Hiroshima nous ne le voyons d'ailleurs pas. Il est évoqué par quelques détails comme on fait parfois pour une description romanesque où il n'est pas besoin d'énumérer toutes les caractéristiques d'un paysage ou d'un événement pour faire prendre conscience de sa totalité."[48] (We do not see the event of Hiroshima itself. It is evoked by a few details, as something one does in a novelistic description where it is not necessary to list all of the features of a landscape or of an event to create awareness of the whole.) This suggestive presentation of the bomb is also a literary one as Resnais compares the selection of a detail for the screen with that of a novelistic description. Such literary collaboration shaped the film from the outset. Duras's screenplay, the first text she wrote for the screen, is neither a traditional novelistic adaptation nor a film script but a sort of hybrid form.

While direct reproduction of the billowing mushroom cloud was avoided, other clouds do appear in the film in archival photographs and a mural on the wall of the museum and, more abstractly, in a final shot of Hiroshima at dawn (fig. 2.3). This cloud of smoke from

Figure 2.3. Cloud at the end of *Hiroshima mon amour*. *Source*: Resnais, Alain, dir. *Hiroshima mon amour*. 1959; Criterion Channel.

a train, as called for in the shooting script, hangs over an empty street.[49] It recalls the aesthetic of *ma*, or the value of negative space, and reminds the viewer of the absence of the spectacular explosion and overly demonstrative mushroom cloud in the film. At the same time, this final cloud reaches beyond the visual register in evoking the lingering spatial and temporal effects of the bomb and the invisible threat of radioactivity in the atmosphere carried by wind.

Risk, as Ulrich Beck has suggested, is not perceptible until it is represented, which is the heart of the problem of representation in *Hiroshima mon amour*.[50] In this vision of Hiroshima through a nuclear lens, the film represents the risk of not being able to represent risk, and the opposite risk of representing it as spectacular or of creating iconic images that come to stand for risk but ultimately evacuate it of its affective dimension. *Hiroshima mon amour* represents risk as uncertainty with the unease that accompanies it. The affective response of unease is central to this new way of envisioning nuclear disaster beyond the visual register and contrasts with responses of shock, awe, or even nonchalance to the mushroom cloud.

The Chronotope of the Nuclear

With a film more interested in the everyday effects of nuclear disaster than in the nuclear spectacle, Resnais and Duras were avant-garde in their approach to the nuclear subject matter of *Hiroshima mon amour*. In this section, I turn the nuclear lens on the treatment of space and time in *Hiroshima mon amour* to bring attention to the ways in which the film addresses the lived experience of nuclear disaster. In doing so, I use the chronotope of the nuclear to describe the film's nuclear spatiotemporality and to show how *Hiroshima mon amour* established a new kind of nuclear film. The concept of *ma* is also consistent with the chronotope of the nuclear. As Croteau writes, "The crux of *ma* is that it conceives of time and space as inextricable. . . . This renders the perception of time and space mutually reliant or correlative, as they are within film, an art comprised of time moving through space, or space moving through time, depending on perspective."[51]

In terms of time, many analyses of *Hiroshima mon amour* have addressed its multiple temporalities. Bernard Pingaud's conception of time in the film is triangular with two pasts in a present that determines their evocation.[52] Robert Benayoun argues that space annihilates time in the film,[53] whereas Marie-Claire Ropars-Wuilleumier suggests that multiple temporalities offer logical continuity to the narrative and historicize Hiroshima by giving it a proper time and space.[54] Still, time in *Hiroshima mon amour* has yet to be thoroughly considered in relation to the atomic bomb. Ropars-Wuilleumier mentions the relationship between the bomb and the film's formal fragmentation, and Pingaud suggests that the film's conception of time reflects a shattering of the notion of history after the bomb. And yet, *Hiroshima mon amour* deals with not only a shattering of the notion of history but also a shift in our understanding of the present.

While the extensive scholarship on this film stops short of deeper analysis of its nuclear subject matter, a few analyses offer useful points of departure for a more sustained study of nuclear time. Gilles Deleuze understands Resnais as an architect of time who constructs his films from layers of past (*nappes de passé*), as opposed to a writer like Alain Robbe-Grillet, who wrote the scenario for Resnais's film *L'année dernière à Marienbad / Last Year at Marienbad* (1962) and who conceives of time in the form of points of present (*points de présent*).[55] A similar division can be discerned in *Hiroshima mon amour*. Duras constructs a written narrative from points of present (most evident in Elle's present-tense narration of the recollected events in Nevers), while Resnais visually conceives of the film as layers of past. However, these layers of past—the aftermath of the bombing in Hiroshima, the visits to the hospital and museum, and the events in Nevers—do not remain in the past. They contaminate the present, transforming points of present into infinite layers and rendering the present at once eternal and impossible.

Bakhtin's chronotope, a concept that looks at how certain spatiotemporal configurations shape narrative in literature, offers another way to understand the relationship between nuclear time and nuclear space in *Hiroshima mon amour*. In Bakhtin's formulation of the chronotope, time and space are considered as interdependent categories for analysis in a text, and the chronotope is "an optic for reading texts as x-rays of the forces at work in the culture system from which they spring."[56] In film studies, Vivian Sobchack has proposed the "chronotope of the film noir," arguing that the chronotope is a more specific classification tool than genre.[57] The chronotope of the nuclear I propose here brings to light the specific nuclear spatiotemporality of films such as *Hiroshima mon amour* and several that follow in its cycle. The notion of the chronotope is a useful prism through which to explore nuclear spatiotemporality as presented in *Hiroshima mon amour*. The chronotope of the nuclear brings to the fore the sense of temporal disorientation in the film's nuclear space, and it distinguishes *Hiroshima mon amour* from other types of nuclear movies that aesthetically and narratively foreground disaster.

The nuclear space of *Hiroshima mon amour* can be understood here as its nuclear background and as space that is not precisely delimited, that extends beyond national borders. Nuclear time in the film can be seen as at once static and cyclical, seemingly infinite in duration yet contaminated or imprinted on by the instant, and above all nonlinear and unstable. The chronotope of the nuclear is an outgrowth of Bakhtin's chronotope of crisis or threshold, which represents a breaking point or life-changing decision or moment of indecision, and in which "time is essentially instantaneous; it is as if it has no duration and falls out of the normal course of biographical time."[58]

A frequent companion to Bakhtin's chronotope of crisis is the ancillary time of the provincial town, "the locus for cyclical everyday time" in which "there are no events, only 'doings' that constantly repeat themselves." The ancillary time of the provincial town cannot be the primary time of the narrative because nothing happens; instead, "it often serves as a contrasting background for temporal sequences that are more charged with energy and event."[59] This type of static background can be seen in the second act of the film. After Lui and Elle awaken in the hotel room, they discuss the past: what the weather was like and how old they were on the day of the bombing of Hiroshima. Their discussion of the past, which interrupts and is then subsumed by the present, ends with a cut to another conversation in the same room. Now, Lui is on the bed. He picks up his watch and, noticing that it has stopped, holds it to his ear as if to confirm that the registration of time's passing has stopped, as if he and Elle were now stuck in an eternal present (fig. 2.4). Here, the duration of the present is punctuated by a suggestion of static time. The chronotope of the nuclear thus merges the chronotope of crisis and its ancillary time of the provincial town (which need not be restricted to the nonmetropolitan place), fuses them, and reverses their roles. In other words, with the chronotope of the nuclear, the crisis becomes the everyday, and sequences "charged with energy and event" are at

Figure 2.4. Lui checking his watch in *Hiroshima mon amour*. *Source*: Resnais, Alain, dir. *Hiroshima mon amour*. 1959; Criterion Channel.

once subsumed by cyclical, infinite duration at the same time that they contaminate and imprint it with crisis.

After Lui winds his watch, the conversation returns to the present as Elle asks, "Qu'est-ce que tu fais, toi, dans la vie?" (What do you do for a living?) The multiple meanings packed into the French present tense of *faire* (to do: habitually; as a general truth; or in this instant) haunt Elle's question as they also evoke the eternal present: the present instant as habitual present and as absolute present. Lui is not in this moment doing what he does in the habitual present, or working as an architect, because his cyclical everyday time has been interrupted by the affair. Time as registered by his watch has come to a standstill. The nuclear space, too, is evoked in Lui's response: he is an architect in a city that has been completely rebuilt after its destruction by the atomic bomb. Here, the affair, "charged with energy and event," is subsumed by the cyclical, infinite duration of daily life while also infusing that duration with event or imprinting it with the instantaneousness of crisis. While the crisis of the affair is not a nuclear crisis, the experience of time—the inescapable present—has been shaped by the nuclear subject matter because the nuclear spatiotemporality of Hiroshima has facilitated the encounter between Lui and Elle.

This sequence further exemplifies the chronotope of the nuclear with the church bells ringing in the background as Lui and Elle converse in the hotel room. The bells ring for nearly five minutes in the film: during the conversation in the hotel room; as Lui and Elle leave the room and descend the stairs; and as they continue their conversation in front of the hotel, where the ringing bells are finally drowned out by the sounds of automobiles in the street. These interminable ringing bells anticipate the church bells that Elle recalls later in the film at the café as she remembers Nevers and the death of the German soldier: "Je suis restée près de son corps toute la journée et puis toute la nuit suivante. Le lendemain matin, on est venu le ramasser et on l'a mis dans un camion. C'est dans cette nuit-là que Nevers a été libérée. Les cloches de l'église Saint-Etienne sonnaient . . . sonnaient . . ." (I stayed by his body all that day and all the following night. The next morning, they came to get him and put him in a truck. Nevers was liberated that night. The Saint-Etienne cathedral bells rang and rang.) The sustained ringing bells in Hiroshima, paralleling those in Nevers, mark thresholds: the end of an occupation, the beginning of a new day, and presumably the end of an affair as Elle refuses to see Lui again. Bakhtin's chronotope of threshold "can be combined with the motif of encounter, but its most fundamental instance is as the chronotope of *crisis* and *break* in a life."[60] The bells in the film both underscore the crisis or break in life—echoing the warning sirens heard in Hiroshima the morning of August 6, 1945, as well as the bells heard in France signaling the end of the war—and reinforce the notion of the cyclical ancillary time of the provincial town. The bells ring every day in Nevers and in Hiroshima. The nuclear event is again the background for both of these breaks or crises, as the atomic bomb marked the end of war around the globe in Nevers at the same time that it destroyed the city of Hiroshima, the background for the present-day affair in the film.

Perhaps the most salient illustration of the chronotope of the nuclear in *Hiroshima mon amour* comes from an observation that has been made many times: with the exception of an ambiguous cry that is heard but not seen during a scene in Nevers, there is no diegetic sound in the narrated past. In analyses of memory and trauma in the film, the lack of diegetic sound is often interpreted as evidence of the entrenchment of the past in the present. Here, I suggest a reading that considers the silent past in *Hiroshima mon amour* in the context of the larger nuclear spatiotemporality of the film. If the chronotope of the nuclear can be understood as the experience of the eternal present in a nuclearized space, for Elle in Hiroshima, there is effectively no past, only continuous present becoming present. Memories of the past become mute visions in the present. In the course of a single enunciation, Elle moves from remembering less well to forgetting to having forgotten: "Ah! . . . c'est horrible! . . . Je commence à moins bien me souvenir de toi . . . Je commence à t'oublier. Je tremble d'avoir oublié tant d'amour." (Oh! . . . It's horrible! I remember you less and less clearly . . . I begin to forget you. I tremble at having forgotten such love.) The nuclear present in Hiroshima renders impossible a full evocation of the past. In the chronotope of the nuclear, past is not just entrenched in the present but it becomes the present, and in doing so it disappears into the eternal present of the nuclear space of Hiroshima.

Jacques Rivette may have been the first to call *Hiroshima mon amour* "un film en boucle . . . une parenthèse dans le temps" (a film in a loop . . . a parenthesis in time).[61] It is the night that never ends, the twenty-four-hour love affair stuck in the perpetual twenty-fourth hour. In French, this twenty-four-hour parenthesis becomes a sort of *temps mort*, a time-out, or literally dead time. The chronotope of the nuclear encourages imagination not of a potential future catastrophe but of actual present disaster, of the *temps mort* inside of which we are all in a sense trapped; it encourages not the fear of future disaster but recognition of living with the present and ongoing one. As such, the chronotope of the nuclear reveals a very different kind of nuclear film, one that refrains from the reproduction of iconic and spectacular nuclear imagery in favor of exploring the effects of nuclear disaster on everyday life.

While in *Typhoon over Nagasaki* the atomic bombing is briefly referenced as a minor plot point, in *Hiroshima mon amour* the bomb destabilizes narrative, interrupts the flow of time, and serves as a new lens through which Western viewers would see Japan. It is the absent centerpiece of the film according to the aesthetic of *ma*, or the "subterranean continuity" of Duras's script, as Ropars-Wuilleumier puts it. It is used "to establish the characters" but "obliterated by the actual film . . . free[ing] the filmic continuity from any explanatory impediment, and thus mak[ing] possible the functioning of an internal discontinuity."[62] In arguing that a nuclear background serves as another sort of "subterranean continuity" for *Hiroshima mon amour*, I have also shown how the nuclear background of the film destabilizes language, form, space, and time.

This film also incites reflection on ongoing nuclear issues in Japan and in France. While *Hiroshima mon amour* may not have immediately mobilized anti-nuclear activists in France, it has carried out background work of disruption and destabilization. Since its release in 1959, the film has inspired numerous cultural productions that pay homage in some way to the original and grapple with enduring and new nuclear concerns. These works suggest the film's own half-life. From Japan, Suwa Nobuhiro's *H Story* (2001) is a remake about the impossibility of remaking the film, and his short film *A Letter from Hiroshima* (2002) explores themes of apology and remembrance from a Korean perspective. Judith Cahen and Masayasu Eguchi's *Le cœur du conflit / Kokoro no katto / The Heart of the Conflict* (2017) is another Franco-Japanese retelling of *Hiroshima mon amour* that features a French woman and Japanese man and reflects on nuclear power in both countries after the 2011 disaster at Fukushima Daiichi while also centering on a personal story. Jun Yang's short film *The Age of Guilt and Forgiveness* (2016) has a similar premise to *The Heart of the Conflict* but focuses on the broader questions of history, its construction, and its culturally inflected retellings.

The seemingly untranslatable title *Hiroshima mon amour* has also been refashioned countless times and co-opted for various purposes, from Ōshima Nagisa's 1986 absurdist film *Max mon amour* to Chantal Montellier's 2006 graphic novel *Tchernobyl mon amour* and Doris Dörrie's 2016 film *Fukushima mon amour* (*Grüße aus Fukushima* in the original German), to name but a few. Chris Marker's *Level Five* (1996) pays tribute to the film by Resnais, Marker's friend and occasional collaborator, when the protagonist Laura suggests titling her own film within the film "Okinawa mon amour." The recycling of this title and the relative failure of the Japanese version "A Twenty-Four-Hour Love Affair" suggest that the concreteness of place better lends itself to recall than does the abstraction of time.[63] But a purely spatial orientation is not enough on its own as images of place risk becoming easily digested and forgotten icons. The cinematic chronotope allows for the perception of time in space, of time shaping space, and of the specific spatiotemporal configurations that distinguish the stories we tell.

And of course, *Hiroshima mon amour* was not made in a temporal vacuum. The geopolitical and environmental stakes in France at the time of the genesis of the film were significant. While France had been capable of producing nuclear energy since 1948 when its first experimental reactor Zoé underwent chain reaction, in the mid-1950s the French Commissariat à l'énergie atomique (CEA) began work on plutonium-producing plants. As Gabrielle Hecht has written, nuclear power allowed France to restore its former sense of glory on a global stage, with radiation evoking the "radiance of France" under the Sun King Louis XIV and the "radiation" (*rayonnement*) of French culture across the colonial empire with the *mission civilisatrice*. "After the deadly explosions at Hiroshima and Nagasaki," Hecht writes, "nuclear technology became a quintessential symbol of modernity and national power."[64] In 1958, the year *Hiroshima mon amour* was written and filmed, the newly formed French Fifth Republic under President Charles de Gaulle formally announced the "decision" to build the French nuclear arsenal. And on February 13, 1960, the *Gerboise bleue* test made known to the world France's status as the fourth nuclear weapon state.

At the same time that the French state turned inward to shield its nuclear ambitions, postwar French cultural policy favorable to transnational coproductions allowed for a Franco-Japanese film like *Hiroshima mon amour* to be made. From this new transnational collaboration in cinema came a turn outward, a gesture of solidarity with Japan around the shared traumas of war, and a gaze reoriented perhaps to better perceive the nuclear situation at home in France.

3

Tu n'as rien vu

Japanese Responses
to *Hiroshima mon amour*

DESPITE ITS SUCCESS in France, *Hiroshima mon amour* was not particularly well received by popular audiences in Japan, where it closed in Tokyo theaters after only one week.[1] However, the film struck a chord with avant-garde Japanese filmmakers Ōshima Nagisa and Suwa Nobuhiro. Decades after the release of *Hiroshima mon amour*, these filmmakers offered responses to it with the films *Max mon amour* (1986) and *H Story* (2001). For Ōshima, a filmmaker associated with the Japanese New Wave and promoted by Shōchiku Studio as "the Japanese Godard," *Max mon amour* marked the near-end of a filmmaking career and a failed attempt to escape the Japanese film industry to work abroad.[2] *H Story*, which had the limited release in Japan of a *film d'auteur*, nevertheless bolstered Suwa's career as a rising international filmmaker who would spend the next two decades abroad and come to be called "le plus français des cinéastes japonais" (the most French of Japanese filmmakers).[3] Suwa, himself, cites Godard as an inspiration for shooting without a screenplay and took this approach in collaboration with French cinematographer Caroline Champetier (who also worked with Godard) in making *H Story*.[4] Like *Hiroshima mon amour*, *H Story* was met with greater fanfare in

France, where it premiered at the 2001 Cannes Film Festival in the Un Certain Regard selection before wide release later that year, than in Japan, where it had a limited release in 2003.

Hiroshima mon amour has inspired numerous artistic responses from around the world. References to the title—one of the most reworked in global cinema—cross artistic mediums, like the original text-turned-film itself. These references are not restricted to avant-garde and experimental work. The popular American family television series *The Wonder Years*, for example, featured an episode about a science class experiment with a hamster entitled "Hiroshima, Mon Frère" (1989). For smaller productions such as Véronique Bréchot's documentary *Irak mon amour* (2014) about persecuted religious minorities in Irak, referencing the title may be a marketing strategy above all. Other reworkings of the title such as Oliver Herbrich's documentary *Bikini mon amour* (1987) about fallout from the US atomic tests in the Bikini Atoll, Chantal Montellier's graphic novel *Tchernobyl mon amour* (2006) about the 1986 nuclear power plant disaster, and Doris Dörrie's film *Fukushima mon amour* (2016) about a young German woman in the Tōhoku region after the 2011 disaster remain closer to the original film's underlying nuclear theme.[5] Still other films, such as Suwa's *H Story* and films that reference and reframe *Hiroshima mon amour* after the nuclear disaster at Fukushima Daiichi (two of which are analyzed in the final chapter of this book) explicitly engage with the narrative of *Hiroshima mon amour*, its formal fragmentation, and themes of memory and trauma that accompany nuclear disaster.

In this chapter on Japanese responses to *Hiroshima mon amour*, I demonstrate the increasingly reciprocal and dialogic nature of Franco-Japanese exchange in cinema by showing how Japanese filmmakers contribute to a transnational film cycle that originated with *Hiroshima mon amour*. *Max mon amour*, *H Story*, and *A Letter from Hiroshima* serve as the principal objects of analysis to better understand how *Hiroshima mon amour* inspired their Japanese filmmakers. Ōshima's engagements with French cinema extend beyond *Max mon amour* and its titular reference to *Hiroshima mon amour*. Suwa's *H Story*, and to a certain extent his related short film *A Letter from Hiroshima* (2002), explicitly engage with *Hiroshima mon amour* and show refracted visions of Japan through a nuclear lens.

The approach of this chapter is accordingly through a refractive critical lens with analysis of the deflection that occurs in passing the story of *Hiroshima mon amour*—a text before it was a film—through the filmic medium and through different cultural filters. The refractive lens can be understood as a Deleuzian crystal that shows the splitting of time into present and past. For Deleuze, the crystal-image is the point of indiscernibility of images of past and present, or when actuality and virtuality become two faces of the same image.[6] These films that respond to and remake *Hiroshima mon amour* show multiple faces in their actuality as original films and as mirrors or virtual images that assume the actuality of *Hiroshima mon amour*.[7] If *Hiroshima mon amour* is a film about the impossibility of making a film about the atomic bombing of Hiroshima, *Max mon amour* refuses the question of Hiroshima altogether, and *H Story*, with its meditation on the impossibility of remaking a film from a more temporally removed perspective, refracts the source film. The nuclear spectacle in these films remains embedded in the background, as it was in *Hiroshima mon amour*. A refractive critical lens, then, reveals traces of nuclear spatiotemporality in these unspectacular films that recall such traces in *Hiroshima mon amour* and shows how nuclear concerns are redirected in linear narratives that still refuse conclusion as they turn to the absurd and to the meta.

Ōshima's Vision of France in *Max mon amour*

Max mon amour follows an extraordinary event in the lives of a British family living in Paris: Margaret (played by Charlotte Rampling), the bourgeois wife, is having an affair with a chimpanzee named Max. After discovering the affair and in an attempt to better understand it, Margaret's husband, Peter (played by Anthony Higgins), who is having an extramarital affair of his own, insists that Max move into the Paris apartment with them and their son Nelson. While the premise of bestiality may be what sticks in viewers' minds, Margaret's affair with Max only occurs offscreen, if it occurs at all, and the film focuses on the responses of Peter and others in their social circle to the unlikely liaison. The relationship between a white woman and a chimpanzee that threatens the white husband suggests a commentary on race in addition to the film's absurdist satire of bourgeois society.

If the title suggests a connection to *Hiroshima mon amour*, this connection is found less in the subject matter than in stylistic references and in the significance of the background and offscreen space. In his review of the film for *Cahiers du cinéma*, Charles Tesson writes, "*Max mon amour* n'est pas une phrase extraite du dialogue, c'est un dit non formulé, sans signataire, qui survole tout le film" (*Max mon amour* is not a phrase taken from the dialogue, it's an unspoken remark without a subject that covers the entire film).[8] In both films, the spectacular or sensational subject matter plays a supporting if invisible role as it is central to the story but absent from the screen. Both avant-garde films shocked audiences not with spectacular or titillating images, as in Ōshima's previous films, but with the understated treatment of such material. Beyond the title, *Max mon amour* stylistically references *Hiroshima mon amour* in a few scenes. The films also suggest a similar ecological politics. As chapter two incorporates an ecocritical reading of *Hiroshima mon amour*, the ecocritical reading of *Max mon amour* in this section draws attention to background, to the human power to kill, and to the ruthlessness with which this power is wielded against other living beings.

Both *Hiroshima mon amour* and *Max mon amour* were made by directors working outside of their home countries on cross-cultural collaborations. *Max mon amour* was released following several Franco-Japanese collaborations including Ōshima's own *Ai no korida / L'empire des sens / In the Realm of the Senses* (1976) and *Ai no bōrei / L'empire de la passion / Empire of Passion* (1978) with Argos Films, known in Japan for their coproduction of *Hiroshima mon amour*, and Chris Marker's travelogue essay film *Sans soleil* (1982) and documentary *A.K.* (1985) about the legendary director Kurosawa Akira, which was shot during the filming of *Ran* (1985). Serge Silberman, the French artistic producer of *Ran*, met with Ōshima in 1982 to discuss a possible collaboration.[9] Jean-Claude Carrière, the screenwriter known for his work with Luis Buñuel, proposed the initial idea for *Max mon amour*, which he ultimately cowrote with Ōshima.[10] Ōshima worked with the renowned French cinematographer Raoul Coutard, who had also worked with Godard on several films. While it was in this sense a true Franco-Japanese collaboration, *Max mon amour* was a fully French production and thus an opportunity for Ōshima to break out of the Japanese film industry against which he had long rebelled by refusing to make films easily understood by Japanese audiences.

After the rise of the Japanese film industry to international prominence in the 1950s and 1960s, the 1980s saw the end of the studio system in Japan, forcing even established directors such as Kurosawa and Ōshima to seek funding abroad. Foreign film imports also doubled from 200–250 per year in the postwar era to 500 per year in the 1980s, creating increased competition for Japanese filmmakers.[11] Although Ōshima had developed an independent production company to continue to make his films (which were often critical of Japan), he still ran into trouble with distribution. Notably, the controversial *In the Realm of the Senses*, Ōshima's "most openly transgressive film" that "attempts to break all the various 'public decency' laws in Japan" was censored internationally and in Japan, where it faced a lengthy trial that concluded with the judgment that it was impossible to clearly define what was considered "obscene."[12] Meanwhile, French censorship law had been relaxed in the late 1960s, which led to growth in pornographic film production in the mid-1970s and the mainstreaming of erotic films.[13] In this context, Argos Films approached Ōshima about making the hard-core art-house film. For Ōshima, it was an opportunity to subvert Japanese censorship laws and national taboos around showing explicit sex and male nudity.[14]

While often compared to Godard for their similar radical approaches to cinema, Ōshima also found inspiration over the course of his filmmaking career from Alain Resnais, and *Max mon amour* was not the first of Ōshima's films to engage with Resnais's work.[15] Ōshima and Resnais were both interested in theater, and both came to be associated with cinematic new waves at the end of the 1950s. Just as *Hiroshima mon amour* launched the French *nouvelle vague*, Ōshima's first feature film *Ai to kibō no machi / A Town of Love and Hope* (1959), released the same year, is cited as one of the first films of the Japanese New Wave.[16] The title of Ōshima's next feature film *Nihon no yoru to kiri / Night and Fog in Japan* (1960) references Resnais's earlier documentary *Nuit et brouillard / Night and Fog* (1955), the short film that led to the commissioning of *Hiroshima mon amour*.[17] And as Scott Nygren points out, "The student activists in Tokyo seen in the background of Ōshima's *Cruel Tales of Youth* [*Seishun zankoku monogatari*] (1960) are part of the same social phenomenon represented in *Hiroshima mon amour* as antiwar protestors at Hiroshima."[18] Like the young Turks at the *Cahiers du cinéma* who rejected the mainstream French *tradition de qualité* films, Ōshima rebelled against old masters of the form in Japan such as Ozu Yasujirō, Mizoguchi Kenji, and Kurosawa Akira. And like other New Wave directors, Ōshima and the overtly political stances in his films indicated a "radical rethinking of . . . society."[19]

Max mon amour is not about Japanese society, nor is it a nuclear film. Accordingly, it warrants a somewhat different approach here. Still, a critical nuclear lens brings to the fore the historical context of the film's genesis in the mid-1980s during heightened US-Soviet nuclear tensions and amid threats of total global destruction.[20] The film premiered at Cannes in 1986, several months before the October Reykjavik Summit between Soviet leader Mikhail Gorbachev and US president Ronald Reagan and the 1987 Intermediate-Range Nuclear Forces (INF) Treaty, the first agreement to reduce nuclear arms.[21] In the final decade of the Cold War, the growing threat of total anni- hilation dominated screens with dramatic made-for-TV movies such as *The Day After* (1983) and *Threads* (1984); Hollywood blockbusters such as *WarGames* (1983) and *The Terminator* (1984); nihilist punk films including *Mad Max* (1979), *Repo Man* (1984), and *Akira* (1989); and survivalist films such as the French *Malevil* (1981) and *Le dernier combat / The Last Battle* (1983).[22] The evocation of the nuclear in the title *Max mon amour* through its intertextual reference to *Hiroshima mon amour* and the glaring absence of nuclear concerns from a film conceived in a geopolitical context that would have made them difficult to ignore suggests a deliberate refusal of the nuclear as the explicit subject matter of the film. This deliberate refusal was further under- scored by the April 26, 1986, accident at the Chernobyl Nuclear Power Plant in the Soviet Union, which was making headlines in France as the worst nuclear disaster in history during the weeks leading up to the premiere of *Max mon amour* at the Cannes Film Festival.

Max mon amour shows a few parallels to *Hiroshima mon amour*. Both were avant-garde films, but if *Hiroshima mon amour* was avant- garde for its dialectic form, *Max mon amour* was more so for its restraint. The title and shocking premise of Ōshima's film are subli- mated into a conventional linear narrative with an absurd storyline, which limits the applicability of the chronotope of the nuclear and the fragmented narratives it tends to describe. Intimate relations between Margaret and Max are never shown but only suggested when Peter finds Margaret in bed with Max. The question of consumma- tion hangs unanswered over the film as a sort of absurd inversion of the missing mushroom cloud in *Hiroshima mon amour* with the same denial of spectacle and of completion. For Tesson, the plot of *Max mon amour* develops around Peter's need to avoid humiliation; however, beyond the plot, the expansive but inaccessible offscreen space is where Ōshima explores the mystery of pleasure.[23] In a more contemporary reading of the film, I argue that Ōshima also exposes a sublimated fear of miscegenation in postcolonial France as well as that of the white man's loss of status in the context of second-wave feminism and women's liberation.

Other less evident parallels between the films appear in significant stylistic echoes. In *Max mon amour*, a tracking shot following Peter in the hallway of his home recalls the tracking shot in the hospital hallway in the prologue of *Hiroshima mon amour*. As Peter advances to the bedroom to confront Margaret with Max, he is blocked from reaching them by a closed door. He speaks through the door to Margaret, who asks him to leave her and Max alone. In *Hiroshima mon amour*, the camera also stops at the door of a hospital room, and while this door is open, the camera does not enter. The patients turn away from the camera, creating a similar visual tension and refusal of the objectifying gaze. In both instances, the voyeuristic gaze is denied, and private life is shielded from view. The denial of the gaze serves as a denial of spectacle, which moves to the background or to offscreen space. With its stylistic echoes of the scene in *Hiroshima mon amour*, this scene in *Max mon amour* does not reenact but rather refracts the parallel scene in a new affective mode and through a different cultural lens.

Later in *Max mon amour*, as Peter continues his obsession with the offscreen affair, he asks Margaret if he can watch her and Max in bed. "I need to know. I need to be sure," he says. "Do you know what would relieve me? To watch you, the two of you when you make love." Margaret scoffs and tells him, "Never." Peter and Margaret then try to rekindle their own relationship, and he anxiously asks her to compare his sexual performance to that of Max, which she also refuses to do. In this scene (fig. 3.1), the framing, camera angles, and mise-en-scène recall the early scene in *Hiroshima mon amour* (fig. 3.2) when Elle watches Lui sleep in the hotel room and experiences a flashback of her former lover.

A comparison of these scenes might begin with the love triangle evoked in each, a love triangle from which a beloved being is physically absent but psychically present. The visual echo appears in the similar minimalist décor of both rooms and the similar physicality of the characters, particularly with respect to their builds and hairstyles, and the nearly identical blocking with the men in bed and the women

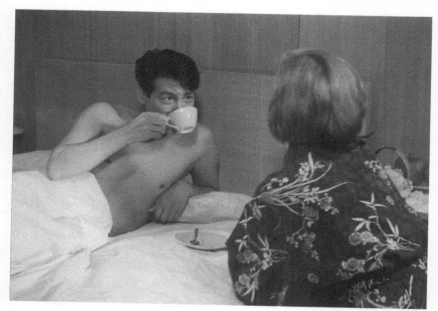

Figure 3.1. Lui and Elle in *Hiroshima mon amour*. *Source*: Resnais, Alain, dir. *Hiroshima mon amour*. 1959; Criterion Channel.

Figure 3.2. Peter and Margaret in *Max mon amour*. *Source*: Ōshima, Nagisa, dir. *Max mon amour*. 1986; Santa Monica, Calif: Lionsgate, 2007. DVD.

above them. However, while Elle looks directly at Lui and crouches to meet him at eye level, Margaret remains standing and looks at the floor as Peter looks up at her and implores her to answer his questions. The hierarchical struggle between Margaret and Peter contrasts with the more horizontal relationship between Elle and Lui. Lui is also first shown sleeping in this scene, while Peter is fully awake. Lui's twitching hand triggers the memory of Elle's German lover at the moment of his death, inserted as a brief, unexplained flashback. Lui rolls over as he wakes up, and Elle asks about his dream, reorienting herself in the hotel room in the present with Lui. While the flashback of the German lover's hand in *Hiroshima mon amour* represents a key temporal shift in triggering the more extensive flashback sequences to come, *Max mon amour* remains firmly in the present, a film without flashback. In this particular scene, Peter and Margaret are fixed in the present rather than drifting between states of consciousness and memories. These stylistic echoes of and departures from *Hiroshima mon amour* suggest that *Max mon amour* is not simply another film using a familiar formula for its title to attract an audience but rather a film that responds cinematically to *Hiroshima mon amour*.

As a response to *Hiroshima mon amour*, *Max mon amour* implicitly evokes the nuclear and calls for broader ecocritical analysis. The film opens on Peter cleaning his rifle, a Chekhovian gun that hangs over the rest of the film and is referenced in conversations prompted by Peter's jealousy. First, Peter threatens to shoot Max unless Margaret allows the chimpanzee to be brought to their apartment. Once Max is living with them, Peter asks Margaret what she would say if he asked her to choose between him and Max. She says that she loves both of them but that Peter could kill Max and get away with it because Max is an animal and her lover. She shows Peter where she keeps the key to Max's room and says, "I know you won't kill Max just to hurt me. But if you do want to kill him, you can. There's no risk for you."

Later, after Peter asks Margaret to compare his sexual performance to that of Max, he demands that Max leave their home. During their next encounter, Max takes Peter's rifle from him, an absurd reversal of the threat of being hunted and an assertion of nonhuman animal intelligence recalling "The Dawn of Man," the opening sequence of Stanley Kubrick's *2001: A Space Odyssey* (1968). The arrival of Max in the Paris apartment recalls the apes' encounter with the monolith, which Garry Leonard frames as the first step in the quest for a point of origin to reverse the dystopic outcomes of progress.[24] At the height of modern civilization, the bourgeois couple, too, seeks a reversal of the dystopic outcomes of progress (e.g., their stultified home life and unsatisfying relationships) by returning to a more primal connection. Toward the end of the film, Max is taken to the countryside and runs off into the forest. Margaret's mother, whom they are visiting and who seems to uphold Romantic values of generations past, cheerfully responds to Max's disappearance by telling the family that animals are happiest when they are free. As the family drives away without Max, gunshots can be heard in the distance, and young Nelson, worried for Max and not yet fully inculcated in the codes of modernity, asks his father why people hunt.

While *Hiroshima mon amour* is celebrated for its ambiguous ending with the open question of whether Lui and Elle will stay together or ever meet again, *Max mon amour* appears, at first glance, to end on a more conclusive note. Margaret and Peter resolve to stay together. The family sits together at the breakfast table with Max, who finally returned with them from the countryside. Peter refuses a telephone call from his mistress. But when he asks Margaret what she is thinking, she says she worries they won't be able to keep Max. The air of uncertainty quickly dissolves as she recounts a fantasy of the police coming to take Max away, another parallel to Elle's story of loss recounted in the present tense in *Hiroshima mon amour*. Just as Elle and Lui confuse modes and temporalities in the café scene, Margaret and Peter in this scene turn speculative fantasy into history: "And what did you do?" Peter asks Margaret. She responds, "Tried holding onto him. I pleaded with them, but it was no use. So I took the gun and I killed him."[25] The film ends with a close-up of Margaret, whose impassive expression turns to a more sinister smile, and then a shot from behind Max's back of the couple and Max at the table, suggesting the chimpanzee's vulnerability at the hands of human beings.

Margaret's brutal outlook in this final scene underscores the film's deeper interest in questions of domination, both in the withering patriarchal family structure and that of humans over nonhumans. With its rarified upper-class world of crystalline environments, this film exemplifies the final Deleuzian state of the crystal in the process of decomposition, "a process of decomposition which eats away at them from within and makes them dark and opaque." In this state, "*something* arrives too late," something that "could perhaps have avoided the natural decomposition and historical dismantling of the crystal-image." For Deleuze, "This something that comes too late is always the perceptual and sensual revelation of a unity of nature and man."[26] In *Max mon amour*, the threat of hunting pervades the film, and the overlooked "unity of nature and man" eats away at the crystal from within. The rifle serves as a reminder that Max could be killed at any moment. In a draft script for the film, the scene with the police coming to take Max away is not just imagined but enacted as Margaret kills Max with the rifle.[27] Like *Hiroshima mon amour*, *Max mon amour*, too, ultimately refuses closure by suggesting uncertainty around Max's safety and by troubling the apparent return to harmony for Margaret and Peter. The rifle is ultimately a red herring, a looming threat that is never carried out, a threat recalling in its absurd way that of total destruction in the nuclear age.

Suwa's Vision of Hiroshima in *H Story*

Suwa Nobuhiro's film *H Story* and the related short *A Letter from Hiroshima* show more explicit ties to *Hiroshima mon amour*. Both films were inspired by the director's encounter with the American filmmaker Robert Kramer in 1999, just months before his untimely death.[28] Kramer's father had been a United States Army doctor in Hiroshima after the atomic bombing, and when he returned home, he was hardly able to speak and shortly after committed suicide.[29] Suwa, who was born in Hiroshima in 1960 and whose grandparents were in the city at the time of the bombing, had never been able to make work about his birthplace. As he explains in *H Story*, "When I thought about making a film here, I had a lot of trouble finding a way in." Kramer and Suwa had planned to film each other in conversation about Hiroshima using two cameras. When Kramer passed away, Suwa found a new interlocutor in the film *Hiroshima mon amour*.[30] The resulting film *H Story*—conceived of as a conversation with *Hiroshima mon amour* and billed as a remake of it—is ultimately a making-of of a failed remake that foregrounds the story of its own breakdown.

Like *Hiroshima mon amour*, *H Story* is a Franco-Japanese collaboration and coproduction.[31] Béatrice Dalle plays the role of the actress Elle in *Hiroshima mon amour* and Umano Hiroaki that of the actor Lui. *H Story* also includes two new central characters: the director

Suwa, who plays himself, and the writer and musician Machida Kō, who plays a writer named Machida who is working on his own project and becomes involved with Béatrice off set. *H Story* announces its relationship to *Hiroshima mon amour* in the opening title "with reference to the motion picture *Hiroshima mon amour*." It also cites *Hiroshima mon amour* with still images (a decision that Suwa made in postproduction) and includes several reenacted scenes from *Hiroshima mon amour* juxtaposed with conversations between Suwa and Machida.[32]

The analysis here of *H Story* and its companion *A Letter from Hiroshima* as nuclear films explicitly responding to *Hiroshima mon amour* requires a different approach than that used for *Max mon amour*. While *Max mon amour* stylistically references a couple of scenes in *Hiroshima mon amour*, *H Story* and *A Letter from Hiroshima* refract the source text in both stylistic and structural ways. Most notably, the nuclear event in the background in *Hiroshima mon amour* is foregrounded in *H Story* as the film is restructured around black-and-white and color archival footage of the aftermath of the atomic bombing. My analysis of Suwa's films through a refractive lens reveals their inversions and deflections of the nuclear event as it is treated in *Hiroshima mon amour.*

The multifaceted approach of a refractive lens synthesizes stylistic inversions identified by Olivier Ammour-Mayeur with Suwa's own broader vision of his hometown Hiroshima refracted through *Hiroshima mon amour.* Ammour-Mayeur focuses on inverted tracking shots, camera angles, and montage, and argues that inversion is an adaptation strategy that Suwa uses to maintain the literary quality of *Hiroshima mon amour.* [33] Building on this stylistic analysis, I draw attention to how Suwa's films disperse the focused concern in *Hiroshima mon amour* around how to speak about the atomic bombing of Hiroshima, as heard in Elle's repeated claim "J'ai tout vu" (I saw everything) and Lui's response "Tu n'as rien vu" (You saw nothing). Through its dispersal in *H Story*, this concern neither lessens nor disappears but comes to pervade the entirety of the film, which itself does not exhaust the question but takes a new form with reflection from different facets in *A Letter from Hiroshima*.

The refractive lens makes visible the Deleuzian crystal-image, in which the actual image becomes virtual and the virtual image becomes actual, as the remake is caught in a circuit of virtual and actual, a mirror that accompanies the source film without exhausting it.[34] In Suwa's films, play with mirrors as well as the mirror relationship of the remake to the source film become instances in which actual and virtual are indivisible. A refractive lens also reveals in these films an unbounded and uncertain nuclear spatiotemporality recalling that in *Hiroshima mon amour*. This is the spatiotemporality of the chronotope of the nuclear, or the intertwined nuclear space and time that come to the fore in a film. In *Hiroshima mon amour*, the chronotope of the nuclear describes the sense of eternal present and nuclear background that haunt the film; in *H Story*, the nuclear past thickens the present but is increasingly inaccessible in an unbounded nuclear space that extends offscreen and beyond view as it evokes the enormity of the nuclear event. The refractive lens is thus a Deleuzian crystal that allows time—and more specifically the splitting of past and present—to be seen.[35]

The refractive lens also brings into focus the increasing narrative instability of *H Story* as a story about the atomic bombing of Hiroshima. While *H Story*, like *Max mon amour*, is a linear film without flashbacks, it shows an even more fundamental breakdown of narrative than seen in *Hiroshima mon amour*. This is due in part to the further collapse of distinction between fiction and nonfiction in *H Story* with actors and the director playing themselves and with the inclusion of meta-filmic elements such as the clapboard and discussion between actors and the cinematographer. The breakdown in linear narrative may also be attributed to the film's increasing temporal distance from the nuclear event, to its reliance on other films and documentary evidence to tell a story, and to its mise-en-abyme structure.

Beyond its explicit engagement with *Hiroshima mon amour*, *H Story* with its remake premise recalls another French film made a few years before: Olivier Assayas's *Irma Vep* (1996), a supposed remake of Louis Feuillade's ten-part film serial *Les Vampires* (1915–16). *Irma Vep* was also conceived of as a cross-cultural collaboration between Assayas, Claire Denis, and Atom Egoyan but became a different kind of collaboration with the Hong Kong film star Maggie Cheung playing herself opposite the *nouvelle vague* icon Jean-Pierre Léaud playing a film director.[36] Like *H Story*, *Irma Vep* is making-of film about a failed remake, and central to both films is the same question: Why remake this film?

Transnational remakes are often "dismissed within critical discourse as unoriginal, derivative and inferior to their source texts."[37] However, as self-reflexive art films that involve cross-cultural collaboration and re-envision their source texts, *H Story* and *Irma Vep* challenge the transnational remake as a one-way cultural translation of secondary importance and destabilize any vertical relationship between remake and source film.[38] Aliza Ma contends that *Irma Vep* "retains a critical and speculative distance from its collage of different subjectivities, reference points, and diegetic realities," which could just as well be said of *H Story*.[39] Both *H Story* and *Irma Vep* experiment with generic and narrative boundaries and imagine new possibilities for the collaborative transnational making-of remake. Made at the turn of the century at the dawn of the digital era and amid accelerating globalization, both films return to canonical twentieth-century films made during or about the world wars, both insist on materiality through the incorporation of archival footage, and both end with unresolved narratives, suggesting that there may be no greater narrative certainty at the start of the twenty-first century.

Although Suwa sets out to remake *Hiroshima mon amour* by following Duras's text word for word, *H Story* is a flawed crystal full of mirrors but cracked, allowing contents to escape. In this state of the crystal for Deleuze, "a new Real will come out beyond the actual and virtual."[40] *H Story* thus transcends the remake and becomes a mirror that accompanies the source film without exhausting it. Understanding *H Story* as a mirror accompanying *Hiroshima mon amour* reveals one of the ways in which this thwarted remake itself refracts the source film. The refraction in *H Story* becomes a hall of mirrors, a mise en abyme, as the remake turns into a self-reflective making-of film. The mise-en-abyme structure of *H Story*, like that of *Irma Vep*, bridges distant temporalities and creates its own narrative depth.

One of the ways in which *H Story* bridges distant temporalities and makes visible the splitting of past and present is through the incorporation of archival footage. Suwa uses the same black-and-white footage from Itō Sueo's documentary *The Effects of the Atomic Bomb on Hiroshima and Nagasaki* (1946) that Resnais used in the first part of *Hiroshima mon amour*. *H Story* also incorporates footage from the only known color reels of the immediate aftermath of the bombings. This footage was shot on 16 mm Kodachrome (and some in Technicolor) by Lieutenant Herbert Sussan and Lieutenant Colonel Daniel A. McGovern's team with the US Army in Japan after the United States dropped the atomic bombs on Hiroshima and Nagasaki. The color reels were immediately seized in 1946 and classified as top secret by

American officials, who buried the film for decades.[41] The affective power of this footage to mobilize viewers against nuclear weapons and against the American decision to use the atomic bombs would have been a primary reason for its suppression by the United States government. Half a century later, Suwa's use of the footage in *H Story* brings to the fore the horrific events of the distant past, making them feel increasingly present again.

In *Hiroshima mon amour*, the black-and-white archival footage in the first act of the film shows the devastation of Hiroshima from the atomic bomb. Resnais's use of the footage from Itō's documentary (which was also censored by the US government and not publicly released until 1967) in *Hiroshima mon amour* in the late 1950s challenged US censorship and "cast serious doubt on the 'official' narrative."[42] Yuko Shibata proposes that *Hiroshima mon amour* was itself a remake of Kamei Fumio's *Ikiteite yokatta / It Is Good to Live* (1956), which was released just after the end of the American occupation of Japan and which also incorporates footage from Itō's documentary.[43] If *Hiroshima mon amour* can be understood as a remake, then *H Story*—a remake of a remake—falls deeper into the intertextual mise en abyme and shows continued Franco-Japanese cooperation in challenging the authorized visualization of the atomic bombing. Just as *Hiroshima mon amour* reconfigures parts of *It Is Good to Live*, *H Story* restructures the use of documentary footage, incorporating it throughout and particularly toward the end of the film rather than concentrating it in the beginning as in *Hiroshima mon amour*. The incorporation of archival footage throughout *H Story*—an inversion and dispersal of its location in *Hiroshima mon amour* as a point of departure—destabilizes the apparently linear narrative of the remake.

This interspersed footage in *H Story* responds to the elusiveness of the past and the continual need for reminding. In *Hiroshima mon amour*, the past intrudes on the present throughout the film in the form of flashback sequences. In *H Story*, by contrast, the narrative is firmly rooted in the present, and the only moving images of the past come from archival footage. The central characters in *H Story* do not show the same direct connection to the past traumas of war that Elle does to her memories in flashback. The documentary footage in *H Story* effectively replaces Elle's flashback scenes in *Hiroshima mon amour* and reorients the film around the destruction of Hiroshima, the "H story." The documentary intrusions in *H Story* thus become flashbacks without a subject and without clear triggers, such as the twitching hand that triggers Elle's flashback in *Hiroshima mon amour*.

In *H Story*, these documentary flashbacks often occur at moments of frustration for Béatrice. Notably, the Itō footage follows a scene between Béatrice and Umano early in the film when Béatrice becomes tired of following the script. In *H Story*, this familiar footage with its slow pan of the devasted Hiroshima landscape after the atomic bombing is echoed by a pan of the contemporary Hiroshima skyline (fig. 3.3). Greg Hainge argues that the shot of the rebuilt Hiroshima skyline in *H Story* shows the impossibility of reconstructing emotions from forty years ago.[44] Still, this shot in color prepares for the immediacy of the color archival footage used later in *H Story*. The distant hills in the hazy background of the contemporary Hiroshima skyline are also a reminder of geological stability and of the brevity of a half century in comparison to the deep future of radioactive materials. In *H Story*, finding a way to access the past—whether through archival traces, memory, or intertextuality—becomes a central preoccupation for multiple characters in the film.

Later in the film, during an attempted reenactment of the café scene in *Hiroshima mon amour*, Béatrice becomes stuck in the present and unable to recall her memorized lines. The mise-en-scène in *H Story* follows Ammour-Mayeur's pattern of inversion with Béatrice on the right side of the frame (Elle was on the left) across the table

Figure 3.3. Contemporary Hiroshima skyline in *H Story*. *Source*: Suwa, Nobuhiro, dir. *H Story*. 2001; Hong Kong: Panorama Entertainment, 2001. DVD.

from Umano on the left side of the frame (Lui was on the right) (fig. 3.4 and fig. 3.5). While Elle's breakdown in the café because she is losing the memory of her former lover is punctuated by flashback

Figure 3.4. Café scene, *Hiroshima mon amour*. *Source*: Resnais, Alain, dir. *Hiroshima mon amour*. 1959; Criterion Channel.

Figure 3.5. Café scene, *H Story*. *Source*: Suwa, Nobuhiro, dir. *H Story*. 2001; Hong Kong: Panorama Entertainment, 2001. DVD.

sequences, Béatrice's parallel breakdown in the café when she cannot remember her lines leaves her firmly rooted in the present. For this film, Suwa worked without a script and without clearly defined characters, leaving much to chance and inspiration in the moment. He left a camera running on set at all times.[45] When Suwa asks in the film about finishing the scene, Béatrice identifies the inaccessibility of the past as the problem, explaining through a translator, "il manque trop de choses. . . . Par exemple, dans le film d'Alain Resnais, au moment du texte difficile, il y a toutes sortes d'images documentaires. Mais il n'y en a pas dans ce film-ci" (too much is missing. . . . For example, in Alain Resnais's film, at the difficult moment in the text, there are all sorts of documentary images. But there are none in this film). Béatrice as the actress in the film within the film and the actual actress Dalle's frustration with the script of *H Story* and its missing elements merge in this moment in the film within the film.[46] However, as actual merges with virtual, a crack appears. This becomes a Deleuzian moment from which a new Real emerges beyond actual and virtual, a moment when "[e]verything happens as if the circuit served to try out roles, as if roles were being tried in it until the right one were found, the one with which we escape to enter a clarified reality."[47] This scene in particular is not only an inversion of the corresponding café scene in *Hiroshima mon amour* but also a turning point in *H Story*: the remake as reflection assumes its independence from *Hiroshima mon amour*, passing from virtual remake to a new Real and revealing the narrative instability of *H Story* as a remake and, moreover, as a story about the atomic bombing of Hiroshima.

Suwa's own uncertainty about *H Story* is reflected in the changing project, which collapses as it evolves into a film independent of the remake. The concept of the mirror, with the remake as a mirror accompanying the source film, is central in upholding the tension between collapse and evolution. A film that was intended to be a conversation between Kramer and Suwa using two cameras becomes a hybrid making-of-remake punctuated by conversations between Suwa and Machida about their own attempts to access the past for their creative work. These conversations are shot with a single camera on Machida. The back of Suwa's head is visible at the side of the frame, and occasionally Suwa's face can be seen in the mirror behind Machida, but Suwa appears ambivalent about his own position on or offscreen in the film.

Machida becomes in these scenes a mirror for Suwa and his own project. Machida tells Suwa about his project on Kobori Rintaro, an artist from Hiroshima who experienced the bombing: "I've read his book and seen his work . . . and I felt that it was very personal, based on his experience of the bombing. I thought that by going to Hiroshima, I could perhaps feel for myself certain things. That's why I came here." Machida's uncertainty that he "could perhaps feel . . . certain things" mirrors Suwa's own uncertain feelings about his hometown, contrasts with Elle's certainty in *Hiroshima mon amour* that she saw everything ("J'ai tout vu") and introduces a greater uncertainty about accessing an increasingly distant past. Suwa's response to this, "So you're wandering around, visiting . . . ," underscores the uncertainty of Machida's seemingly aimless project and the difficulty of accessing the past while also describing Suwa's own process in making *H Story* as he wanders between sources of inspiration.

Yet Machida is not a perfect mirror for Suwa but rather a refraction of the director. While Machida admits that he does not have "precise goals" for his project on Kobori, Suwa does begin with concrete plans for his film: first the conversation with Kramer, then the remake of *Hiroshima mon amour*. Both plans rely on outside perspectives to offer Suwa a way in to making a film about Hiroshima. As he explains to Machida, it was Duras's text that particularly preoccupied him: "But in actual fact, from the moment I encountered this text, I couldn't get it out of my head. Every time I searched for new ideas, I couldn't remove it from inside myself." While Suwa can't get Duras's text out of his head, his remake is undermined by Béatrice's inability to remember the same text. She ultimately rejects the word-for-word remake because she finds that it is missing too much.

H Story assumes its independence from *Hiroshima mon amour* as a flawed crystal. A new Real emerges from the indiscernible actual and virtual of the crystal-image as Machida takes over the role of Lui in the extradiegetic diegetic world within the film, or the world in *H Story* that is outside of the remake. After the remake breaks down, Machida takes Béatrice to the Hiroshima City Museum of Contemporary Art, where they take a guided tour in Japanese. The guide Ms. Suhama tells them about the museum's collection of Hiroshima-themed work and recently commissioned pieces by fifty artists for the 50th anniversary of the bombing. The abstract artworks offer other ways of knowing about the atomic bombing of Hiroshima. Machida is interested in how artists who were affected by the bombing responded to it in their work. Béatrice, who does not understand Japanese, moves listlessly through the room without stopping to reflect on the artwork. As Machida and Suhama discuss the artists' fascination with fire after the bombing, Béatrice leaves the room, and her footsteps can be heard as she exits the museum, foregrounding her offscreen presence.

The museum becomes a stage for the breakdown of interaction between Béatrice and Machida, which is due, in part, to linguistic and cultural barriers.[48] Not only does Béatrice not understand what the guide is saying, but she also appears uninterested in engaging with the art, which demands cultural if not linguistic proficiency. Earlier in the film, she spoke of her experience at the Hiroshima Peace Memorial Museum as one of shame because the exhibit prompted her to think about her personal life. This trip to the museum with Machida may have represented for Béatrice an opportunity for a more engaged experience, but she once again retreats to herself, much as Elle in *Hiroshima mon amour* retreats to her traumatic wartime memories when confronted with the atrocities of the atomic bombing. The Museum of Contemporary Art and its Hiroshima-themed work refract the historical artifacts at the Hiroshima Peace Memorial Museum that Elle visits in *Hiroshima mon amour* through aesthetic abstraction. While Elle insists that she saw everything during multiple trips to the museum, Béatrice leaves the museum shortly after arriving and without having spent time with the artwork responding to the atomic bombing.

The substitution of the Hiroshima City Museum of Contemporary Art in *H Story* for the Hiroshima Peace Memorial Museum introduces a new aesthetic epistemology. In *Hiroshima mon amour*, the Peace Memorial Museum offers the illusion of understanding to a foreign visitor (or to viewers of the film) who has encountered its artifacts, documentary photography, and scientific explanations. In *H Story*, the Museum of Contemporary Art engages with the history of the bombing through abstract artistic responses to it, responses such as a large metal sculpture that extends beyond the space of the frame, refusing both figurative signification and full apprehension by the museum visitors and by viewers of the film. Like Béatrice's offscreen footsteps, the extension of the sculpture beyond the frame also evokes offscreen space and refuses the viewer's full apprehension.

When Béatrice recounts her visit to the Peace Memorial Museum and the shame she felt for thinking of her personal life, she also describes finding the archival documents, testimony, and artifacts—such as a broken watch—incredibly moving: "Et la moindre photo, vraie photo, image de reportage, une personne qui peut témoigner, tu vois, des choses comme ça, sont tellement plus émouvantes que—ou des détails aussi, même il y a un détail d'une montre qui est cassée, tu sais, ça c'est terrible, ça c'est terrible je trouve" (And the slightest photo, true photo, image from a news report, a witness, you see, things like that, are much more moving than—or details too, even the detail of a broken watch, you know, that is terrible, I find that terrible). As she describes the details she finds moving—photos, newsreels, witness testimony—she does not finish the comparison, and her silence allows space for summoning the missing image of terror and total destruction: the mushroom cloud. She then interrupts herself with the memory of another small detail that troubles her above all: a broken watch and the temporal rupture by the bomb it represents. This unmooring in time is reinforced in other details in the film as well: the color archival footage of the iconic clock stopped at 8:15, the time of the atomic blast on August 6, 1945, and Béatrice's own watch with an obscured face (fig. 3.6), which recalls Lui's stopped watch in *Hiroshima mon amour*. These broken and illegible measures of time continue to evoke the eternal nuclear present of the chronotope of the nuclear and contribute to a new nuclear iconography that emerges from the refusal to reproduce the nuclear spectacle.

Figure 3.6. Béatrice's illegible watch, *H Story*. *Source*: Suwa, Nobuhiro, dir. *H Story*. 2001; Hong Kong: Panorama Entertainment, 2001. DVD.

The importance of offscreen space is underscored again at the end of *H Story* when Béatrice and Machida visit ruins that recall the atomic bombing. In this scene, the characters stand at the threshold of a skeleton brick building (fig. 3.7). Béatrice walks from the entryway behind the ruins and reappears in the open spaces where windows would have been. Neither Béatrice nor Machida enters the structure, the interior of which is strewn with rocks and debris with greenery growing in the interstices. The tight focus on the dilapidated building creates visual tension and reinforces the presence of offscreen space, of what cannot be directly perceived, as Béatrice walks behind the building and as the city in the distance can be glimpsed through the open space of the windows.

The structural displacement of the museum and ruins sequences from the opening of *Hiroshima mon amour* to the second half of *H Story* follows the pattern of inversion that Ammour-Mayeur identifies, shifting these institutions and monuments of collective public memory from the first part of the source film to the interior and ending of the remake. If the museum and ruins sequences from which Elle and Lui are absent contextualize the love affair in *Hiroshima mon amour*, they appear in *H Story* as key sites of interaction for Béatrice and Machida, as a past that must be engaged with in order to continue to be remembered, as crystal-images in which past and present, virtual

Figure 3.7. Béatrice and Machida in the ruins, *H Story*. *Source*: Suwa, Nobuhiro, dir. *H Story*. 2001; Hong Kong: Panorama Entertainment, 2001. DVD.

and actual, are two sides of the same image. Structural inversion brings new meaning to these sequences in *H Story*, underscoring the role of the remake as a mirror that accompanies and refracts the source text.

The final sequence in the ruins also insists on a connection between offscreen space and the past. Both are beyond the immediate frame and not directly perceptible but rather evoked as attention is drawn to what cannot be seen. After an establishing shot of Béatrice and Machida in the ruins of a brick building that recalls the iconic Atomic Bomb Dome, Béatrice wanders outside the frame. As the camera pans away from Machida, Béatrice reappears briefly framed by window openings in the walls. Like the abstract painting and sculpture at the Museum of Contemporary Art, the ruins serve as a reminder of the city's nuclear history while foreclosing the possibility of direct experience of it. As a resident of Hiroshima whose grandparents experienced the bombing, Suwa would seem to have more direct access to the event; however, like Machida and Béatrice, Suwa struggles with the atomic bombing as the central subject of his work. Instead, he mobilizes inaccessible but evocative offscreen space and time past for their potential to offer different angles of approach. In decentering the nuclear spectacle and foregrounding nuclear space and time, Suwa adopts a similar approach to that of Duras and Resnais in *Hiroshima mon amour*.

The offscreen space and distant perspectives Suwa makes use of in his work suggest the unboundedness of nuclear space and the trauma of the atomic bombing that extends beyond the boundaries of the city. Temporally, the consequences of the atomic bombing on August 6, 1945, extend well beyond that date, particularly for hibakusha and their descendants experiencing effects of radiation for generations to come. The temporal continuity of nuclear disaster is evoked in the mise-en-abyme structure of *H Story*, a temporal abyss that both maintains connections to the past—the atomic bombing fifty-five years earlier and the release of *Hiroshima mon amour* over forty years prior—and reveals how increasingly tenuous those connections are. Suwa explained in an interview, "Finally, I think that I made a phantom film, against the oppression of History and against the necessity of forgetting it."[49]

The closing credits of *H Story* feature black text on a white background, offering yet another inversion of the credits in white against a black background in *Hiroshima mon amour*. This final inversion of light and dark recalls the filmic negative and echoes the white flashes integrated throughout *H Story* that evoke the blinding white flash of the atomic explosion. Suwa's formal inversions and refractions in *H Story* create crystal-images in which actual and virtual crystallize, crack, and allow for a new Real to emerge. The film resists the fossilization of the nuclear event and maintains its uncertainty in a way that a word-for-word remake of *Hiroshima mon amour*, an exhaustion of the source text, would not.

Another Refraction of *Hiroshima mon amour*

Suwa's subsequent film *A Letter from Hiroshima* (2002), a prequel of sorts to *H Story*, is another story of an unfinished film about the atomic bombing of Hiroshima. The short film was released the year after *H Story* as part of the compilation film *After War*, financed by the Jeonju Digital Project of the Jeonju International Film Festival in South Korea.[50] This film also developed from Suwa's correspondence with Robert Kramer. However, the titular letter from Hiroshima is not Kramer's letter to Suwa in Hiroshima but a letter written to Suwa from a Korean actress in the film who is in Hiroshima at Suwa's invitation. While Kramer's letter is incorporated into voiceover narration in *A Letter from Hiroshima*, the film centers on the Korean woman's experience of Hiroshima, which she articulates in her letter to Suwa. While neither a remake of *Hiroshima mon amour* nor of *H Story*, *A Letter from Hiroshima* can be seen as yet another refraction of the nuclear event and its telling.

Like *H Story*, *A Letter from Hiroshima* features Suwa as himself, a director from Hiroshima who intends to make a film about the atomic bombing of the city. *Hiroshima mon amour* is no longer the entry point or interlocutor for Suwa in this short film; instead, he has invited the Korean actress Kim Ho-jung to Hiroshima to write a film with him. However, once Kim arrives in the city Suwa cannot bring himself to meet with her, so he sends Lee Faji, a young Korean national who grew up in Hiroshima, in his place. Conversations between Kim and Lee about the atomic bombing of Hiroshima, how they learned about it, and what it has meant to them—particularly in the context of Japan's historical colonization of Korea—are juxtaposed with scenes of Suwa reflecting on the film he intends to make (and is in the process of making) and sharing memories with his young son. After a week in Hiroshima without contact from Suwa, Kim sends him a letter thanking him for the invitation and telling him that she will return to Korea. It is only as she is leaving her hotel room in the final sequence of the film that Suwa and his son arrive to meet her. They speak to each other in English in the hallway, and Suwa apologizes for his absence, explaining that he was confused but is now okay and that he hopes she will stay in Hiroshima.

A Letter from Hiroshima, like H Story, is marked by inversion. First, there is the inversion of the short and feature-length film, as shorts often precede related features and serve as opportunities to work out thematic and stylistic concerns and to attract financial support. Premiering the year after H Story, A Letter from Hiroshima shares with the feature the pretext of Robert Kramer's letter and preoccupation with the memory of the atomic bombing. However, A Letter from Hiroshima is neither a remake of nor a blueprint for H Story but another refraction of its subject matter, an approach from a different cultural and historical angle to the problem of making a film about the atomic bombing of Hiroshima. Instead of responding to Hiroshima mon amour, A Letter from Hiroshima represents another turn of the crystal, recasting the memory of the bombing through the perspectives of two Korean women. While H Story and A Letter from Hiroshima are not paired films and were neither released nor distributed together, they can be productively read in conversation to show yet another refraction of the story of the atomic bombing of Hiroshima.[51]

Formal inversion in A Letter from Hiroshima appears most clearly in discussions between the Korean women that mirror those between Suwa and Machida in H Story (fig. 3.8 and fig. 3.9). The mise-en-scène of both scenes is nearly identical with the settings in small rooms and actors seated beside a window and across from one another. Both scenes rely on natural light from the window to illuminate the room, and both include the same wall sconces and a mirror behind one of the speakers. The mirror behind Machida in H Story, who is seated on the left side of the frame, shows Suwa's face, which is partly obscured by Machida for much of the scene. Two photographs are affixed to the mirror and appear in clear focus: in the bottom left corner, a still of Elle and Lui in Hiroshima mon amour; several inches above, a photograph of Suwa and Kramer. As Suwa and Machida discuss their motivations for making work about

Figure 3.8. Machida and Suwa, *H Story*. *Source*: Suwa, Nobuhiro, dir. *H Story*. 2001; Hong Kong: Panorama Entertainment, 2001. DVD.

Figure 3.9. Lee and Kim, *A Letter from Hiroshima*. *Source*: Suwa, Nobuhiro, dir. *A Letter from Hiroshima*. 2002; YouTube.

Hiroshima, the photographs recall two sources of inspiration for Suwa for the film he is making. When Machida's head eclipses Suwa's face in the mirror, Machida becomes a mirror for Suwa. Machida's own struggle to make work about Hiroshima for reasons that he cannot yet articulate mirrors Suwa's struggle with his film.

In *A Letter from Hiroshima*, the mirror behind Kim, seated on the right side of the frame, shows Lee unobscured. There are no photographs in this mirror, and the focus remains on the two women. This clear focus is enhanced by warm light from the window reflected by Kim's off-white sweater. (By contrast, a softer light on Machida is absorbed by his dark clothing.) The inversion in *A Letter from Hiroshima* from the partly obscured and dimly lit conversation between the Japanese men in *H Story* to the brighter, clearer conversation between the Korean women in *A Letter from Hiroshima*, as well as the shift of the camera from the left to the right side, underscores the change in perspective from one film to the other. The Korean women's experiences of history differ from those of the Japanese men and allow for more open and transparent discussion of the atomic bombing of Hiroshima.

The replacement of the Japanese men in *H Story* with Korean women in *A Letter from Hiroshima* recasts the atomic bombing and history of Hiroshima through a refractive lens. If Suwa's preoccupation in *H Story* was remaking *Hiroshima mon amour* and the impossibility of understanding what people felt forty years ago, it is redirected in *A Letter from Hiroshima* to different generational and cultural responses to the bombing itself. In both films, Suwa questions his own motivation for making a film about Hiroshima, undermining any sort of conclusion these films might offer. In *A Letter from Hiroshima*, Suwa's shift to Korean perspectives acknowledges the Japanese colonization of Korea. This acknowledgment is significant as stories of Korean victims of the atomic bombing of Hiroshima—victims who Lisa Yoneyama cites "comprised between 10 and 20 percent of those killed immediately in the Hiroshima bombing"—rarely figured in official Japanese accounts at the end of the twentieth century.[52] In *The Wages of Guilt: Memories of War in Germany and in Japan* published a few years prior to *H Story* and *A Letter from Hiroshima*, Ian Buruma points out how the city's "status as the exclusive site of Japanese victimhood" excludes Korean victims, many of whom were forced laborers in Japan during the war and suffered in the atomic bombing.[53] This attitude was concretized in the Monument in Memory of the Korean Victims of the A-bomb erected in 1970 by the South Korean residents' association in Japan. The monument was "[t]ucked away in a corner, outside the [Peace Memorial] park" until it was relocated inside the park in 1999 after pressure from various groups.[54] Yoneyama underscores the importance of the monument's location in determining its meaning and explains that its isolation from the official commemorative site and the controversies over its relocation are "symptomatic of the subaltern status of Korean residents in Japan" and of the Japanese government's resistance to taking responsibility for its colonization and invasion of Korea.[55]

Despite the relocation of the Korean monument just a few years before Suwa's films were made, the monument does not feature in *A Letter from Hiroshima* or in Kim's account of her visit to museum. Her visit to the Hiroshima Peace Memorial Museum does, however, mark a return to the institution foregrounded in *Hiroshima mon amour* and refracted through the Hiroshima City Museum of Contemporary Art in *H Story*. The return to the Hiroshima Peace Memorial Museum in *A Letter from Hiroshima* at the start of the twenty-first century with the approach of the sixtieth anniversary of the atomic bombing of Hiroshima reveals a room filled with Western visitors. Footage of the Enola Gay aircraft that dropped the bomb code-named Little Boy replays on television screens above visitors' heads, beyond eye level with voiceover explaining, "Here in this place it is always August 6, 1945." Suwa's camera lingers on a photograph on the wall of a severely wounded victim of the bomb. During a nine-second fixed shot, three visitors walk past the eye-level photograph without stopping to look at it, recalling Béatrice's hurried visit to the Museum of Contemporary Art in *H Story*. In *A Letter from Hiroshima*, the focus on intergenerational memory and the present-day meaning of Hiroshima to people such as visitors at the museum destabilizes the seemingly eternal present of nuclear disaster as seen in the chronotope of the nuclear. In the museum, it may always be August 6, 1945, but do the hurried, uncomfortable visitors experience this sense of the nuclear present? The Hiroshima Peace Memorial Museum in *Hiroshima mon amour*—a spacious building full of evocative artifacts such as victims' hair under glass cases and abstract objects such as a disco ball representation of the bomb—becomes in the early twenty-first century a crowded space with virtual images that force a more explicit confrontation with the horrors of the atomic bomb attack as it recedes into history.

The two letters in *A Letter from Hiroshima* are introduced toward the end of the film. First, Suwa reads the letter from Kramer in voiceover, and then Kim reads her letter to Suwa, also in voiceover. She thanks him for the chance to go to Hiroshima to better understand the city's history, and she writes of her position outside of Japan and the different perspective it affords:

> You have inherited your ancestors' suffering. I was born in Korea. Indirectly, I know the pain my ancestors felt under Japanese colonial rule. So many lives were lost in Hiroshima. Soon afterwards, our country was freed from yours. Isn't it an ironic circumstance of history? Now I have seen another Hiroshima, a new city with a painful past. We live at the edge of history with pain in our hearts. Our lives seem so small. But this trip has made me feel the weight and dignity of every single "small" life.

Kim's distance from the pain of the war allows her a perspective on Hiroshima that is not dominated by the mushroom cloud, perhaps a symbol of liberation for her ancestors. She connects her personal, indirect knowledge of the suffering of her ancestors under Japanese colonial rule to the painful history of Hiroshima and the younger generation's indirect experience of it while living in the "new city." Kim's indirect experience of the historical trauma recalls that of Elle in *Hiroshima mon amour*; and yet, with her position "at the edge of history" Kim has a wider perspective on the event than Elle did and a recognition of the "weight and dignity of every single 'small' life," a perspective that Elle may have sought but did not attain despite her claim to have seen everything in Hiroshima. Kim's letter is also refracted through Lee's translation of it into Japanese for Suwa. And it is the indirect reception of the letter that prompts Suwa to visit Kim at the hotel to begin work on the film that they will write together.

The multiple inversions, refractions, and translations that occur from *Hiroshima mon amour* to *H Story* and *A Letter from Hiroshima* lead to the latter's increasingly tenuous relationship to the former. Suwa's films show a preoccupation with the question of how to pass along history to future generations. In *A Letter from Hiroshima*, the presence of Suwa's son and Kramer's letter about his father, who never spoke of his time in Hiroshima after the bombing, underscore this concern. Kramer's letter to Suwa shows his own hope for the younger generation: "To tell you the truth, I'm only interested in young people living in the past's shadow, living here and now in an uncertain and troubled Japan, a place that is not as we think. Hiroshima's youth. Follow them in life, work with them like actors. [. . .] Hiroshima is their city. They don't say much to us. But they lead us to what needs to be seen."

A Letter from Hiroshima is neither a remake nor a revision of *H Story* but a refraction of the nuclear event through multiple perspectives: Kramer's, Suwa's, and then Kim's. While *H Story* concludes in ruins and in a certain resignation to the failed film it was supposed to be, *A Letter from Hiroshima* ends with possibility. Possibility begins in Kramer's final line in the letter to Suwa: "Tell me what you understand of what I write, where you have problems, and what your needs and expectations are." Kim's letter expresses what she has come to understand about Hiroshima during her time there and gives new life to Suwa's project. While the film Suwa may have initially thought he was making remains unmade, *H Story* and *A Letter from Hiroshima* offer new and unexpected perspectives on Suwa's concerns. These films enter into conversation with one another, with *Hiroshima mon amour*, and with artists and filmmakers like Robert Kramer and Kobori Rintaro who continue to engage with the eternal nuclear present. Suwa's own memories and understanding of Hiroshima are refracted through these different lenses and ultimately through the crystal of cinema itself as Suwa contends that cinema is not about illustrating a script but about capturing a common experience. These films illustrate his understanding of cinema as a form of artistic and human investigation on film.[56]

The three responses to *Hiroshima mon amour* explored in this chapter—*Max mon amour*, a Franco-American coproduction with a Japanese director; *H Story*, a Japanese film based on a French script and made with the French cinematographer Caroline Champetier and actress Béatrice Dalle; and *A Letter from Hiroshima*, a Japanese-Korean collaboration and part of a transnational compilation film—suggest not only the continued importance of *Hiroshima mon amour* in global art cinema decades after its release but also its significance for transnational cinema as one of the first feature-length Franco-Japanese coproductions. In Mette Hjort's typology of transnationalisms, *affinitive transnationalism* describes relationships based on ethnic, linguistic, and cultural affinity or shared commitments and concerns. Hjort's distinction serves as a reminder that ongoing cross-cultural collaboration in cinema can be based on more than opportunistic financial incentives but also around "the discovery of features of other national contexts that are deemed to be potentially relevant to key problems experienced within a home context."[57] Two such problems for France and Japan are those of wartime memory and of nuclear risk. These transnational coproductions, I argue, extend the global reach of French and Japanese cinemas and underscore the soft power of these industries in shaping alternative narratives to those put forth by the US government or by Hollywood.

Across the three films analyzed in this chapter and most evidently in *H Story* and *A Letter from Hiroshima*, the chronotope of the nuclear reveals a fading eternal nuclear present in relationship to an increasingly distant nuclear past and a need for continual reminders as well as different angles of approach. The specter of the nuclear in these films extends beyond the frame to offscreen space, seemingly expanding the already unbounded nuclear space that served as the background of *Hiroshima mon amour*. While these films show the increasingly global nature of nuclear concerns, they also underscore with their different cultural angles of approach the specificity of sites and cultures of impact beyond nuclear targets and moments of explosion.

Things That Quicken the Heart

Sensing the Nuclear in Chris Marker's Japan

Je reviens d'Hokkaido, l'île du nord. Les Japonais riches et pressés prennent l'avion, les autres prennent le ferry. L'attente, l'immobilité, le sommeil morcelé, tout ça curieusement me renvoie à une guerre passée ou future: trains de nuit, fins d'alerte, abris atomiques, de petits fragments de guerre enchâssés dans la vie courante.

(I'm just back from Hokkaido, the northern island. Rich and hurried Japanese take the plane, others take the ferry: waiting, immobility, snatches of sleep. Curiously all of that makes me think of a past or future war: night trains, air raids, fallout shelters, small fragments of war enshrined in everyday life.)

—Sandor Krasna, *Sans soleil*

Il faut prévenir le spectateur contre l'obsession de "comprendre" à tout prix, comme s'il n'y avait à chaque film qu'une seule réponse.

(The viewer must be warned against the obsession of "understanding" at any cost, as if there were only one response to every film.)

—Chris Marker

∾

I N SEVERAL OF CHRIS MARKER'S films, there is a miss-it-if-you-blink
    moment when the nuclear specter comes to the fore. In *Description
d'un combat / Description of a Struggle* (1960), Marker's essay portrait
of Israel twelve years after its foundation, this moment is the film's
atomic nucleus: exactly halfway through the film, at twenty-seven
minutes, Marker describes in voiceover narration an image of the
still and silent Dead Sea as "a stretch of lunar landscape embedded
into the earth . . . the site, according to a Russian, of the first atomic
blast, on a Judean Hiroshima named Sodom." In *La Jetée* (1962), the
postapocalyptic science-fiction photo-film of a Paris destroyed in a
third world war, this moment is the sudden transition from photographic stills to moving images, a climactic moment in the narrative,
at precisely nineteen minutes and forty-five seconds, a reference to
the year of the first atomic bomb explosions. In the short film *2084*
(1984), a synthesized image of a red outline of a mushroom cloud
appears on a screen in the background as a narrator mentions the
possibility of a nuclear explosion as an ultimate conclusion to the labor
crisis. The nuclear fragments enshrined in these films need not be
interpreted as keys to understanding the films themselves but rather
as traces of a broader nuclear anxiety, or as "things that quicken the
heart" in the words of Japanese court poet Sei Shōnagon as cited in
Marker's *Sans soleil* (1982). The nuclear fragments, like radioactivity
itself, may not be visible and thus their detection, I argue, requires
different modes of sensory perception.

     In 1960, the year Marker began embedding nuclear fragments in
his films, France became the world's fourth nuclear weapons state. In
his films since that time, Marker seemed to be taking the temperature
of nuclear anxiety in France and around the globe.[1] A filmmaker better
known for his penchant for travel, Marker made films on five continents and several islands, shooting in as far-flung locations as Japan,
China, North Korea, Vietnam, the Soviet Union, Israel, Chile, Cuba,
Finland, Iceland, Cape Verde, and Guinea Bissau. In the photo-film
Si j'avais quatre dromadaires / If I Had Four Dromedaries (1966), still
images are apparently shown from twenty-six different countries.[2] In
his creative work, Marker returned to some places more than others.
Most notable was his sustained interest in Japan.

     This chapter offers an extended study of the recurrence of Japan
in Marker's work, a recurrence many have previously noted.[3] To the
work of scholars such as Grace An and Chiba Fumio I add detail and

analysis of the evolving nuclear vision of Japan across Marker's work. His first recorded vision of Japan was supposed to be a documentary about the 1964 Summer Olympics in Tokyo. Ichikawa Kon ended up making the documentary *Tōkyō orinpikku / Tokyo Olympiad* (1965), and Marker, like Resnais, turned his commissioned documentary into the more experimental *Le mystère Koumiko / The Koumiko Mystery* (1965), a personal essay film and portrait of his guide in Tokyo. In *The Koumiko Mystery*, the Olympic Games fade into the background as an offscreen Marker interviews Koumiko about everyday life in Tokyo and metaphysical concerns. While the film might "dall[y] with the clichés of the mysterious feminine Orient,"[4] Koumiko also resists easy categorization, commenting, for example, that she does not find her face to be totally Japanese. For Chris Darke, the film was also a sketch for the more fully realized portrait of Japan in *Sans soleil*.[5]

The short photo-film *La Jetée*, made on the eve of the Cuban Missile Crisis and dealing with time travel after a nuclear apocalypse, is the most explicitly nuclear and the least evidently Japanese film analyzed in this chapter. Nuclear anxieties resurface at several points in *Sans soleil*, a film that shows formal and temporal instability similar to that seen in other nuclear films that emerge from the chronotope of the nuclear. As the first epigraph to this chapter announces, Marker's fictitious cameraman Sandor Krasna (which is also one of Marker's pseudonyms) awaits the ferry from Hokkaido to Honshu and is reminded of "une guerre passée ou future" (a past or future war), revealing from the start of the film an unmooring in time. This past or future war and the landscape of atomic shelters it evokes for Krasna also recalls the black-and-white post-apocalyptic landscape of *La Jetée*. And the "petits fragments de guerre enchâssées dans la vie courante" (small fragments of war enshrined in everyday life) that Krasna mentions in *Sans soleil* anticipate the more careful consideration Marker gives to war with his focus on the Battle of Okinawa in *Level Five* (1996), one of the final productions from Argos Films and a film that An has called "an indirect re-make of *Hiroshima mon amour*."[6] As the Battle of Okinawa was overshadowed in the historical archive by the atomic bombings of Hiroshima and Nagasaki, *Level Five* was seen as provocative in its treatment of the historical event. The Japanese distributor (and friend of Argos Films president Anatole Dauman) Shibata Hayao warned of the sensitivity of Okinawa for Japanese audiences, comparing its weight for Japanese intellectuals to that of

Algeria for the French.[7] In both *Sans soleil* and *Level Five*, Marker not only evokes the nuclear specter but also explores the culture that exists around and as a result of global demands for energy, demands that have been chiefly met in France and Japan by nuclear power.

Marker's cinematic style—evocative, pensive, unstable—is particularly well suited to addressing nuclear concerns, which for decades have remained in the margins of French cinema, literature, and philosophy. In Marker's work, images are juxtaposed and manipulated in innovative ways such as with the image synthesizer in *Sans soleil*. Sometimes visual association is enough to transport the viewer into an oneiric viewing experience similar to the one induced in *Sans soleil* with the juxtaposition of people sleeping on a train and their imagined dreams. Often, the viewer is left to question the ontological status of the images themselves. Jacques Rancière situates Marker in "the generation of artists and intellectuals concerned with teaching people how to see instead of stupidly looking," with commentary and voiceover in his films "saying look at the image, don't trust the image, look behind, look for deception in the image."[8] André Bazin, too, questioned the status of the image in Marker's oeuvre, describing the montage style in his early films as horizontal, with the ear leading the eye in movement "from the audio element to the visual."[9] The relationship between the ontological uncertainty of images and the way Marker's films challenge memory call to mind Rancière's thoughts on the ontology of cinema: "Cinema is not only an art; cinema is a specific sensorium, cinema is a way of living in the shadows. I think it is very important that a film is never given as a whole. So the film is a sensation, the sensation of an apparition, of shadows, and it lives in our memories."[10] This understanding of a film and the viewer's experience of it as a sensation that "lives in our memories" extends beyond the visual regime and thus requires multisensory perception.

In this chapter, I expand the scope of the nuclear lens by taking a multisensory approach to Chris Marker's visions of Japan in order to perceive the nuclear, which cannot always be seen. The chronotope of the nuclear and the nuclear lens serve as tools in this multisensory analysis. The chronotope of the nuclear, a concept used to bring together narrative types or genres by their common nuclear spatio-temporalities, manifests in Marker's work as an impossible present in an invisible nuclear space in which nuclear concerns are evoked in sounds and rhythms and as shadows cast over history.[11] The nuclear lens brings into focus instances of nuclear instability, uncertainty, and anxiety in *La Jetée, The Koumiko Mystery, Sans soleil,* and *Level Five.* It also serves as a filter through which nuclear visual evidence and aural and rhythmic sensations can be perceived. Sensing the nuclear in Marker's works allows for recognition of nuclear concerns beyond the spectacle of disaster by bringing attention to the lives, events, and histories overshadowed or erased by it.

The multisensory approach to these works follows Vivian Sobchack's phenomenological approach to film and her definition of film as "an act of seeing that makes itself seen, an act of hearing that makes itself heard, an act of physical and reflective movement that makes itself reflexively felt and understood."[12] I join Sobchack and Jenny Chamarette in their embodied approaches to films such as *La Jetée* and *Sans soleil* with special attention to the nuclear fragments enshrined in them.[13] Approaching Marker's films through the senses and using a nuclear lens to focus not only on visual elements but also on acoustic and rhythmic elements allows for an illumination of the nuclear undercurrents that have been overlooked in Marker's work. This method could open the door to new ways of perceiving the nuclear in a wide range of cultural productions.

This chapter also serves as a bridge between the historical periods spanning this book, from Hiroshima to Fukushima. Several French documentaries and telefilms about nuclear issues have been made during the intervening period, and a few of these works focused on the Pacific region, such as René Vautier's *Mission pacifique / Pacific Mission* (1989) on the effects of atomic testing in the Pacific Islands and *Hirochirac 1995* (1995), which was filmed during the fiftieth anniversary of the bombings and documents the announcement made by President Jacques Chirac that France would reengage in nuclear testing in the South Pacific. This chapter focuses on Marker's films from the 1960s through the 1990s that deal with nuclear issues and are made in Japan or in collaboration with Japanese people and images. I show how Marker's visions of Japan through a nuclear lens have been ongoing and attentive to nuclear fragments buried underground and enshrined in everyday life in the years between nuclear disasters in Japan. These French visions of a nuclear Japan also underscore anxieties about a nuclear France, if not destroyed by nuclear explosions as imagined in *La Jetée,* then defined in many ways by a dependence on nuclear energy.

Chris Marker's interest in Japan was sustained and more intentional than that of fellow Left Bank filmmaker and occasional collaborator Alain Resnais. Marker found in Japan a source of creative inspiration over the course of his career and created more work there than perhaps any other French filmmaker. Other Marker films made in and about Japan include *A.K.* (1985), a Franco-Japanese coproduction documenting Kurosawa Akira on the set of his film *Ran* (1985); the short films *Tokyo Days* (1991) and *Bullfight / Okinawa* (1992), part of the *Zapping Zone* (1990–1994) installation; and *Immemory* (1997), an encyclopedic multimedia project on CD-ROM and now online that recycles images of Japan from Marker's previous work. Japan is the subject of a sequence on the Minamata mercury poisoning protests in *Le fond de l'air est rouge / A Grin without a Cat* (1977), and it is mentioned in passing in episodes of the thirteen-part series *L'héritage de la chouette / The Owl's Legacy* (1989) and in the very short *3 Video Haikus* ("Petite ceinture," "Tchaïka," and "Owl Gets in Your Eyes," 1994). Marker also made *Vive la baleine / Three Cheers for the Whale* (1972), an Argos Films documentary about whaling in Japan and the Soviet Union, and wrote the screenplay for *Kashima Paradise* (1973), a documentary directed by Yann Le Masson and Bénie Deswarte about protests against the construction of Narita Airport.[14] Inescapably influenced by the tradition of Japonisme, the visions of Japan throughout Marker's oeuvre are also complex, heterogenous, and evolving. Of particular interest here are Marker's politically inflected interrogations of images and expressions of solidarity with people who are often forgotten at the margins of the historical record.

Japan in a Nuclear Paris

La Jetée, a story of time travel told in still images, offers a bleak portrait of the present. The time traveler, a prisoner held captive in an underground refuge in Paris, is sent backward and forward in time to find a way out of the post-apocalyptic present. As he travels through time, however, he finds refuge in the past and develops his own mission. Drawn by a childhood memory of a woman he saw on the observation deck at the Paris Orly Airport on the same day that a man was shot there, he finally returns to the deck at Orly only to discover that the scene he had witnessed as a child was that of his own death as a time-traveling adult.

While Japan is not explicitly represented in *La Jetée*, it is evoked in images of the imagined post-apocalyptic Paris, the real-world analogs of which are the Japanese cities destroyed by the atomic bomb (fig. 4.1). Made after the atomic bombings of Hiroshima and Nagasaki and on the eve of the Cuban Missile Crisis in October 1962, *La Jetée* summons contemporary global anxieties about the possibility of nuclear war through the lens of those who have experienced it in Japan. Darke's monograph on the film recalls this historical context in his comparison of the visions of Paris in *La Jetée* and the contemporaneous documentary *Le joli mai / The Lovely Month of May* (1963): "In *Le Joli mai* Marker probes and praises Paris. In *La Jetée* he blows it up. Why? The obvious answer is out of fidelity to the times, to push the anxieties of the historical moment to their all too conceivable conclusion. Anxiety abounded as the dark backing to the period's increasing economic prosperity. . . . Fears of nuclear catastrophe were heightened by the Cuban Missile Crisis in October 1962. And the memory of World War II lingered."[15]

In *La Jetée*, conceptions of space and time are ontologically uncertain. The narrative skips between the past (the man's childhood in peacetime Paris), the present (underground Paris after nuclear war), and a deep future (a dark and indefinite space). The images used in

Figure 4.1. Paris destroyed in *La Jetée*. *Source*: Marker, Chris, dir. *La Jetée*. 1962; Criterion Channel.

the photo-film to represent a destroyed Paris are those of other cities bombed out during the Second World War. The viewer is led to perceive the destruction of Paris in nuclear war through the rhythm of dissolving images of the city intact with those of other cities destroyed beyond recognition. The time traveler is thus unmoored in ontologically uncertain time and the viewer in ontologically uncertain space.

While in *Hiroshima mon amour* the nuclear present can be understood as eternal and inescapable, in *La Jetée* the present conveyed in still images is static, unchanging, and impossible. The impossible present can be seen in the film's situation in the future. For the time traveler who exists in the post-nuclear present as a prisoner and subject of the scientists' experiments, the present is a void. His life (and death) is in the past. For Janet Harbord, *La Jetée* is "a view of what the present will look like from [the future]. It is, in a sense, an othering of the present, a making strange of its objects, people, thoughts and landscapes in order to bring them into view, to provide a frame through which the ineffable present may be described."[16] This "othering of the present" makes it at once strange and impossible as well as definable and knowable as an "other" time, a past from the perspective of the future, or a present always in the process of slipping away. However, the present in *La Jetée* could just as well be understood as eternal. The man's desire to return to the past in order to make it present, to subsume the past rather than to be subsumed by it (as the past for Elle is subsumed by the present in *Hiroshima mon amour*), allows for an understanding of the past in which a kind of eternal present is inherent. The time traveler finally dies in the past, thus turning the underground present into an impossible future.

Nuclear space and time are as intimately entwined in *La Jetée* as they were in *Hiroshima mon amour*. This spatiotemporal configuration fits with the chronotope of the nuclear as an outgrowth of Bakhtin's chronotope of crisis and cyclical ancillary time, which "often serves as a contrasting background for temporal sequences that are more charged with energy and event."[17] The still images of the impossible nuclear present in *La Jetée* are the cyclical ancillary time that is background to the one sequence in the past that is "more charged with energy and event." In this particular sequence in the past, the woman whom the time traveler has been following is shown awakening in bed. Still images of her lying in bed, looking toward the camera, and smiling dissolve into one another. One image contaminates the next until the rhythm accelerates such that the still images become moving pictures. Birdsong in the background becomes louder and more insistent. The woman blinks. Then the rhythm slows and the still images return. The force of this moment can be felt through its visual, aural, and kinetic elements. In this moment is the suggestion that life (as movement) existed in the past but is missing in the present. The photographic form of *La Jetée* thus evokes the sense of a temporally impossible present, which is instead made up of isolated moments, of still photographs with irregular and unpredictable durations, as opposed to the steady flow of twenty-four frames per second of cinema.

This single instance of moving images takes on nuclear significance both in the form and structure of *La Jetée*. The moment suggests a rediscovery of cinema as the flow of still images creates the illusion of movement and kinetically recalls the era's recent realization of the atomic bomb with the chain reaction of a nucleus splitting to create nuclear fission. As Darke has observed of this sequence in *La Jetée*, "It lasts all of six seconds, this moment. Nineteen minutes (and forty-five seconds, precisely) into the film, we watch Chatelain [the woman] waking. . . . The impact of this moment is out of all proportion to its screen time because it manages to impress us with something of the wonder that the first audiences must have experienced at the birth of cinema."[18] The ontologically uncertain images in *La Jetée* and the invisible nuclear elements of the film, such as the chain reaction of moving images lasting six seconds and occurring at 19:45, can be more fully appreciated with a multisensory approach to the film. Multisensory perception brings attention to both the meaning and experience created by the rhythm and durations of the still images. Thus, the force of the moving image for six seconds starting at 19:45 is significant in relation to nuclear history and is also an experience of stimulation and wonder for the viewer accustomed to the preceding still images and steady offscreen narration.

What *La Jetée* offers is less a vision of Japan than a vision of France through a nuclear lens, through images of nuclear destruction that recall the destruction of Hiroshima and Nagasaki. Marker was solicited by many in Hollywood for the rights to remake the film, notably by a producer who wrote to Marker several times and cited American ignorance of nuclear war in an attempt to persuade him to sell the rights: "I am wondering if, perhaps, I have misjudged you [sic] intentions from the beginning. I thought La Jette [sic] was a warning about the consequences of nuclear war. If you do not feel that such a warning is more necessary now than ever, you must not be reading the news reports that I am."[19] By turning the lens on France and invoking the viewer's visual, auditory, and kinetic senses, the photo-film can be seen as an expression of solidarity with Japanese victims of nuclear attacks by offering a multisensory experience of listening and feeling that goes beyond voyeurism. *La Jetée* also lays a foundation for Marker's own evolving visions of Japan, from the one presented in *The Koumiko Mystery* during his first trip to Japan in 1964 to the more complex and extended reflections on images of Japan in *Sans soleil* and *Level Five*.

Sensing the Nuclear in Marker's Tokyo

If the portrait of Japan in *The Koumiko Mystery*, one of Marker's earlier and less well-known films, is said to have been replaced by that in *Sans soleil*, the films share many similarities, not least the reflective, experimental montage and abiding interest in faces.[20] In *Sans soleil* and later in Marker's book of photographs *Staring Back* (2007), the gaze is returned, updating or replacing the unidirectional male filmmaker's gaze in *The Koumiko Mystery*. *Sans soleil* also returns to the nuclear fragments enshrined in *The Koumiko Mystery*.

A nuclear fragment in *The Koumiko Mystery* arises during a short news briefing in French heard ten minutes into the film over the image of Koumiko's face (fig. 4.2) and people sitting and sleeping on benches in a square in Tokyo: "Tokyo, 17 octobre. Neuf étudiants ont été arrêtés au cœur de la manifestation pour protester contre la visite au Japon des sous-marins américains, porteurs de bombes atomiques." (Tokyo, October 17. Nine students were arrested at the demonstration for protesting the visit of American submarines carrying atomic bombs.) The anti-nuclear demonstration was peaceful, the reporter says, and most people did not notice that it was happening because they were watching the Olympics on television. During this sequence, the demonstration is not shown but remarked upon for being overshadowed by the Olympics. The inclusion of this nuclear fragment in *The Koumiko Mystery* attests to a broader underlying anxiety around Cold War nuclear aggression, represented here by the nuclear-armed American submarines visiting Japan nearly two decades after the

Figure 4.2. Close-up of Koumiko during news briefing in French in *The Koumiko Mystery*. *Source*: Marker, Chris, dir. *Le mystère Koumiko / The Koumiko Mystery*. 1965; YouTube.

atomic bombings of Hiroshima and Nagasaki and one decade after the end of the American occupation of Japan and the Lucky Dragon Number Five incident. The submarines, a mostly invisible nuclear threat, are made perceptible by the demonstration. However, as the demonstration is overshadowed by the Olympic Games, the nuclear concern is again pushed to the background.

In *The Koumiko Mystery*, this background concern is represented by embedding nuclear references in the audio track accompanying images of a city square in Tokyo. Here, it cannot be seen but must be heard. While contemporaneous nuclear films such as Honda Ishirō's *Mothra* (1961) and Stanley Kubrick's *Dr. Strangelove or: How I Learned to Stop Worrying and Love the Bomb* (1964) explicitly and visually address nuclear concerns in spectacular fashion, *The Koumiko Mystery* requires a multisensory approach to perceive its embedded nuclear concerns. David Deamer refers to such embedded concerns as "trace elements" that allowed Japanese directors in particular to address nuclear issues while avoiding censorship and prohibition during the postwar American occupation of Japan.[21] For French filmmakers such as Marker and Resnais, embedding the nuclear in the background of the film may also be as much a political concern as an aesthetic and ethical one. For these filmmakers, background nuclear fragments are more destabilizing and disconcerting than a central, spectacular nuclear explosion.

Following this brief nuclear fragment in *The Koumiko Mystery* is a shot of a billboard with a quotation from Pierre de Coubertin, the French founder and second president of the International Olympic Committee (fig. 4.3): "Le plus important aux Jeux Olympiques n'est pas d'y vaincre mais d'y prendre part, car l'essentiel dans la vie n'est pas tant de conquérir que de lutter." (The most important thing in the Olympic Games is not to win but to take part, just as the most important thing in life is not the triumph but the struggle.) This is followed by footage of a Japanese wrestler competing in the games who was accused of lacking aggressiveness by his manager. In an idealized view, the Olympic Games become an antidote to the aggression of

Figure 4.3. Citation from Pierre de Coubertin on billboard in *The Koumiko Mystery*. *Source*: Marker, Chris, dir. *Le mystère Koumiko / The Koumiko Mystery*. 1965; YouTube.

the Cold War. Juxtaposing the message from Coubertin that privileges participation over triumph with a portrait of the insufficiently aggressive wrestler, Marker expresses his own geopolitical view promoting engagement and exchange over conquest.[22]

In *Sans soleil*, a film made nearly twenty years later by a now "disillusioned militant filmmaker,"[23] Marker's portrait of Japan is revised and complicated. Here, Marker compares his visions of Japan with those of other places around the world, and primarily of Guinea Bissau, using footage shot during his travels in the preceding years as well as archival and synthesized images. The film takes the form of an epistolary travelogue with metaphysical reflection on time, space, travel, and visual representation. An offscreen narrator reads letters from an invisible correspondent named Sandor Krasna who writes from the year 4001.

Heralded as a "triumphant return to personal filmmaking" and a "return to the quirky and digressive style of his early essay-films following a decade of close involvement with militant political film collectives,"[24] *Sans soleil* nevertheless offers critical reflection on history and politics through its interrogation of images. A John F. Kennedy mannequin outside of a shopping mall in Tokyo is accompanied by a recording of voices singing in English. "Ask not what your country can do for you" becomes a playful melody on the streets of Tokyo, and Kennedy is transformed from a Cold War commander to an American celebrity icon of men's fashion. A similar transformation of historical significance occurs in a later sequence in which Marker acknowledges the Battle of Okinawa. Krasna writes of a hill where "two hundred girls had used grenades to commit suicide in 1945 rather than fall alive into the hands of the Americans," which has become a photo op for tourists, a destination where "souvenir lighters are sold shaped like grenades."

Beyond its recurring interest in nuclear history, *Sans soleil* also enshrines nuclear concerns in its treatment of space and time, which are finally its central objects of contemplation. In Chiba Fumio's view, *Sans soleil* is not about Japan but about the weaving of time and temporalities, of the infra-ordinary and the extraordinary and apocalyptic.[25] The chronotope of the nuclear manifests in this film in an impossible present and in the imagination of a place outside of time as an alternative for existence. While in *La Jetée* the present is the temporality of imprisoned stasis and death, in *Sans soleil* the present is a grammatical impossibility. The narration of the film is in the past tense, with the narrator's common refrain, "He told me . . ." "He wrote me . . ." "He spoke to me. . . ." This was a deliberate choice by Marker, for whom narration "is always a nightmare but with *Sans soleil* it was particularly difficult." In a rare interview Marker explained, "For more than a month, I did not know what to do and I was working with the present tense and then I tried the past tense and it worked."[26] While the narrator recollects in the past tense, Krasna's letters are narrated in the present tense. As in *La Jetée*, the vitality of the present is preserved in the past while the present during which the narrator reads Krasna's letters recalls the static present in the underground refuge in Paris. The female narrator in *Sans soleil* is never shown on screen and exists in a time between the past recollected in the letters and the future position of Krasna in 4001. The present of the narration is thus absent from *Sans soleil*.

The impossible present can also be seen in Hayao Yamaneko's Zone, a place where images of the past are synthesized and manipulated. In altering these images, the Zone facilitates temporal transformations. For David Montero, the Zone is "a cinematic space in which images are divested of their iconic quality in an attempt to turn them into the direct representation of human memories, that is images that are temporally marked. These images are external to time; they have escaped the flow and remain frozen, ready to be rewritten and manipulated."[27] By divesting images of their iconic quality and creating new images that are external to time, Yamaneko's Zone in *Sans soleil* functions as a different sort of time machine than the low-tech time-travel apparatus in *La Jetée* but a time machine that also originates in this impossible present.

Midway through *Sans soleil* and during a shot of Yamaneko's control boards, the narrator describes a point outside of time from Krasna's letter. He writes, "J'envie Hayao et sa Zone. Il joue avec les signes de sa mémoire. Il les épingle et les décore comme des insectes qui se seraient envolé du temps et qu'il pourrait contempler d'un point situé à l'extérieur du temps—la seule éternité qui nous reste." (I envy Hayao and his Zone. He plays with the signs of his memory. He pins them down and decorates them like insects that would have flown beyond time, and which he could contemplate from a point outside of time—the only eternity we have left.) In both *Sans soleil* and *La Jetée*, time travel is possible, and a complementary notion of a place outside of time emerges. This place outside of time is a space for reflection and creation, as in Yamaneko's Zone, but also a place for possible existence and thus an alternative to the present. The impossible present in *Sans soleil* develops from that in *La Jetée*; thus, while time and space are less directly connected to nuclear concerns in *Sans soleil* as they are in *La Jetée*, they nevertheless continue the nuclear spatiotemporality first explored in *La Jetée*.

A multisensory approach becomes particularly important in order to consider how invisible elements of concern, such as radioactivity or contamination, can be perceived in the film. In *Sans soleil*, the viewer is led to multisensory perception through attention to rhythm and juxtaposition of "things that quicken the heart." Over an archival image of the launching of a Polaris missile (fig. 4.4), the first US submarine-launched ballistic missile, the narrator introduces Sei Shōnagon, who wrote a collection of lists, poetry, and observations entitled *The Pillow Book* and served as lady-in-waiting to the Princess Sadako at the start of the eleventh century. Of the imperial court, Krasna writes, "ce

Figure 4.4. Polaris missile in *Sans soleil*. *Source*: Marker, Chris, dir. *Sans soleil*. 1982; Criterion Channel.

petit groupe d'oisifs a laissé dans la sensibilité japonaise une trace autrement profonde que toutes les imprécations de la classe politique, en apprenant à tirer de la contemplation des choses les plus ténues une sorte de réconfort mélancolique." ([T]his small group of idlers left a mark on Japanese sensibility much deeper than the mediocre thundering of the politicians by learning to draw a sort of melancholy comfort from the contemplation of the tiniest things.)

The narrator continues: "Shōnagon avait la manie des listes: liste des 'choses élégantes,' des 'choses désolantes' ou encore des 'choses qu'il ne vaut pas la peine de faire.' Elle eut un jour l'idée d'écrire la liste des 'choses qui font battre le cœur.' Ce n'est pas un mauvais critère, je m'en aperçois quand je filme." (Shōnagon had a passion for lists: the list of "elegant things," "distressing things," or even of "things not worth doing." One day she got the idea of drawing up a list of "things that quicken the heart." Not a bad criterion I realize when I'm filming.) During the voiceover narration, a small military aircraft is shown flying over a larger plane (fig. 4.5). This is not a neutral or calming image but one that evokes aggression, distress, and wonder. The things that quicken the filmmaker's heart are never

Figure 4.5. Military aircraft in *Sans soleil*. *Source*: Marker, Chris, dir. *Sans soleil*. 1982; Criterion Channel.

named but suggested in Marker's images. The experience of the film is oriented toward these moments of quickening of the heart with flashes of surprising images, such as a boat at sea and the head of an emu that appear for a second each during a parade sequence in Tokyo, the imagined dreams of passengers on a train juxtaposed with their sleeping faces, and a split second of the elusive filmmaker inserted between frames of a shot of televisions and camera operators on the street in Tokyo.

While these instances allow for perception of the anxiety and uncertainty of living in the nuclear era—particularly on the eve of Ronald Reagan's Strategic Defense Initiative in the early 1980s—the most explicit nuclear reference in *Sans soleil* is a playful one: a Doraemon balloon in a festival parade in the streets of Tokyo. Doraemon, a time-traveling, nuclear-powered, animated robotic cat, first appeared in a manga series in the 1970s to promote the peaceful use of nuclear power, and it has been one of Japan's most popular cultural exports.[28] The Doraemon balloon appears onscreen for four seconds between shots of a girl dancing and a woman playing shamisen (fig. 4.6). When the balloon passes by the camera, a man in festival attire carrying the

Figure 4.6. Doraemon balloon in *Sans soleil*. *Source*: Marker, Chris, dir. *Sans soleil*. 1982; Criterion Channel.

Figure 4.7. Man behind Doraemon balloon in *Sans soleil*. *Source*: Marker, Chris, dir. *Sans soleil*. 1982; Criterion Channel.

balloon is revealed (fig. 4.7). The camera lingers on the Doraemon balloon for four seconds, a brief but captivating distraction.

Unlike the inserted shots of the boat and emu during this parade, the Doraemon balloon is part of the festival. Its inclusion might be interpreted as an example of Marker's affinity for the ludic, for cats, or for animation, which he himself practiced and included in many of his films. It was likely a chance appearance. As Marker the narrator says in *A Grin without a Cat*, "On ne sait jamais ce qu'on filme." (One never knows what one films.)

This shot of the Doraemon balloon can be perceived differently than the shots of the dancing girl, the woman playing shamisen, and the one-second inserts during the parade. Across the series of shots, the noises of the festival begin to merge with the Doraemon publicity jingle as the camera lingers on the balloon. This moment serves as a sonic transition from the diegetic sound to synthesized sounds with the entrance of Doraemon signaling a transition into a new nuclear era. The juxtaposition of traditional and popular culture attests to the ubiquity and banality of nuclear culture as it becomes embedded in the festival with the jingle and promotional character. The brief shot of the man behind the balloon draws attention to the human presence behind advertising and propaganda. The blending of soundtracks is subtle enough that the jingle could easily go unnoticed. In this way, Marker exposes the use of subliminal messages in advertising and suggests the need for multisensory perception to become fully aware of them. Jon Kear proposes that themes emerge cyclically in *Sans soleil* and that the film is structured by a series of "'shifting dominants,' in which each moment of the film acquires a relative equality."[29] A structure of shifting dominants grants the same status to the Doraemon balloon in the parade sequence as to an image in a more prominent place in the film such as the opening shot of the children on a road in Iceland, the closing images of the city of Heimaey covered in volcanic ash, or the startling moment when a woman at the market in Guinea Bissau returns the camera's gaze.

In *Sans soleil*, Marker's vision of Japan is multiple. It is a revision of the portrait of Japan as a stage for global engagement and peaceful competition in *The Koumiko Mystery*. Japan in *Sans soleil* is juxtaposed with Guinea Bissau as an "extreme pole of survival." For Lupton, this Japan is a "world of appearances." The viewer is asked to trust it and recognize it as deceptive and requiring time to be understood.[30] The Zone alters the familiar images of Japan that inform outside visions and forces the viewer to reconsider them in their essential form as images.

Krasna writes, "Il m'a montré les bagarres des Sixties traitées par son synthétiseur. Des images moins menteuses, dit-il avec la conviction des fanatiques, que celles que tu vois à la télévision. Au moins elles se donnent pour ce qu'elles sont, des images, pas la forme transportable et compacte d'une réalité déjà inaccessible." (He showed me the clashes of the Sixties treated by his synthesizer: pictures that are less deceptive, he says with the conviction of a fanatic, than those you see on television. At least they proclaim themselves to be what they are: images, not the portable and compact form of an already inaccessible reality.) The recognition in *Sans soleil* that images are constructions and not a "portable and compact form of . . . inaccessible reality" acknowledges their potential use to deceive and suggests that sight alone should not be privileged in attempting to make sense of a film. A nuclear lens that facilitates multisensory perception enhances awareness of invisible and inaudible nuclear undercurrents.

Level Five and the Shadow
of the Mushroom Cloud

Examining Marker's films about Japan through a nuclear lens magnifies another less explicitly nuclear concern in his work: the Battle of Okinawa, an event that led to and was overshadowed in the archive by the bombings of Hiroshima and Nagasaki. The Battle of Okinawa is briefly mentioned in *Sans soleil* and further developed as the central focus in *Level Five*, in which the viewer is told that the battle killed as many as 150,000 Okinawan civilians, or a third of the island's population. As the Battle of Okinawa is overshadowed by the more spectacular nuclear holocausts at Hiroshima and Nagasaki, *Level Five* might also be seen as overshadowed in Marker's oeuvre as a lower budget, more personal project. *Level Five* was Marker's final feature-length film about Japan and "the last of his 'cinema films.'"[31]

Unlike *Sans soleil*, *Level Five* was not shot in Japan, but it includes archival images of Japan and interviews with Japanese figures such as filmmaker Ōshima Nagisa and writer Tokitsu Kenji. The film revives many concerns central to *Sans soleil* such as memory, history, and the use of images to construct and make sense of both. In *Level Five*, a French woman named Laura sits in a small room at a computer trying to finish a game that her late companion started to create about the Battle of Okinawa. The title of the film refers to the final level of the game, which has not yet been completed. As Laura progresses through the game, she learns more about the events through video interviews with Japanese witnesses and experts, and she reflects broadly on war, memory, and humanity. In learning about this event that is marginalized in many accounts of the war, and in light of her own experience of personal loss, Laura empathizes with the victims of the Battle of Okinawa, recalling the conflation of personal and collective trauma in *Hiroshima mon amour*. Completing the game becomes both an expression of solidarity with these victims and an attempt to appease her own ghosts.

Raymond Bellour calls *Level Five* "un film moins harmonieux que *Sans soleil* dont il est une continuation"[32] (a less harmonious film than *Sans soleil*, of which it is a continuation) as it returns to the history of the Battle of Okinawa, mentioned during a five-minute sequence in *Sans soleil*. In *Sans soleil*, the dates and circumstances of the battle are given before a brief discussion of Ryūkyū civilization, about which Krasna admits he, like the American soldiers, knew very little. In this sequence, attention is drawn to "the faces of the market ladies at Itoman" which remind Krasna "more of Gauguin than of Utamaro," or more of France (or French Polynesia) than of Japan. But as Gauguin was also inspired by Japanese art, Marker seems to be seeing Japan through Gauguin's eyes, implicating himself in the tradition of Japonisme.

As in *Sans soleil*, nuclear anxiety is revealed in fragments enshrined in *Level Five*. When Laura appears wearing a gas mask, her face is superimposed over and intercut with those of young Okinawans, and a synthesized voice from the computer game provides narration:

> En d'autre temps, pour lester la puissance de l'abonné, on avait cherché une matière dense, lourde et rare qui pourrait en être le gage au fond des coffres, et on avait trouvé l'or. Maintenant, l'argent était devenu invisible et volatile et pour gager la nouvelle puissance, on avait cherché une matière invisible et volatile, et on avait trouvé le savoir. C'étaient les atomes de savoir qui traversaient nos écrans. C'était des trous noirs de savoir où s'engouffraient les rêves de puissance de ce siècle qui n'en finissait pas.

> (In past times, to support the value of money, a dense, rare material was sought as a guarantee in the safe, and gold was chosen. Now, money had become invisible and volatile, so the new source of power needed collateral that was invisible and volatile too, and we found knowledge. Atoms of knowledge crossed our screens. And this unending century's dreams of power fell into the black holes of knowledge.)

Using a critical nuclear lens, I propose a reading of these "invisible and volatile" "atoms of knowledge" as a polysemic evocation of nuclear power. This passage as a whole merits consideration for its analysis of the system of capital that is both dependent upon and threatened by knowledge. Nuclear energy is also invisible and volatile, dependent upon both capital and knowledge and often at odds with them, as seen in the swelling budgets of nuclear construction and disaster management as well as the concealment of nuclear incidents and accidents from public awareness. In *Level Five*, Laura questions the stability of the material world—of gold, of nuclear materials—and explores possibilities for transformation.

Appropriations from *Hiroshima mon amour* in *Level Five* further reveal the film's underlying nuclear anxiety. An early title proposed for this film was "Okinawa, mon amour." The phrase instead made its way into *Level Five* along with a few borrowed seconds of the sorrowful refrain from *Hiroshima mon amour* as Laura says, "Je peux me reconnaitre dans cette petite île parce que ma souffrance la plus unique, la plus intime est aussi la plus banale, la plus facile à baptiser. Alors, autant lui donner un nom qui sonne comme une chanson, comme un film. Okinawa mon amour." (I can recognize myself in that little island because my most unique and intimate suffering is also the most banal, the easiest to name. So, let's give it a name that sounds like a song, like a film, Okinawa mon amour.) This melodic echo brings the past into the present and underscores the eternal present of cinema in which a work like *Hiroshima mon amour* continues to resonate across time. Laura also resembles Elle in *Hiroshima mon amour* in that both have lost their lovers and seek to console themselves by relating their personal suffering to broader historical suffering and, more specifically, to Japanese victims in the Second World War. With its parallel evocation of underlying nuclear anxieties and its engagement with nuclear spatiotemporality *Level Five*, too, joins the transnational film cycle initiated by *Hiroshima mon amour*.

The chronotope of the nuclear describing a nuclear present in crisis is characteristic of this film cycle beginning with *Hiroshima mon amour*, in which the present is eternal and inescapable. In *La Jetée*, the present is existentially impossible, and in *Sans soleil* it is grammatically impossible. In Marker's films, the impossible present leads to awareness of a place of existence outside of time. This idea is further developed in *Level Five* as the computer game developed to teach about the Battle of Okinawa has no temporal constraints. It is a game without a timer or stopwatch. Despite the evocation of progression in the title *Level Five*, the game turns out to be rhizomatic rather than linear. It is a network, a virtual world that resembles

Marker's CD-ROM *Immemory* and allows for a rhizomatic exploration of history. In the confined space in which Laura works, she too seems to exist in a place outside of linear time. Her final speech in the film explores temporal alternatives to the present: "J'aurais pensé qu'il y a eu un temps où. Mais depuis, il y avait eu un autre temps, celui de la liste, celui des mensonges et de la jalousie, et ce temps-là aurait assourdi notre temps. Il aurait assourdi l'écho de notre propre vie. Et tout se serait passé comme à travers un mur. Ça aurait été à peine audible." (I would have thought: 'There was a time when . . .' But then there was another time, the time of the list, of jealousy and deceptions, and that time would mute our time. It would mute the echo of our life. Everything would have been as though through a wall, barely audible.) The present in *Level Five* is thus imagined as muted or suppressed by the past. Laura continues the monologue by comparing death to a dream from which one does not awaken. The camera closes in on her face, then on her mouth and a remote control she holds in front of her face as the image blurs before finally cutting to black. Marker's voice narrates a coda over an image of the empty room in which he says that Laura was never seen again, as though Laura entered a time outside of time, outside of the present.

When nuclear time in the chronotope of the nuclear is only understood as the eternal present, the chronotope risks becoming an overly optimistic concept. The idea of an eternal nuclear present ignores some of the greatest problems nuclear power presents: how to pass along responsibility, how to communicate its dangers in a language that a future world will understand, and how to remember. The eternal present could suggest a constant awareness of danger or the inability to forget. As Krasna remarks in *Sans soleil*, "total recall is memory anesthetized." A position outside of time, however, allows for a broader perspective on the present. Such a perspective might come from the post-apocalyptic time traveler in *La Jetée*, the letter-writing traveler from the future in *Sans soleil*, or the virtual time traveler in *Level Five*.

Marker's films do not support the platitude that by simply learning history we will avoid repeating it. *Level Five* concludes, "Laura avait compris que le jeu ne servirait jamais à refaire l'Histoire. Il se contenterait de la répéter en boucle, avec une obstination méritoire et probablement inutile. Mémoriser le passé pour ne pas le revivre

était une illusion du vingtième siècle." (Laura had understood that
the game would never be used to remake History. It would settle for
repeating it over and over, with a commendable and probably futile
persistence. Learning the past in order to not relive it was an illusion
of the twentieth century.) Still, Marker's work insists on revisiting
history and reconsidering the relationship between images and reality.

Across these films, Marker creates a larger portrait of the multifaceted, mediated Japan he knew from art, film, literature, and his
own time spent there. In *La Jetée*, images of Japan are subsumed
into those of post-apocalyptic Paris. In *The Koumiko Mystery*, they are
restless, distracted images. In *Sans soleil*, images of Japan are modified
by the image synthesizer. In *Level Five*, they are mediated through
a computer game. Significantly, the focus on the Battle of Okinawa
shifts attention to the southern extremity of Japan, an island that only
officially became Japanese after annexation in 1879, after Japonisme
had already taken root in the West. *Level Five* thus presents a broader
vision beyond Tokyo extending to the margins of Japan and of the
historical archive.

It is not possible to remember everything in Marker's films
because they are not constructed to be remembered in this way.
Unstable images and uncertain spatial and temporal boundaries
become sources of strength in this work. Nuclear undercurrents haunt
La Jetée, *The Koumiko Mystery*, *Sans soleil*, and *Level Five* as they are
woven into everyday life, which Marker was intent on exploring. A
film's twenty-four images per second pass too quickly for the viewer
to take in each frame. These films, and particularly *Sans soleil* with its
frequently discordant images and sound, exploit the sensorial overload
that cinema can offer and leave the viewer on ontologically uncertain
ground, not unlike that of memory or a dream. Fragments, flashes,
whispers, and echoes lodge in the subconsciousness provoking instability
and uncertainty in the viewer's mind. The uncertain forms of these
films encourage multisensory perception and reward repeat viewing.
At first, one might be hard pressed to say anything definitive about
these films. Even upon multiple viewings, new questions and doubts
surface. But it is precisely such uncertainty and instability that allow
for mobility of the mind. Viewers remain active and engage senses
beyond the visual: listening and feeling and observing the heart quicken.

Beyond Marker's work, multisensory perception is useful for
detecting undercurrents of nuclear anxiety in France in the second half
of the twentieth century. Despite the acceleration of nuclear production

in France under the 1974 Messmer Plan, anti-nuclear sentiment among the population was growing. In the 1970s, *soixante-huitards* and local communities mobilized against nuclear energy and the construction of power plants in their regions. In 1981, François Mitterrand rose to power on the left and deceived supporters who opposed nuclear energy by violating anti-nuclear promises.[33] In 1985, French government operatives bombed the Greenpeace ship *Rainbow Warrior* while it was moored in New Zealand in protest of ongoing nuclear tests in French Polynesia. While nuclear energy has always been considered a "peaceful use" of the atom, it has inflicted significant social and environmental violence in accidents such as the Kyshtym nuclear disaster, the disaster at Three Mile Island, the Chernobyl disaster, and the disaster at Fukushima Daiichi. Rather than providing indictments of those responsible for nuclear mishaps and disaster, Marker's films register the undercurrent of nuclear anxiety in France. They remind viewers of the nuclear fragments enshrined in everyday life, the Doraemon balloon in the street parade, the things that quicken the heart.

As for the French visions of Japan they present, Marker's films are more engaged with the tradition of Franco-Japanese exchange than was *Hiroshima mon amour*. While Resnais was commissioned to make a film in Japan, Marker chose to work in Japan, and he chose to do so several times. Marker's sustained engagement with Japan, from his first trip in 1964 through his many returns throughout his life, shows a deep affinity for the place and its many cultures. In the documentary *Chris Marker: Never Explain, Never Complain* (2015), Wim Wenders compares his own experience traveling to Japan with Marker's deeper physical, intellectual, and spiritual connections there. Marker returned to Japan and to his work about Japan to revise and update his impressions. In filming a visit to "le petit bar de Shinjuku" (a bar called La Jetée, after his film, owned by the cinephile and French-speaking Kawai Tomoyo) in *Sans soleil*, Marker allusively cites himself as part of the tradition of Franco-Japanese cultural exchange.

Japanese interest in Marker's films has also grown over the years. After his death in 2012, the 2013 Yamagata International Documentary Film Festival organized a retrospective featuring forty-five of his films accompanied by the catalog *Memories of the Future. Chris Marker's Travels and Trials*. Kaneko Yu and Higashi Chiho edited the collection *Chris Marker: cinéaste nomade et engagé* which was followed by a 2015 colloquium on his work.[34] And the La Jetée bar (fig. 4.8) in Tokyo is a pilgrimage site for international filmmakers and cinephiles alike.

Figure 4.8. Entrance to La Jetée bar in Tokyo. *Source*: Photograph by author.

5

Interaction and Solidarity through a Digital Nuclear Lens

K EIKO COURDY's web-documentary and film *Au-delà du nuage °Yonaoshi 3.11 / Beyond the Cloud* (2013) begin with footage of the tsunami triggered by the Great East Japan Earthquake on March 11, 2011. A man with a mobile phone on a balcony at Miyako City Hall records the tsunami as it crests and overflows the floodwall while the people standing beside him narrate the destruction and cry out in disbelief.[1] In the long edit version of this footage, the camera pans to reveal water overtaking the city and several other people on the balcony, at least one of whom is also recording the disaster on a mobile phone.[2]

While many amateur photographers and citizen filmmakers in Japan took to their smartphones to document the 2011 triple disaster, Courdy, along with Philippe Rouy, are two of several French filmmakers who also responded to the disaster by making films about it. Courdy's web-documentary and film include interviews with people in Japan affected by the triple disaster: nuclear refugees and people who have chosen to remain in highly radioactive areas; journalists, artists, and filmmakers; medical professionals; and political actors such as Kan Naoto, the prime minister at the time of the disaster who has since become an anti-nuclear spokesperson. Courdy followed the cross-platform project *Beyond the Cloud* with two additional documentaries about the ongoing nuclear disaster, *A Safe Place* (2017) and

L'île invisible / The Invisible Island (2021), both with the participation
of the renowned Japanese composer Ryuichi Sakamoto. Rouy made
a different kind of trilogy of non-narrative films about the nuclear
disaster at Fukushima Daiichi. The films *4 bâtiments, face à la mer / 4
Buildings, Facing the Sea* (2012), *Machine to Machine* (2013), and *Fovea
centralis* (2014) were made in France using found footage from the
Tokyo Electric Power Company's (TEPCO) live-stream webcams and
surveillance cameras as well as from YouTube. While these films do
not explicitly reference *Hiroshima mon amour*, they join the tradition of
Franco-Japanese collaboration in cinema around nuclear issues initiated
by the earlier work. This chapter will focus on the visions of Japan
through a nuclear lens presented in these two French filmmakers'
work and consider how the digital age offers filmmakers increased
opportunities for transnational collaboration and for the expression
of solidarity through their work.

Other experimental films from France responding to the nuclear
disaster at Fukushima Daiichi include Jean-Luc Vilmouth's *Lunch Time*
(2011/2014/2018), Angela Melitopoulos and Maurizio Lazzarato's
*L'incommensurable: une recherche audio-visuelle après Fukushima / The
Incommensurable: An Audiovisual Study after Fukushima* (2012), Pierre
Huyghe's *Sans titre (masque humain) / Untitled (Human Mask)* (2014),
Mark Olexa and Francesca Scalisi's *Demi-vie à Fukushima / Half-Life
in Fukushima* (2016), and Judith Cahen and Masayasu Eguchi's *Le
cœur du conflit / Kokoro no katto / The Heart of the Conflict* (2017), the
latter of which is analyzed in the final chapter of this book. Several
traditional documentaries about the disaster have also been made by
French and Belgian filmmakers such as Alain de Halleux's *Récits de
Fukushima / Stories from Fukushima* (2012), *Welcome to Fukushima* (2013),
and *Beyond the Waves* (2018), which was co-directed with Tanaka Aya;
Jean-Paul Jaud's *Tous cobayes? / All of Us Guinea-Pigs Now?* (2012) and
Libres! / Free! (2015); Thierry Ribault and Alain Saulière's *Gambarō /
Courage! / Stay Strong!* (2014), Claude-Julie Parisot and Gil Rabier's
Fukushima, des particules et des hommes / Fukushima, Particles and Men
(2014), and Marc Petitjean's *De Hiroshima à Fukushima / From Hiroshima to Fukushima* (2015). Documentaries by some of these filmmakers
made prior to 2011—most notably de Halleux's *R.A.S. nucléaire, rien
à signaler / Nuclear Energy, Nothing to Report* (2009) and Petitjean's
Blessures atomiques / Atomic Wounds (2006)—attest to a pre-2011 interest
in nuclear issues among French-speaking filmmakers working in the

twenty-first century. This work responding to the 2011 disaster is informed by earlier documentaries about nuclear issues with Petitjean, for example, returning to interviews from *Atomic Wounds* with Dr. Hida Shuntaro in *From Hiroshima to Fukushima*. Employing very different narrative and aesthetic strategies, these French-language films express a common concern for and solidarity with victims of the triple disaster in Japan. Many of the filmmakers also turn a critical eye toward France and its continued use and development of nuclear energy. The majority of these French-language films about the triple disaster in Japan are also transnational coproductions and involve collaboration with Japanese participants.

On the other side of the exchange, Japanese films about the disaster such as Fujiwara Toshi's *Mujin chitai / No Man's Zone* (2012) and Kenichi Watanabe's *Fukko, histoires de résistance / Fukko, Stories of Resistance* (2021), *Notre ami, l'atome: Un siècle de radioactivité / Our Friend the Atom: A Century of Radioactivity* (2020), *Terres nucléaires: une histoire du plutonium / Nuclear Lands: A History of Plutonium* (2015), and *Le monde après Fukushima / The World after Fukushima* (2012) have been made with support from French production companies. KAMI Productions, a company based in Paris and led by Christine and Kenichi Watanabe, has produced many of Watanabe's documentaries as well as documentaries about the disaster and its aftermath by Marie Linton entitled *Revenir à Fukushima / Return to Fukushima* (2017) and *La grande muraille du Japon / The Great Wall of Japan* (2018). KAMI Productions also supported an unfinished web-documentary project by Jérémie Souteyrat and Alissa Descotes-Toyosaki entitled "Road Fukushima."[3] Other internationally well-received Japanese documentaries about the 2011 nuclear disaster such as Matsubayashi Yojyu's *Soma Kanka / Fukushima: Memories of the Lost Landscape* (2011) and *Matsuri no uma / The Horses of Fukushima* (2013) and Funahashi Atsushi's *Futuba kara toku hanarete dainibu / Nuclear Nation II* (2014) have been successful on the documentary festival circuit in France.[4]

Many of these films about the nuclear disaster at Fukushima Daiichi share themes of uncertainty, invisibility, and risk, as well as recurring motifs such as roadblocks and empty streets, workers in hazmat suits and nuclear refugees, face masks and Geiger counters, maps showing concentric circles and wind patterns, wild and stray animals, citizen organizations and protests, and droning machines and silence.[5] Films made a few years after the disaster, such as Courdy's

The Invisible Island, emphasize the ongoing effects on everyday life for nuclear refugees and returnees as well as the continuing cleanup of the site. Black bags of radioactive dirt pile up in fields alongside public roads, populated neighborhoods, and deserted shopping malls.

Kan Naoto, interviewed in Courdy's earlier work, appears in several other documentaries about the disaster as well, lending his political authority to the films. In contrast to earlier French visions of Japan through a nuclear lens, these documentaries were made relatively soon after the 2011 nuclear disaster, and they explicitly foreground nuclear concerns. While films made in the aftermath of the atomic bombings in 1945 were censored and suppressed during the American occupation of Japan, and while censorship and suppression of sensitive information continue after the nuclear disaster at Fukushima Daiichi, the ubiquity of digital tools and platforms available today such as live stream cameras, smartphone video, and social media have led to greater transparency and circulation of knowledge. In the digital age, art and information move quickly.

The digital age has also facilitated the incorporation of borrowed and found footage into films. The found webcam footage in Rouy's film and the tsunami footage from a smartphone in Courdy's work—like the footage from the documentary *The Effects of the Atomic Bomb on Hiroshima and Nagasaki* (1946) used in *Hiroshima mon amour* (1959)—come from databases of existing images. Yet the analog images Resnais consulted for *Hiroshima mon amour,* some of the only remaining footage taken in the immediate aftermath of the bombings, were extremely limited, especially compared with the countless digital images available to filmmakers today. The proliferation of digital images adds a new layer of uncertainty regarding authorship and selection criteria for nuclear films made in the digital age. While such questions have always been a part of filmmaking, in the digital age they are amplified by technologies that facilitate processes of image creation and circulation.

Both Courdy and Rouy use found footage in their work and both take as their primary subject matter the nuclear disaster at Fukushima Daiichi. However, their films present rather different visions of Japan as their responses are shaped by distinct formal approaches as well as by different levels of access to Japanese culture. Courdy expresses an ambivalent optimism in her initial vision of a post-3.11 Japan. The title *Au-delà du nuage °Yonaoshi 3.11 / Beyond the Cloud* recalls the iconic mushroom cloud associated with the atomic bomb as well as the plumes from the 2011 explosions at Fukushima Daiichi and suggests the possibility of moving "beyond" these moments of explosion. *Yonaoshi*, Japanese for "renewal of the world," offers a hopeful frame for nuclear disaster and a gesture of solidarity with victims in Japan, one that is reinforced by the film's bilingual title, transnational collaboration, and global distribution.[6] Courdy's proficiency in Japanese allows her greater access for her interview-based work in Japan. She also promotes her work on social media and crowdfunding sites, encouraging viewers to "partager sans modération" (share widely).[7] If this optimism is tempered several years later in *The Invisible Island*, Courdy's commitment to the nuclear refugees and cleanup workers remains steady.

Rouy does not speak Japanese and did not go to Japan to make his films. In his work, language is de-emphasized as the human element is either abstracted or absent. Instead, a machine-operated world shows the fractures and fragments of societies that have put technological progress ahead of human well-being. Firmly entrenched in the ongoing disaster, these films offer no vision of renewal or moving beyond it. While Rouy's mostly nonverbal films are more accessible to an international, multilingual audience, they do not seem to be aimed at a wide viewership, having been shown mostly at festivals, museums, and colloquia.[8]

These more recent French visions of Japan through a nuclear lens recall certain aspects of earlier French visions analyzed in previous chapters in this book with one notable difference: in these films, nuclear concerns move to the foreground where they become the central subject matter. Courdy was not in Japan in March 2011 to witness the disaster. Yet, as she explains in an early scene in the film, she felt she had to go there "to take part, help, do something." On May 1, she took a nearly empty flight to Tokyo armed with a mask, gloves, and her camera. Because she did not witness the beginning of the triple disaster, Courdy relies on local accounts of the earthquake, tsunami, and nuclear meltdowns.

Working at a much greater spatial distance in France, Rouy made his trilogy of films from found footage, bringing attention to the enormous amount of publicly available material about the nuclear disaster and questioning the apparent transparency of mass dissemination of information. A key tension arises in the digital age between increased transparency through greater quantities of and access to information and the obscuring of that which is intended to be revealed through a profusion of digital fragments. Rouy's films focus on the institutions and technologies involved in the nuclear disaster at Fukushima Daiichi and its aftermath with particular attention to issues of transparency and obscurity, recasting the paradoxical problems of visibility and invisibility that are associated with nuclear disaster.

Given the accelerated production and distribution of information in the digital age, it is difficult to say how long these films will last, or whether they, too, will be lost in a sea of data and disaster media. Will these films matter in the long run as *Hiroshima mon amour* continues to matter today? Whether or not they have the same cultural reach, Courdy's and Rouy's films join a tradition of Franco-Japanese cinema through a nuclear lens, and like their filmic forebears they explore nuclear spatiotemporality and have increasingly unstable forms.

Voices from the Zone

The French artist and filmmaker Keiko Courdy was born in Japan, lived there until the age of twelve, and returned at twenty-one to earn a doctoral degree at the University of Tokyo. Her knowledge of Japanese culture and ability to speak the language allow her to engage directly with victims of the 2011 triple disaster. Her feature-length documentary film *Beyond the Cloud* began as a web-documentary of short video interviews with local residents and public figures about the triple disaster. Courdy later made the short film *A Safe Place* (2017) about the zone around the Fukushima Daiichi power plant. Her most recent documentary, *The Invisible Island* premiered at the International Uranium Film Festival in 2021 in commemoration of the tenth anniversary of the triple disaster. This section will focus primarily on the web-documentary and film *Beyond the Cloud*.

While the web-documentary is no longer available online in its original form, fragments of it remain on YouTube. The original web-documentary included short video interviews as well as contextual information about the disaster and Courdy's project, a collection of still images, a map of Japan, a calendar of screenings and events, and an interactive space where viewers could post messages on digital *ema*, the small wooden plaques on which people write wishes at Japanese shrines. In the film, which incorporates most of the interviews from the web-documentary, Courdy's voiceover narration provides contextual information about her work and the places she filmed. The film does not have the same invitation for direct viewer interaction as the web-documentary, although in 2017 it was made publicly available on YouTube and viewers continue to respond to it in the comments section.

All of these works have been transnational collaborations with Japanese artists and technicians. Most notably, composer Ryuichi Sakamoto contributed music to *A Safe Place* and *The Invisible Island*. The web-documentary offered a new kind of transnational collaboration by inviting viewers from around the world to add messages to the wish tree. The interviews in *Beyond the Cloud* were conducted in Japan between 2011 and 2012 with public figures, media professionals, artists, activists, and residents near Fukushima Daiichi. Courdy can occasionally be heard offscreen asking questions. She also credits Japanese translators for their work on the narration and on the web-documentary. In the web-documentary, the interview videos were in black and white, while in the film the same interviews are shown in color. Because the web-documentary was made earlier and thus at a shorter temporal distance from the events, Courdy explains that she preferred black and white as a minimalist, discreet, and respectful response to the immediate shock and trauma of the triple disaster. When working with a Japanese producer on the feature-length documentary, she was encouraged to use color in order to differentiate it from the web-documentary.[9]

The web-documentary also included an additional interview that was not used in the film with Gérard Aleton, a retired French nuclear engineer who worked for an unnamed French public multinational conglomerate and with an unnamed Japanese company on the development of a Franco-Japanese reactor. In Aleton's view, nuclear power is a transitional energy that we are stuck with for generations to come, even if we stop using it. Aleton was the only French interview subject in the web-documentary. His transnational work with the Japanese company shows Franco-Japanese collaboration beyond the cultural sphere, and the inclusion of his interview in the web-documentary serves to explain the accident in Japan and to remind viewers of France's own deep investment in nuclear energy. In the other interviews, the disaster in Japan is spoken about in Japanese, perhaps creating cultural if not spatial distance from the disaster to viewers watching from outside of Japan. Aleton, though, reminds viewers that once a core melts down, a nuclear accident becomes a borderless threat open to the vicissitudes of unpredictable and uncontrollable elements such as wind and rain.

While the web-documentary is no longer available in its original form online, it remains an interesting object for analysis in this study as it embodied nuclear spatiotemporality through its spatial and temporal loops and its non-linear database form. And while the chronotope of the nuclear remains useful as a tool for distinguishing these digital nuclear films from more spectacular and traditional visions of nuclear disaster, it takes a new form in the digital age as representations of nuclear space and time are reshaped by digital technologies.

In earlier French cinematic visions of Japan, nuclear spatiotemporality served as the background for romance, recollection, travel, and historical study. After the 2011 disaster at Fukushima Daiichi, nuclear space and time move from the background to become central concerns. The title *Au-delà du nuage °Yonaoshi 3.11 / Beyond the Cloud* expresses these key concerns with the reference to an abstract spatial notion of "beyond" and an implicit recognition of the area in the Tōhoku region below the "cloud" of radioactive contamination. The 3.11 date establishes the triple disaster as a fixed moment in time that will shape any possible future renewal, suggested by the word *yonaoshi*, or "renewal of the world."

The locations of the interviews are identified by their distance in kilometers from Fukushima Daiichi: the ghost town of Iitate, forty kilometers away from the power plant where a retired farmer drinks purifying herbs and continues to farm; Minami-Soma, twenty kilometers away where two women and their children return to their abandoned home for a few hours; a family inside the twenty-kilometer exclusion zone who were moved to a gymnasium just four kilometers away from their home. This spatially demarcated tour through the region does not serve to orient viewers unfamiliar with the region but rather to show the uncertain and unreliable safety determinations based on a concentric-circles model of contamination zones. Under this model, a woman forced to leave her home inside the twenty-kilometer exclusion zone goes well outside of it to Fukushima City where radiation levels are higher than those in her home. Courdy continues this spatial identification in *The Invisible Island*. In this feature-length documentary, Courdy returns to locations such as Minami-Soma and visits new sites closer to the Fukushima Daiichi, such as the floating citizen Umi Labo, which tests radioactivity levels in fish one and a half kilometers away from the plant and the Fukushima Daini plant twelve kilometers away from Fukushima Daiichi (fig. 5.1). Footage is also shown from ten meters below the damaged reactor core.

This uncertainty extends to time as well. Miyata Miho, an interviewee in *Beyond the Cloud*, explains that she lives in the present and continues to live as she did before the triple disaster but with more daily stress and fear. Several interview subjects mention fear, recalling that of the postwar era in Japan as dramatized, for example, in Kurosawa Akira's *Ikimono no kiroku / I Live in Fear* (1955). For today's survivors, age calculations are considered in relocation decisions, and the uncertain stress of moving is balanced with what Molly Wallace deems "the highly ambivalent concept of 'resilience,'" a concept that appeals "to ecologists and activists who might wish to envision a world of salutary adaptations."[10]

The change in representations of nuclear time in the digital age is perhaps best illustrated by the viewer's experience of the time of the web-documentary compared with that of the film. In the web-

Figure 5.1. Umi Labo, 1.5 km from Fukushima Daiichi in *The Invisible Island*. *Source*: Courdy, Keiko, dir. *L'île invisible / The Invisible Island*. 2021; Screened May 19–29, 2022, 11th International Uranium Film Festival.

documentary and the fragments of it that remain on YouTube, the duration of each video is visible in the progress bar and the time code at the bottom of the image, but like the game in Chris Marker's *Level Five* there is no temporal boundary for the experience of the entire web-documentary or the fragments of it that remain on YouTube. One viewer might watch a few interviews, while another could spend hours interacting with the different sections of the web-documentary and following links to social media platforms and related news and events. The web-documentary and feature-length film were also linked across platforms as the screenings announced on the web-documentary were for the feature-length film. The viewer of the film could rewatch parts of it and then leave a message about the film on the web-documentary wish tree. The film, on the other hand, has a fixed duration of ninety-five minutes. The viewer does not see the lengths of the individual interviews, which vary between three and eight and a half minutes. The uncertain time of the web-documentary thus extends beyond the uncertain nuclear time presented in the diegetic world of the film and invites viewers to participate in that temporal uncertainty.

Nuclear space and time are also uncertain in new ways in these visions of Japan in the digital age. Digital technologies offer new possibilities for the cinematic representation of nuclear spatiotemporality and allow for different manifestations of the chronotope of the nuclear. With *Hiroshima mon amour*, the chronotope of the nuclear describes the experience of an eternal present against a nuclear background. In Marker's films, the chronotope of the nuclear involves an impossible present in invisible and hypervisible nuclear spaces. In these contemporary visions of Japan through a digital lens, conceptions of an inescapable nuclear present and unbounded nuclear space stretch into a new spatiotemporal form: the loop.

In the digital age, the loop emerges as a new form of temporality.[11] The loop form is intimately related to the origins of cinema and its proto-cinematic devices, while the narrative cinema that developed from them "puts forward a notion of human existence as a linear progression through numerous unique events."[12] In the twenty-first century, Lev Manovich identifies concrete uses of the loop in new media: a looped moving image, loops in animation and video games, and loops as computer programming structures. The loop form and sequential progression also need not be mutually exclusive.[13] In the digital films in this chapter, the loop becomes an abstract form that contains spatial and temporal potential. For example, the home page of Courdy's web-documentary included looped sound and animation that became part of the narrative once the viewer interacted with the site. The videos in the web-documentary existed independently of one another and could be watched on loop in contrast to their linear placement in the film, which leads the viewer toward a conclusion.

While the film and web-documentary present essentially the same subject matter (the interviews), the nonlinear database form of the web-documentary was at once flexible, uncertain, and unstable, and more so than the unstable forms of films by Resnais, Suwa, and Marker discussed in previous chapters. The analog footage Resnais incorporated into *Hiroshima mon amour* was relatively limited compared with the countless digital images and videos available to filmmakers today. This ever-expanding database adds a new layer of uncertainty to audiovisual work in the digital age: Where do the images come from? Who created them? Why are certain images chosen and not others? (Resnais, by contrast, had a single choice for documentary footage of the immediate aftermath of the bombing of Hiroshima.) These questions have always been central to filmmaking, but in the digital age they are amplified by technologies that facilitate the process of image creation and expand access to images.

Coudy's web-documentary, a database of video interviews and still images that could be viewed in any order, upends cause-and-effect narrative structure. The web-documentary presents the diegetic world as thematically grouped categories with each image and video offering a micro-narrative. The film, on the other hand, presents a more structured, linear narrative of Courdy's trip to Japan and the people she met with there. In destabilizing the notion of linear cause-and-effect narrative, the web-documentary offers the possibility of a film in which a more dynamic relationship exists between the parts, perhaps best illustrated by the opportunity viewers have to participate in the ordering of fragments.

The web-documentary as a relatively new digital form is even more ontologically unstable than the filmic medium. In June 2017, the digital infrastructure of Courdy's web-documentary began to break down. First, the host website no longer supported video, but other elements such as photographs, wishes, and credits were still accessible to viewers. However, shortly after the videos disappeared from the web-documentary, the entire website became inaccessible due to issues with the server.[14] The individual interviews are now only available on YouTube, where the feature-length documentary can also be viewed. In its shift across the internet, from the website hosting the web-documentary to YouTube, the web-documentary itself underwent a sort of decay. While YouTube offers a less curated experience for viewers, the larger social media platform potentially reaches a broad audience and presents new possibilities for interaction. Algorithmically recommended related content appears on the side of the screen introducing different perspectives on the triple disaster as do additional videos listed on Courdy's FUKUSHIMA DOCUMENTARY PROJECT YouTube channel, from eyewitness footage to news broadcasts and interviews with Courdy. The web-documentary thus has its own metanarrative of decay, migration, revival, and reconfiguration. This metanarrative offers a new way of thinking about the instability of these nuclear films in the digital age.

Filmmaking has always been a collective endeavor. Digital technologies facilitate increasingly independent production and distribution while also providing new opportunities for transnational collaboration. While all of the films in this study have significant transnational components, those by Courdy and Rouy are deeply transnational and exploit collective strategies in different ways than did films by Resnais and Marker. In the digital age, crowd funding websites and crowd-sourced footage allow for collaboration in production. Digital distribution platforms reach wider global audiences, allowing for greater visibility and possible expressions of solidarity. Additionally, digital ecosystems allow for viewer interactivity with the works themselves.

Courdy's own transnational engagements are evident in her work. Her multilingualism provides cultural and linguistic access that also facilitates transnational work. She interviews Japanese people, foregrounding their voices in her work, and uses footage of the tsunami borrowed from a Japanese eyewitness. The credits of *Beyond the Cloud* list support from French, Japanese, and Franco-Japanese individuals and institutions, including forty-six crowd funding contributors from around the world. Courdy also anticipated multilingual audiences, offering French, English, and Japanese versions of the web-documentary and the film.

Courdy's engagement with viewers and solidarity with victims of the triple disaster are also evident in the work itself. In the "about" section on the web-documentary, Courdy invited viewers to join in solidarity: "Si vous explorez ce Webdoc, peut-être êtes-vous prêts à vous laisser inspirer, et à participer au changement" (In exploring this webdoc, perhaps you too will be inspired to take part in this change).[15] Becoming involved gives a viewer a greater stake in the work. Viewers contributing funding or footage are credited as contributors or participants. Viewers of the web-documentary were also able to leave a virtual footprint and offer a gesture of solidarity by leaving a message on a digital *ema* on the wish tree, thus responding to and becoming part of the online work.

Courdy's work, like that of other filmmakers discussed in this book, exemplifies Mette Hjort's affinitive transnationalism. This form of transnationalism is not one based on opportunistic or financial imperatives but rather one that expresses cultural affinity and "arise[s] in connection to shared problems and commitments."[16] For Hjort, this is a valuable form of transnationalism in its commitment to political values over financial ones. Courdy's own investment in Japan and Japanese culture give rise to this affinity "in connection to shared problems and commitments" such as concern over the release of radioactive water into the Pacific Ocean evoked at the end of *The Invisible Island*. Her approach remains resolutely transnational in this second feature-length documentary as signaled in the opening title in Japanese above French (fig. 5.2) and acknowledged in the closing credits (in English): "This film was shot building a trust relationship on

Figure 5.2. Bilingual film title over the sea in *The Invisible Island*. *Source*: Courdy, Keiko, dir. *L'île invisible / The Invisible Island*. 2021; Screened from May 19–29, 2022, 11th International Uranium Film Festival.

the long term with local people and nuclear workers, in the exclusion zone around Fukushima Daiichi Nuclear Power plant. Keiko Courdy is extremely grateful to everyone in Japan and France who helped this film come to life." Courdy collaborates with Japanese creators such as Ryuichi Sakamoto and Ono Seigen, who contributed music to *The Invisible Island*, and she receives crowd-funded support for her films from around the world. As a French filmmaker, she is also joining a tradition of Franco-Japanese cultural collaboration and exchange that has shifted in the nuclear era to account for French engagement with Japan as a way to understand France's own problematic investments in nuclear power.

Visions from Afar

Unlike Courdy, Philippe Rouy does not speak Japanese and did not go to Japan to make his films. Working in France, Rouy made three films about the nuclear disaster at Fukushima Daiichi using found footage, bringing attention to the enormous amount of publicly available material documenting the disaster while questioning the apparent transparency of its mass dissemination. Rouy's films focus on the institutions, technologies, and tools involved in the nuclear disaster at Fukushima Daiichi and its aftermath with particular attention to questions of visuality. His physical distance from the disaster also allows him to reflect on it in broader terms. Referring to the TEPCO live stream feed he relies on for some of his footage, he explains, "Grâce à cette caméra j'avais la possibilité d'exprimer l'inquiétude d'une catastrophe nucléaire; à distance, en observant—ce qui correspondait à ma manière de faire. Il n'était pas question pour moi d'aller au Japon." (This camera gave me the possibility of expressing the anxiety of a nuclear disaster. At a distance, through observation. This corresponded to my way of doing things. There was no question of my going to Japan.)[17] Rouy suggests that if he went to Japan to make a film, it would not be about the nuclear disaster: "J'y verrais une forme d'obscénité à laquelle le travail à distance sur ces images m'a permis, j'espère en tout cas, d'échapper." (I would see in that a kind of obscenity that working on these images from afar allowed me to escape, at least I hope.)[18]

The first film in Philippe Rouy's trilogy, *4 bâtiments, face à la mer / 4 Buildings, Facing the Sea*, is tripartite itself, with three sections recalling the tripartite sequence of earthquake, tsunami, and nuclear disaster and thus evoking a temporal dimension. The film is also explicit in its spatial orientation with the "four buildings" in a position "facing the sea." The open sea before the buildings evokes future radioactive contamination from the damaged plants located on the coast of the Pacific Ocean. The sea suggests both a spatial and temporal "beyond": unbounded, uncontained, seemingly infinite, and continuously contaminated.

The first part of the film entitled "l'invisible et le caché" (the invisible and the hidden) provides a sequence of views of one of the damaged reactors at Fukushima Daiichi from June 2011 through January 2012. In the second part of the film, "squelettes enveloppés de soie" (skeletons shrouded in silk), an anonymous worker stands in front of TEPCO's live stream camera at the reactor and points at it for nearly twenty-four minutes. This gesture, reminiscent of Vito Acconci's performance art *Centers* (1971), was the spark for the entire trilogy of films. Rouy had seen thirty seconds of the footage on Stéphane du Mesnildot's blog in September 2011 and then found the entire sequence on the YouTube channel Fuku1live.[19] On YouTube, Rouy also found live stream TEPCO footage dating back to June 2011, which he combined with his own recordings from the ongoing live stream camera shown on the TEPCO website.[20] In the third part of the film entitled "j'écouterai le reste du chant au pays des morts" (I will listen to the rest of the song in the land of the dead), narration from a 1985 promotional film by TEPCO subtitled in French plays over a cycle of footage of the damaged reactor similar to what was shown in parts one and two.

Rouy's second film, *Machine to Machine*, is the shortest in the trilogy with a running time of thirty-two minutes. It is also the most abstract and demanding of the viewer. *Machine to Machine* uses images from drones, cranes, robots, and probes that have been sent into the highly radioactive reactors to document damage. Ghostly images of ruins haunt what Rouy calls an "environnement minéral dont toute humanité est absente et dans lequel il est difficile de se réparer spatialement" (mineral environment devoid of all humanity and in which it is difficult to obtain spatial reference points).[21] The only intermittent sounds are those of machines. *Machine to Machine* offers a non-human vision of the disaster and shows human non-mastery of tools and machines used in an attempt to manage the situation.

The third film in the trilogy, *Fovea centralis*, takes its title from the anatomical term for the center of the field of vision in the eye where visual acuity is highest. *Fovea centralis* presents a multi-image mosaic of videoconference footage from eight TEPCO boardrooms in Tokyo and the Fukushima Daiichi region during the days and weeks following the nuclear disaster (fig. 5.3). TEPCO made this footage available to the public while also extensively censoring it by blurring faces and bleeping or entirely removing the sound. Rouy's film acknowledges and reframes these "blind spots," juxtaposing blurred boardroom footage with his own selection of text and sound. At times, all eight boardrooms share the screen, creating a sense of visual and informational overload; other times, one or two frames fill the screen and offer no greater clarity on the situation.

Rouy's vision of the nuclear disaster at Fukushima Daiichi is thus constructed through these "views" from afar. The first view

Figure 5.3. Apparent transparency in *Fovea centralis. Source*: Rouy, Philippe, dir. *Fovea centralis*. 2014; Vimeo.

in *4 Buildings, Facing the Sea* opens on what appears to be a still image of the damaged reactor with a date and time code at the top (2011-06-08 15:14:38) along with a "Tokyo Electric Power Company, Incorporated" copyright. The apparently still image is revealed to be a moving one as the time code advances and slight movement can be discerned in the distance as a hose sprays over exposed scaffolding of the damaged structure. The webcam image changes every minute or so to show new views of the same reactor at different times of day and in various atmospheric conditions from June 2011 through January 2012. In June, the camera shakes from continued aftershocks. Footage from November shows orange and brown foliage. In January, the site is covered with a light dusting of snow. In the early morning, fog obscures the buildings, while at night they are illuminated by an offscreen source of light. In place of a cause-and-effect linear narrative, several independent micro-events are shown: crows fly across the screen and land on part of the reactor; the camera zooms in on a tower and zooms back out; footage is sped up, showing hyperreal atmospheric movement against a night sky; construction cranes add and remove parts of the structure, which dangle uncertainly before the camera; the sun rises and sets. Four and a half minutes into the film, the first sounds can be heard: faint bell tones and eerie instrumentals. Sonic transitions provide an unsettling sense of progression. Synthesized instrumentals fade to silence or are overtaken by crackling feedback or deep rumbling, which are in turn interrupted by a buzzing drone, sounds that evoke the imperceptible radioactivity.

The second view, "squelettes enveloppés de soie" (skeletons shrouded in silk), contains the footage of the worker pointing at the live stream camera for nearly twenty-four minutes on August 28, 2011. The worker is dressed in a full-body hazmat suit with personal identifying marks removed. The name "Finger Pointing Worker" (*yubisashi sagyōin*) was bestowed on the laboring activist by the artist Takeuchi Kota, who claims to represent the worker and who displayed video of the performance in a solo exhibition at XYZ collective in Tokyo in March 2012. Takeuchi, a graduate of Tokyo University of the Arts, was also a temporary cleanup worker at the plant at the same time that the pointing action was undertaken. He does not confirm or deny that he, himself, is the Finger Pointing Worker saying only, "Even if I said it was me, it would in fact be very difficult for you to confirm that I was telling the truth."[22]

This second section begins with the worker (or "skeleton," evoking the worker's mortality and the potentially life-threatening conditions at the damaged power plant) in a white hazmat suit entering the frame, walking toward the camera and getting positioned in front of the live stream camera using the screen on a smartphone, which is also used to watch the live stream of the act. With the other hand, the worker points first to the reactor and then at the camera, a gesture that is held for over twenty minutes (fig. 5.4). A few minutes into the film's second view, the screen splits into two frames, literally providing two views. Micro-events of other workers at the site appear on the left, while on the right, the worker remains fixed in position, so immobile that the viewer might check the time code to confirm that it continues to progress. On the left, other workers move quickly through the highly radioactive area, underscoring the duration of the pointing worker's act (fig. 5.5).

The juxtaposition of footage draws attention to the unchanging shot and fixes the moment in the present. Nearly twenty-four minutes

Figure 5.4. Finger Pointing Worker in *4 Buildings, Facing the Sea*. Source: Rouy, Philippe, dir. *4 bâtiments, face à la mer / 4 Buildings, Facing the Sea*. 2012; Vimeo.

Figure 5.5. Split screen in *4 Buildings, Facing the Sea*. Source: Rouy, Philippe, dir. *4 bâtiments, face à la mer / 4 Buildings, Facing the Sea*. 2012; Vimeo.

in a highly radioactive zone begins to feel like an eternity. The shot also holds attention on the worker long enough for this subject to become interesting. The worker standing in front of the camera for ten seconds or one minute may be unremarkable; at five minutes, the act is notable; at over twenty minutes it becomes striking.

At one point, the same footage of the worker plays in both frames and a beating sound intensifies, suggesting a heartbeat and thus the humanity of the worker. This moment creates a sense of urgency and a climax of sorts for the non-narrative film. It also requires multisensory perception as the viewer not only sees the worker but hears and feels the heartbeat. Later in this section, a different worker who can be distinguished by a yellow helmet, appears in the left frame. This worker also stands in front of the camera but points at something offscreen, gesturing urgently, which calls attention to the dangerous labor conditions at the plant and underscores the intentionality of the Finger Pointing Worker's steady, accusatory gesture. At the end of this section, the left frame disappears and the right moves forward into its place. After pointing at the camera for over twenty minutes, the worker walks out of the frame and returns seconds later directly in front of the camera to point at it again. In closer framing, the worker's face, partially obscured by the pointing hand, becomes almost visible through the mask (fig. 5.6). After several seconds, the worker's hand drops again, and the worker walks out of the frame.

In a blog post published shortly after the act, someone claiming to be the Finger Pointing Worker admits to being a contract worker for TEPCO who came to Fukushima Daiichi on a day off to carry out the action. This person explains that in pointing at the

Figure 5.6. Finger Pointing Worker in closer framing in *4 Buildings, Facing the Sea*. Source: Rouy, Philippe, dir. *4 bâtiments, face à la mer / 4 Buildings, Facing the Sea*. 2012; Vimeo.

camera, the worker was symbolically pointing at TEPCO in order to draw attention to unsafe labor conditions. The worker was also pointing at the Japanese government, which was keeping information from Japanese residents, and at viewers of the live stream (or of the recorded excerpt on YouTube) so that they might share a sense of responsibility rather than simply participate as voyeurs, and so that they might begin to understand the workers as heroes rather than as lowly laborers. Finally, the gesture was a reflexive one, pointing at the self in what is described as an act of "self-sacrifice by narcissism."[23] In her analysis of this act as performance art, Anna Volkmar writes that the gesture can be read as "not only making the (Japanese) viewer complicit in having used the disaster-generating technology, but on a much simpler, material level, of being exposed to its fallout (radioactive, political, social) too."[24]

The third view, "j'écouterai le reste du chant au pays des morts" (I will listen to the rest of the song in the land of the dead), returns to a single frame of the same reactor. In this section, voiceover narration from a 1985 TEPCO promotional film describes the genesis and construction of Fukushima Daiichi and extols the economic benefits it brings to the region, adding a historical lens through which to view the footage. The title of this section suggests an ominous future in which we may have more clarity about the situation at Fukushima Daiichi, just as the filmmaker in 2012 more clearly perceives the naïve arrogance and irony of TEPCO's 1985 promotional film.

During the ten minutes of narration in this third section of the film, several micro-events take place: a racoon wanders across the frame, a cat walks alongside the damaged reactor, a fly crawls on the camera lens, and a crow lands on a long pipe. The voiceover narration in Japanese concludes, "The new energy that has come into existence here will be a great energy. It will improve all of our lives." Then, the narration stops, and the film ends with a final ninety-second micro-event: a breeze ripples through the vegetation and an inchworm crosses the lens.

The three views of Rouy's *4 Buildings, Facing the Sea* suggest a new structural possibility for digital nuclear visions. In this new structure, independent digital fragments such as these micro-events can be brought together to provide multifaceted visions of Japan through a nuclear lens. The fragments in this film have their own temporal limits made explicit by the time code at the top of the frame. The footage segments are chronologically arranged within the three views, and all three views cycle through the same eight months of footage.

The superstructure of this film, too, creates a temporal loop, an inescapable eight months. This loop of live stream footage recalls the inescapable eternal nuclear present in *Hiroshima mon amour* as well as the impossible present in *La Jetée*. In the digital age, however, the eternal and impossible present alone no longer define the chronotope of the nuclear. As in the electron's nuclear orbit, in the digital age, the temporal loop comes to indicate nuclear potential. To break the temporal loop, then, is to release time from infinity and allow it to unfold as a very long duration. As Timothy Morton writes of the hyperobject, "gigantic timescales are truly humiliating in the sense that they force us to realize how close to Earth we are. Infinity is far easier to cope with . . . I can think in infinity. But I can't count up to one hundred thousand."[25]

One can imagine in the abstract a worker at a destroyed nuclear reactor pointing at a camera for an infinite amount of time. But imagining infinity allows us to look away. Infinity diminishes human agency and dehumanizes the subject. We know we cannot watch anything for an infinite amount of time. We can, however, watch the worker pointing at the camera for nearly twenty-four minutes. These minutes begin to feel extremely long as workers in the adjacent frame move quickly in and out of the frame; twenty-four minutes is a very long duration for any shot in cinema; twenty-four minutes in a highly radioactive site comes to feel that much longer, especially without the relief offered by fictional remove or by the abstraction of infinity.

4 Buildings, Facing the Sea, with a time code always visible at the top of the frame, has an explicit temporal framework that also announces its digital identity. The cycle of the same eight months of footage in the three parts of the film evokes different temporal strata. Rouy explains:

> [C]ette structure en modules autonomes permet de faire advenir ces strates temporelles dont je parlais. Un temps plutôt terrestre, géologique, est évoqué dans la première, un autre plus historico-politique dans la dernière. Et puis le temps du présent, de l'immédiateté, du direct—qui est aussi le temps de l'exposition du corps humain aux radiations—dans la partie centrale.

> ([T]his structure of autonomous modules allows these temporal strata I'm talking about to emerge. A more terrestrial, geological time is evoked in the first part, another more historico-political time in the last. And then the time of the present, of immediacy, of the direct—which is also the time of exposure of the human body to radiation—in the middle part.)[26]

Placed between the geological, terrestrial time evoking the past and the historico-political time projecting an unpromising forecast for the future, the present—the Finger Pointing Worker—is thus at the heart of *4 Buildings, Facing the Sea*.

The long durations of seemingly static shots in Rouy's work offer opportunities to reflect on the passage of time, on the slow work of repair, and on the dispersal of radiation as wind blows through overgrown vegetation and unsuspecting wildlife move at their own paces through the zone. Wildlife and atmospheric forces such as wind bridge what have been determined to be "contaminated" and "safe" spaces, carrying radioactivity between them. They also operate according to different timescales. Wind speed is independent of time, and nonhuman animals may experience the passage of time in very different ways than humans do.[27]

The loop can also be understood in spatial terms as a perimeter or contamination zone, an attempt at mastery over the reality of the borderless space of radioactive contamination. The spatial loop can be seen in the concentric circles marking the exclusion zones around Fukushima Daiichi. These abstract and imprecise loops are challenged by reports showing the uneven and unpredictable spread of radioactive contamination. Areas beyond the loop may be more highly radioactive than areas inside of it. When the illusory spatial loop is broken, peripheral narratives emerge undermining the centralized political accounts of orderly containment.

In Rouy's work, live stream cameras break the loop of containment around the Fukushima Daiichi reactors and mediatize the situation allowing access to anyone with an unobstructed internet connection. Narrative in these films comes from broken spatial and temporal loops. The porous spatial boundaries of the exclusion zone are revealed in shots of the unrestricted movement of atmospheric elements and wildlife. Rouy breaks the chronological loop using nonlinear temporal montage. In the digital age, spatial and temporal loops are shown to be illusory as they break down in representations of nuclear disaster. As hyperobjects, nuclear materials cannot be contained by borders, continents, or bodies of water. For Morton, hyperobjects "end the idea that time and space are empty containers that entities sit in."[28] Digital technologies and platforms allow nuclear disaster to be virtually seen and felt around the world at the same time that it is experienced by those in proximity to the disaster site. Nuclear materials extend beyond the nuclearized site, beyond the spatial container suggested by the place name *Fukushima* and the temporal container suggested by the date *3.11*. Nuclear spatiotemporality moves to the foreground and gives form to these digital nuclear narratives.

The long durations in Rouy's films also encourage viewers to reflect on the imperceptible danger of radiation. In *Machine to Machine* and *Fovea centralis*, the second and third films in the trilogy, Rouy challenges the notion that radiation is invisible by showing radioactive dots and filaments that twinkle against a dark grainy background. These images recall the common origins and contemporaneous discovery of radioactivity and cinema, and they show that digital cameras are also vulnerable to the radioactivity that Henri Becquerel observed in 1896 on photographic plates from the Lumière factory. Cinema in the digital age remains what Akira Lippit calls a "technolog[y] for visualizing the inside, for imagining interiority."[29] *Machine to Machine* takes the viewer inside reactor ruins, often to enclosed spaces alive with radioactivity. *Fovea centralis* includes in its mosaic of videoconferences a black frame that sparkles with radioactivity. The visualization of radioactivity in Rouy's films may offer a suggestion of control over it, but seeing radioactivity also renders more uncertain the filmic spaces in which radioactivity is not visible.

The superstructures of Rouy's films allow for fragments accessible on YouTube to be seen in a broader context. Fragments stitched together in Rouy's work allow, for example, the Finger Pointing Worker to be seen in relationship to other workers at the power plant, to other life forms, and to atmospheric conditions changing over time at the same site. Together in Rouy's films, these fragments of surveillance footage take on new significance and tell a larger story of nuclear disaster. Rouy's visions of Japan through a digital nuclear lens are also increasingly unstable as the film fragments do not necessarily depend on one another for meaning and can easily come apart, leading to a breakdown of narrative.

Rouy's films rely on a different kind of transnational collaboration than do Courdy's. The footage he uses comes from TEPCO and the Fuku1live YouTube channel. Rouy intentionally remains distant from the disaster. He began a career as a journalist but is shy and does not want to intrude on people, so he moved to filmmaking.[30] In his trilogy of films, Rouy does not tell others' stories but observes and responds to them. His work suggests that solidarity is as much in listening, watching, and reflecting as it is in translating and telling. Solidarity is in the act of working though thousands of hours of live stream footage to find significant moments and then highlighting them to create meaning. Meaning is created in the pairing of video of a raccoon walking alongside the damaged reactor while an audio recording extols the virtues of nuclear energy, and of footage of a worker in a white hazmat suit standing in front of a surveillance camera and pointing for nearly twenty-four minutes with the sound of a heartbeat in the background.

Rouy's films are visual essays in the tradition of Marker's essay film in which meaning is created through montage and sound is as important as image. In Rouy's work, though, verbal language is almost completely removed, and Rouy himself does not provide voiceover narration. His films are essays on visibility and invisibility and on anonymity in the secretive nuclear industry.[31] As such, these films are explicit in their criticism of this industry and the institutions that support it. Having grown up in France through Cold War threats of apocalypse and the Chernobyl disaster in 1986, Rouy is familiar with nuclear anxiety. In these filmic critiques, Rouy implicitly expresses solidarity with all people whose lives and well-being are subordinated to the economic imperatives of capitalism and technological progress. Rouy did not contact the internet user whose footage he borrowed from the Fuku1live YouTube channel, but he credits the channel in the film, explaining, "Être isolé, à distance, me convient. J'aime conserver mon statut de regardeur non informé. Me dire que ces images sont lancées par un émetteur, et que j'y réponds à ma manière ; que je relaie le signal sous une autre forme." (I liked the idea of being isolated, at a distance. I like preserving my status as uninformed viewer. Telling myself that these images were made available by someone and I respond to them in my way; that I broadcast the signal in another form.)[32]

As transnational collaborations of a different kind, Rouy's films about the nuclear disaster at Fukushima Daiichi arise neither from financial imperatives nor from a desire to create a lasting network but as an "artistically cogent and necessary thing to do at a given moment in time."[33] In Hjort's typology of transnationalisms, his work might thus be considered as a form of *experimental transnationalism*, in which broader social and political values are secondary to aesthetic commitments, which reveal their own politics. Takeuchi frames the central pointing act as performance art while Rouy understands his own work as a more personal political act: "Les gens qui viennent les voir ont déjà une conscience politique affirmée. Mes films relèvent d'abord d'un geste politique que je me dois de faire pour moi. . . . Je n'ai pas fait ces films pour dénoncer quoi que ce soit" (People who come to watch these movies already have a strong political conscience. My films are first and foremost a political act that I owe to myself to make. . . . I did not make these films to denounce anything at all).[34]

Perhaps more so than any other French visions of Japan since *Hiroshima mon amour*, Rouy's visions of Japan through a nuclear lens are as much if not more about France itself in their implicit critiques of French investments in nuclear power. The visions of Japan in these films also return in a way to the tradition of Japonisme with Rouy's long takes of seemingly static landscapes recalling the ukiyo-e landscapes that so inspired French Impressionist painters. At the same time, the Finger Pointing Worker's accusatory gesture in Rouy's film recalls the closing question of Resnais's postwar documentary *Nuit et brouillard / Night and Fog*: "Alors qui est responsable?" (Then who is responsible?)

With digital media it is easier than ever to become aware of global concerns and to interact with one another. But do awareness and connection lead to action? The films studied in this chapter offer two different visions of potential action their works might inspire. In the web-documentary, Courdy explicitly encourages viewers to join in the action:

Ne serait-ce pas l'occasion de repartir sur des bases plus saines dans notre rapport au monde, à l'environnement, à l'énergie? Beaucoup en rêvent. Mais est-ce possible? Peut-on changer nos comportements? Les Japonais pourront-ils le faire, ou nous inciter à le faire ? Comment ? En dépit des apparences et de l'impuissance que beaucoup ressentent, le changement est profond. Partout des individus s'activent pour lutter contre l'inertie. Si vous explorez ce Webdoc, peut-être êtes-vous prêts à vous laisser inspirer, et à participer au changement.

(Might not this be the opportunity to start anew, with a healthier approach in our relationship to the world, the environment and energy production? Many dream of this. But is it possible? Can we change our behavior? Will the Japanese be able to change, or persuade us to change? And if so, how? Contrary to appearances and the impotence felt by many, the change is profound. Throughout Japan, individual people are standing up and fighting against this inertia. In exploring this Webdoc, perhaps you too will be inspired to take part in this change.)

Rouy, on the other hand, does not expect that his work will directly inspire political action. His viewers, he assumes, already have a developed political consciousness. However, in the making and sharing of his films, Rouy models significant acts of environmentalism. He did not travel to make these films, and he uses relatively little material in the production and distribution of his work. These films have relatively small carbon footprints. If Rouy does not directly ask viewers to act, he offers his work and his methods as possibilities for action. Since making this trilogy of films, Rouy's work has become increasingly oriented toward Japan with a 2021–22 residency at the Villa Kujoyama in Kyoto for a project on the Ukishima Collective, a Japanese filmmaking collective formed immediately after the nuclear disaster at Fukushima Daiichi.[35]

Finally, the digital media employed in these films destabilize the ontological status of the digital works themselves. Websites disappear. Links are broken. Servers come down. It may no longer make sense to pay to keep work online. Just three years after its launch, Courdy's web-documentary began to break down. The Nos Voisins Lointains 3.11 model is more collaborative and has remained active, but this association's website has also migrated to a new platform. What does it mean for a film to last now? Is a film still a film if its material traces break down, disappear, or are rendered functionally invisible? Or is this breakdown, not unlike that of radioactive decay, an essential quality of these nuclear films? Whether or not they last, these French visions of Japan through a digital nuclear lens are more easily modified and more open to dialogic transnational exchange, from conception and production through distribution and reception. Whether or not these films will be inscribed in the tradition of Franco-Japanese exchange for generations to come is, perhaps, beside the point. These are not fixed visions of an exotic floating world halfway around the globe; they are immediate and ephemeral visions of half-life after a nuclear disaster.

6

Reframing *Hiroshima mon amour* after Fukushima

Pourtant, j'ai envie d'essayer de comparer.
(And yet, I want to try to compare)

—Judith Cahen, *The Heart of the Conflict*

THE AUGUST 1945 ATOMIC bombings of Hiroshima and Nagasaki and the March 2011 nuclear meltdowns and explosions at Fukushima Daiichi were nuclear disasters of very different orders. The former were intentional acts of war that entailed the mass killing of human beings, and the latter, a series of events resulting from a sequence of natural disasters and that have ongoing but less easily detectable harms. Serious health impacts from both nuclear disasters are linked to radiological exposure, but the type of exposure is different: in Hiroshima and Nagasaki, exposure was predominantly external from gamma waves, while in the Fukushima Daiichi disaster, the risks and impacts have come primarily from internal exposure with the ingestion of alpha-emitting or beta particles, or what is termed fallout.[1]

While the names Hiroshima and Fukushima, often used as shorthand for these distinct disasters, should not be confused, Jean-

167

Luc Nancy remarks that their rhyme nevertheless suggests a common concern about nuclear energy.[2] As Robert Jacobs has argued, nuclear power was "born violent" in that it was "invented as part of the manufacturing process of nuclear weaponry."[3] This common concern around nuclear technologies, their risks, and the enduring harms they have caused is brought to the fore in two films made after the Fukushima Daiichi nuclear disaster that reference and reframe *Hiroshima mon amour*. The first, *The Age of Guilt and Forgiveness* (Jun Yang, 2016), is a twenty-three-minute single-channel video and part of an installation that opened at the Mori Art Museum in Tokyo. The short film reprises the relationship between a young European woman (played by Alexandra Faust) and a Japanese man (played by Michael Mishima) in Hiroshima after the nuclear disaster at Fukushima Daiichi and widens its lens beyond nuclear disaster to broader environmental concerns. The second, *Le cœur du conflit / Kokoro no katto / The Heart of the Conflict* (Judith Cahen and Masayasu Eguchi, 2017), is a feature-length film that contains several references to *Hiroshima mon amour* and centers on the Franco-Japanese couple Judith and Masa (played by the filmmakers) who explore questions of nuclear energy, sustainability, and reproduction after the 2011 disaster. These films extend the cycle of Franco-Japanese nuclear cinema initiated by *Hiroshima mon amour*, a cycle that resists iconic imagery and spectacle in favor of the nuclear mundane. In referencing and reframing *Hiroshima mon amour* after Fukushima, these filmmakers reinforce the sinister rhyme of the place names, revealing their interconnection while interrogating, after Nancy, the "equivalence of catastrophes."[4]

This chapter, like the last, examines art and experimental films made in the aftermath of the 2011 nuclear disaster. As both *The Age of Guilt and Forgiveness* and *The Heart of the Conflict* explicitly reference and reframe *Hiroshima mon amour*, this final chapter also reprises discussions in previous chapters about *Hiroshima mon amour* and responses to it. While chapter three analyzes Japanese responses to *Hiroshima mon amour*, this chapter focuses on repetition and the comparison that it invites. Repetition, as Deleuze notes, is significant for the change or difference it introduces in the mind of the thinker or viewer.[5] The repetition of nuclear disaster in Japan provides an opportunity to distinguish between disasters, to interrogate attempts to establish their equivalence, and to reflect on the incommensurability of personal and collective traumas and of military attack and cascading natural and sociotechnical disasters.

The films in this chapter engage with the historical repetition of nuclear disaster in Japan through formal repetition of *Hiroshima mon amour*, the film that provided the prototypical French vision of Japan through a nuclear lens. The repeated returns to *Hiroshima mon amour* suggest that this film itself is a sort of cinematic trauma that many filmmakers—particularly those working between France and Japan—feel compelled to repeat. In referencing and reframing this film, *The Age of Guilt and Forgiveness* and *The Heart of the Conflict* reveal similar conceptions of nuclear spatiotemporality that arise from both disasters and underscore the fundamental interconnection of military and civil applications of nuclear materials and technologies. These films also use repetition to return to the problem of comparison, a problem that is implicit in the film *Hiroshima mon amour* and one that has been discussed at length by scholars and critics of the film. Comparison remains a contested practice in these recent films as well. When Masa in *The Heart of the Conflict* tells Judith that certain things cannot be compared, she responds, "Pourtant, j'ai envie d'essayer de comparer" (And yet, I want to try to compare).

If the nuclear disasters at Hiroshima and Fukushima Daiichi and the collective and individual traumas they have provoked are incommensurable, these recent films suggest that insights for the future might nevertheless be revealed in their comparison. As Linda Gordon has argued, "Comparisons do not have to be equations of value; they do not require comparing commensurate objects."[6] Gordon proposes "light comparison," an admittedly unbalanced, unequal, and partial use of comparative thinking that allows for "observations from one situation [to raise] questions of another, questions one might not have thought to ask otherwise."[7] Light comparison of the incommensurable disasters in these films that reference and reframe *Hiroshima mon amour* reveals a continued interest in the nuclear mundane, reaffirms a conception of nuclear spatiotemporality as unbounded and uncertain, and introduces new transnational engagements around broader environmental concerns.

The Age of Guilt and Forgiveness and *The Heart of the Conflict*, selected for analysis primarily for their explicit engagement with *Hiroshima mon amour*, share similarities between themselves as well.

Both incorporate footage of the 2011 disaster at Fukushima Daichi: silent, grainy, distant black-and-white footage of the explosions in *The Age of Guilt and Forgiveness*, and a slightly different framing in color and with the sound of the explosion in *The Heart of the Conflict*. Both films present an alternative post-nuclear landscape to the scorched city of ruins after the atomic bombings. While the bomb, concealed from the public eye until it was hypervisible at the moment of explosion, represents one form of nuclear threat, the nuclear contamination landscape introduces a more pervasive and enduring one. The visualization of this invisible threat entails different strategies to register nuclear traces such as Geiger counters and images of decomposing bags of radioactive dirt. If the iconic mushroom cloud has been stripped of its evocative power through overuse, these other images contribute to a new iconography of nuclear disaster, a future-oriented one that includes a broader focus on elements such as water and earth as represented by *hibakujumoku*, the trees that survived the atomic bombings in Japan.

The critical nuclear lens in this chapter shows how this other kind of nuclear cinema that emerges from the chronotope of the nuclear continues to resist the nuclear spectacle in favor of the nuclear mundane, which is often embedded in the films' nuclear spatiotemporalities. These more recent films retain a sense of the eternal present of ongoing nuclear disaster at and around Fukushima Daiichi while gesturing toward a future if not beyond radiological risk then in a new relationship to it. The films in this chapter also sustain interest in landscapes and seascapes and engage with broader environmental concerns around energy and resilience. Their visions of Japan open a wider transnational lens on nuclear concerns and implicitly call for global action.

The Future Looks the Same as the Past

The Age of Guilt and Forgiveness opens on waves crashing under a dense cloudy sky in a palette of whites, grays, and blues. A low horizon divides the clouds from the breaking waves and underlines the film's title, which appears first in English before fading to Japanese. There is a cut to a profile shot of a man standing on the shore gazing at the sea. While Philippe Rouy's films in the previous chapter offer distant and remediated views of the reactors, the opening seascape of Jun Yang's film shot in Japan signals proximity to the nuclear disaster.

The seascape is followed by aerial color shots of black bags of radioactive dirt that line roads and fill fields near Fukushima Daiichi and archival footage of the tsunami in muted color that fades to black and white. In voiceover narration in Japanese, a man describes the incinerated victims of the atomic bomb as "etched into memory": "They will disperse and infiltrate everything, like a shadow, a cloud that will cover everything." As the tsunami footage fades to black and white, it is defamiliarized and infiltrated by the memory of the incineration of the atomic bombs, the memory of which covers the opening of this film like a shadow or a cloud.

The filmmaker Jun Yang was born in mainland China and works out of Vienna, Taipei, and Yokohama. His work, a product of his international upbringing, "examines the influence of clichés and media images on identity politics."[8] Yang describes the twenty-three-minute film *The Age of Guilt and Forgiveness* as taking *Hiroshima mon amour* "as a reference and starting point."[9] *The Age of Guilt and Forgiveness*, an Austro-Japanese coproduction, was shot primarily in Hiroshima with an international cast and crew. It incorporates documentary footage from Fukushima, and the final sequence occurs at the Observatory of Jantar Mantar in Jaipur, India, a location with no immediate geographic or cultural connection to *Hiroshima mon amour*. While *The Age of Guilt and Forgiveness* is not a French production, Yang has had several previous engagements with France in his work, including a performance piece entitled *Paris* (2000), and a group of works produced since 2007 under the title *Paris Syndrome*.[10]

The archival footage incorporated in the prologue of this film recalls the documentary prologue of *Hiroshima mon amour*. In *The Age of Guilt and Forgiveness* this footage is followed by another familiar black-and-white shot of a man's hands on a woman's bare back. In contrast to the ash-covered and glistening skin of the embracing bodies in the opening dissolves of *Hiroshima mon amour* and the accompanying mournful score, the movement of bodies in *The Age of Guilt and Forgiveness* is rigid and minimal in a short, silent scene. While the intertextuality with *Hiroshima mon amour* is evident, the divergent style of the repeated shot in *The Age of Guilt and Forgiveness* draws attention to its difference. Although these films, like the nuclear disasters they contemplate, are not to be mistaken as equivalent, the use of *Hiroshima mon amour* as an intertext nevertheless establishes Yang's vision of Japan after the nuclear disaster at Fukushima Daiichi as mediated through that film and its eternal nuclear present. While a central concern in *Hiroshima mon amour* is of memory and forgetting with an orientation toward the past, the question in Yang's film is how to deal with guilt and forgiveness from the past and in the present and how they will shape the future.

The Age of Guilt and Forgiveness centers on the embracing couple mentioned above, a European woman who is in Hiroshima as a student of comparative cultural studies and history and the Japanese man on the beach in the opening scene (fig. 6.1). The two are confronted with personal issues including his infidelity and her pending departure from Japan. They are also interested in the history of the Second World War, their generation's relationship to that history, and the relationship of the atomic bomb to the nuclear disaster at Fukushima Daiichi. The couple is shown together in a bedroom, walking through the streets of the city, at a bar, at the Hiroshima Peace Memorial Park, and at the Hiroshima City Museum of Contemporary Art. The film contains several explicit parallels to *Hiroshima mon amour*, including the shared locations and the opening embrace. Like Elle and Lui in *Hiroshima mon amour*, the couple in Yang's film are a European woman and a Japanese man who are dealing with questions of personal and collective guilt around the memory of the war.

Figure 6.1. The couple in *The Age of Guilt and Forgiveness*, recalling *Hiroshima mon amour*. *Source:* Yang, Jun, dir. *The Age of Guilt and Forgiveness*. 2016; Vimeo.

Despite its thematic echoes and reenactments of scenes from *Hiroshima mon amour*, *The Age of Guilt and Forgiveness* is not an attempted remake, as was *H Story*. Yang's film extends reflection to Japan's role as aggressor in the Second World War, and it highlights parallels between the atomic bombing of Hiroshima and the aftermath of the nuclear disaster at Fukushima with a broader focus on the environment. If *H Story* deals with the question of memory and the meaning of *Hiroshima mon amour* forty years after its release, Yang's film in color and black and white examines the burden of history in Japan seventy years after the atomic bombings of Hiroshima and Nagasaki and five years after the March 2011 earthquake, tsunami, and nuclear disaster in Japan. While references to the 2011 triple disaster in Japan are explicit in the archival images of the tsunami, hydrogen explosions at the power plant, and aftermath of the nuclear meltdowns as seen in the shots of black bags of radioactive dirt, the history of this disaster is largely yet to be written.

Yang's distinct cultural approach extends to the language used in the film as well. Unlike the mostly French dialogue in *Hiroshima mon amour*, the dialogue in *The Age of Guilt and Forgiveness* is entirely in Japanese (with English subtitles). Reflecting a more highly developed cultural competence than that of Elle in *Hiroshima mon amour* and Béatrice in *H Story*, the European protagonist in Yang's film speaks Japanese and is in Hiroshima to learn about the city's history. While the cultural encounter between Elle and Lui in *Hiroshima mon amour* is based on the shared trauma of war and the incommensurability of their experiences, the protagonists in *The Age of Guilt and Forgiveness* are interested in exploring the problem of comparison. When the man asks the woman about her interest in comparative cultural studies and history, for example, she responds, "It is useless to compare histories. It's only interesting how [cultures] deal with their past, their guilt and forgiveness, how they interpret it, how each of us tells the story." If the direct comparison of histories is unlikely to produce new knowledge or insight, the woman underscores the value of interpretation.

This chapter, too, is interested in comparison and its role in storytelling and interpretation. Analysis of Yang's film as a vision not *of* but *for* the future through the lens of *Hiroshima mon amour* reveals the continuities and evolutions of nuclear spatiotemporality from Hiroshima to Fukushima and opens a wider transnational lens on a nuclear Japan. With its conception of unbounded and uncertain nuclear space and time, *The Age of Guilt and Forgiveness* exemplifies the chronotope of the nuclear developed over the course of this study while also showing how the concept evolves as it allows for projections into the future.

The de-emphasis of national identification and geographic specificity in *The Age of Guilt and Forgiveness* invites broader diachronic reflection on the film. Neither the man nor the woman says where they are from, though they speak Japanese together. From the film's title that evokes the problem of memory and an atemporal "age of guilt and forgiveness" to its engagement with a tradition of cross-cultural exchange (most notably with *Hiroshima mon amour*), its use of archival material that acknowledges the global dimensions of nuclear disaster in Japan, and its final sequence at the Observatory of Jantar Mantar in Jaipur, India, *The Age of Guilt and Forgiveness* ultimately demands a confrontation with time, a reckoning with the past and its repetitions that is needed for a sustainable future. The film thus invites reflection on the diachronic effects of war and radioactive contamination.

The confrontation with time is underscored in the film's juxtaposition of black-and-white and color footage. The aerial color shots of bags of radioactive dirt piled high create a new anthropogenic stratum and suggest the fragility and vulnerability of our current geological era. The man narrating in voiceover connects this stratum to the atomic bombing of Hiroshima: "like shadows of the past, burnt into history." Over color footage of the tsunami, he continues, "They do not stay burnt but will disperse and infiltrate everything like a shadow, a cloud that will cover everything and leave everything shadow." The color footage of the tsunami changes to black and white, and the grainy image of a flooding landscape becomes indistinct. The man describes the burnt people and burnt landscape, evoking Hiroshima without saying the name. "This time the burn will not be visible," he says, a reference to the invisible radioactive contamination from the explosions at Fukushima Daiichi, which is shown in black and white. Billowing clouds from the explosions are juxtaposed with a burst of flames in color as the man continues, "We don't need others. We will destroy ourselves. The burning of the past. The burning of the present." The implicit references to Hiroshima and explicit references to the Fukushima disaster in this opening sequence underscore the repetition of nuclear disasters in Japan and the eternal nuclear present.

The eternal nuclear present and the background nuclear space of the chronotope of the nuclear appear in the haunting of the present by the past and in the juxtaposition of footage from the disaster at Fukushima Daiichi with present-day Hiroshima. The past and present become entwined as the footage of the 2011 disaster alternates between color and black and white, recalling images of the 1945 destruction of Hiroshima such as those from Itō Sueo's *The Effects of the Atomic Bomb on Hiroshima and Nagasaki* used in the prologue of *Hiroshima mon amour*. Moments after the hydrogen explosion at Fukushima Daiichi shown in *The Age of Guilt and Forgiveness*, images of the protagonists in bed are intercut with a tree branch tied with wishes and a *hibakujumoku* on a playground in Hiroshima.

As in other films that exemplify the chronotope of the nuclear, linear time in *The Age of Guilt and Forgiveness* is interrupted. The 2011 triple disaster is shown out of order with the black bags—part of the decontamination effort in the aftermath of the meltdowns and explosions at Fukushima Daiichi—preceding the tsunami and explosions. The grainy black-and-white footage of the explosions creates temporal distance similar to that evoked by the use of documentary footage in the opening of *Hiroshima mon amour* juxtaposed with the present-day reality of Elle and Lui. Time is further unmoored by the atemporal title "The Age of Guilt and Forgiveness," referring not to a specific date in history as "Hiroshima" might to August 6, 1945, but to a present and future shaped by past events.

The title of the film also evokes the political problem of memory in Japan. Yang includes footage of prime minister Abe Shinzo speaking on television in which he says, "In Japan, the postwar generations now exceed 80% of its population. We must not let our children, grandchildren, and even further generations to come, who have nothing to do with that war, be predestined to apologize. Still, even so, we Japanese, across generations, must squarely face the history of the past. We have the responsibility to inherit the past, in all humbleness, and pass it on to the future." Abe describes the titular age of guilt and calls for acceptance of the past, a responsibility not for past events but for their inheritance. In Yang's film, the remediation of the speech through the television lessens its didacticism and invites the viewer's reflection on Abe's perspective on responsibility without apology. The man and woman do not respond directly to the speech. The man turns off the television and asks the woman why she is in Japan. She answers, "to study," suggesting an effort to understand history if not to squarely face it. Her position is rather different than that of Elle in *Hiroshima mon amour*, who was in Hiroshima to make a peace film and was convinced that after a few trips to the museum she had seen everything. She is also different from Béatrice in *H Story*, who seemed to resist understanding.

The tension between engaging the past and moving on from it continues in a scene of the couple visiting the Hiroshima City Museum of Contemporary Art. While Elle is never shown in the Hiroshima Peace Memorial Museum and Béatrice moves wordlessly and uncomfortably through the Museum of Contemporary Art and leaves shortly after arriving, the woman in *The Age of Guilt and Forgiveness* walks calmly through the Museum of Contemporary Art alongside the man. As they stroll through the space with their gaze directed at what appear to be empty walls, they never stop to contemplate. The continuous sound of footsteps reinforces this sense of action without reflection and a refusal of both past and present in an orientation toward the future. This scene raises questions about what kind of future is possible if the past is not left behind but also what future is imaginable beyond the shadow of the past, beyond the eternal nuclear present. A future that leaves the past completely behind might resemble a cursory walk past blank walls of an exhibition space.

If the protagonists skim the surface of history and refuse political interpretations of it, their conversations about their own relationship evoke these larger concerns and establish an implicit comparison between personal and collective experience. After the trip to the museum, the two sit at a bar and have a conversation that on one level is about their relationship and on another is about the history of the atomic bombing. The man asks if the woman will forgive him. She says she will in time but proposes they let it go and not continue the suffering. "You are neither here nor there, neither in time nor in space . . . Not with her, not with me. Not here. Not there. Somewhere, sometime," she says. The man explains his inability to leave the past behind: "I feel I am trapped. . . . Even if I tell you, you would not understand. A shadow will always be there like a maze." She responds, "You try to interpret the past and predict the future. But you are not in the present." He asks her to stay in Hiroshima, stay with him, and she looks down at bar. On the surface a conversation about his infidelity, this abstract discussion of space and time and of past and future offers another level for interpretation regarding the weight of history and suffering in Hiroshima. His evocation of history as a shadow that traps him as if in a maze references the installation *A Maze and an Observatory as a Memorial of the Past* of which this film is a part. The installation does not include a maze, but a staircase modeled after the sundial at Jantar Mantar that figures at the end of the film. In the exhibition space, the staircase leads to nothing but serves as another viewpoint from which to watch the film. This metaphorical maze suggests a temporal period that cannot be directly accessed and that requires a certain amount of puzzling out, of comparison with the present, to arrive at a point of clarity such as that offered by the observatory.

Beyond its evocation of the historical shadow cast by the atomic bombing of Hiroshima, *The Age of Guilt and Forgiveness* shows sustained interest in the elements as they relate to the nuclear disasters: water in shots of the ocean and tsunami; earth in the stacked bags of dirt and *hibakujumoku*; and fire and air in the billowing clouds from the explosions and in a low angle shot of the sky at Jantar Mantar at the end of the film. With its evocation of the broader effects of radioactive contamination on the natural world, this film contributes to a new, elemental iconography of nuclear disaster. In the twenty-first century, images of explosions offer little new knowledge of nuclear disaster and its long-term radioactive contamination. Yang's turn to the elements recalls that of other artists and filmmakers in the aftermath of the 2011 disaster who have sought new ways to visualize the invisible and evoke the specter of radioactive contamination through natural elements that can spread and contain it.

The film's closing sequence expands the elemental iconography and opens a wider transnational lens on the environmental and historical questions evoked in Japan. In this sequence, the woman is at the Observatory of Jantar Mantar, an eighteenth-century astronomical observatory maintained as a monument and UNESCO World Heritage Site that contains Brihat Samrat Yantra, one of the largest stone sundials in the world, amongst its twenty instruments for measuring time. The observatory is a space of cultural exchange representing the adoption of astronomical data from Islamic and Persian civilization into ancient Hindu tradition. The transition from Japan to India is bridged by the woman's voiceover in Japanese: "We live with the sense of no end but a projection of a future, of our future, and a sense of historic continuation and narration. We look up at the stars, look back into the past—we try to make sense of it, looking for clues to predict the future." The voiceover about the future paired with the change in location to India suggests that such a projection of the future takes place elsewhere, beyond Japan. The woman walks around the observatory site alone, looking for a window on the future from the past at a historical astronomical site.

The final low angle shot of the film is of the Brihat Samrat Yantra sundial (fig. 6.2). The monument is a large staircase that leads to a *chhatri*, a small cupola at the top of the structure. Birds flock to the *chhatri*, perch on the structure, and fly away. At one point, just as the birds are about to land, the shot is reversed and they appear to fly away in reverse, a final disruption of the notion of linear time. This long take of the sundial—over seventy seconds—leads into the end credits. The low angle shot does not show the structure's function as a sundial nor the shadow it produces but emphasizes its projection into the sky where it offers an expansive view above ground level. The sundial evokes a different form of radiation, that of sunlight. The camera becomes a management tool for the visible spectrum, but the scene also requires chronoception to appreciate its layered temporal dimensions. The sky is at once a window on the past through the

Figure 6.2. Brihat Samrat Yantra at Jantar Mantar, Jaipur, India, *The Age of Guilt and Forgiveness*. *Source*: Yang, Jun, dir. *The Age of Guilt and Forgiveness*. 2016; Vimeo.

stars and a canvas for projections of the future. The final shot of an observatory that is also a sundial, the function of which is to tell time in the present, underscores the scrambling of temporalities in a film looking to the future to escape from the shadow of the past.

The choice of Jantar Mantar as the location for this final scene is perhaps the most unexpected aspect of the film. The location has no clear connection to *Hiroshima mon amour* or to the nuclear disasters at Hiroshima or Fukushima. However, Yang again references the tradition of East-West cinematic exchange with the use of Ryuichi Sakamoto's theme from *Furyo / Merry Christmas, Mr. Lawrence* (Ōshima Nagisa, 1983) in the soundtrack over the final images and closing credits, reprising its earlier use in the last scene of the film shot in Hiroshima. The soundtrack retains a connection to Japan in an ending that represents a geographical departure from it. Away from Japan and beyond the immediacy of radioactive contamination after the nuclear disaster at Fukushima Daiichi, the film closes by turning to the sun as a different source of radiation and of energy for a future beyond the eternal nuclear present.

The Heart of the Problem

The Heart of the Conflict offers another reframing of *Hiroshima mon amour* after the nuclear disaster at Fukushima Daiichi. It is a literal and figurative reframing as the filmmaker-protagonists Judith Cahen (Judith) and Masayasu Eguchi (Masa), a Franco-Japanese couple like Elle and Lui, watch *Hiroshima on amour* on a laptop in front of a window open on one of the reactors at the Saint-Laurent-des-Eaux Nuclear Power Plant in France, as presented on the cover of this book. *The Heart of the Conflict* is a self-reflexive making-of film about how to create in a nuclearized world that may be coming to an end. It incorporates multiple perspectives on reproduction, contamination, and mortality, Like *Hiroshima mon amour*, it is a multilocal film shot in France (Paris and Saint-Laurent-des-Eaux) and Japan (Fukushima and Saga Prefectures and the city of Hiroshima), and it contains archival material from decades past alongside images from the 2011 triple disaster and its aftermath. Like many of the films in the alternative kind of nuclear cinema that emerges from the chronotope of the nuclear, *The Heart of the Conflict* is a nonlinear, hybrid documentary-fiction film. In referencing and reframing *Hiroshima mon amour* after Fukushima, *The Heart of the Conflict* reconnects France and Japan around nuclear concerns and renews a fading eternal nuclear present with attention to the 2011 nuclear disaster and its resonances with and differences from the atomic bombings.

Intertextuality in *The Heart of the Conflict* underscores the film's central organizing principles: repetition and conflict. The film's use of repetition, in particular, offers a new way of understanding the nuclear spatiotemporality at the foundation of the chronotope of the nuclear. *Hiroshima mon amour* is but one of the filmic intertexts of *The Heart of the Conflict*. In reference to its predecessor, *The Heart of the Conflict* includes archival footage and audio from an interview with Marguerite Duras by her son Jean Mascolo. Traces of Eguchi's previous documentary *Le printemps de Hanamiyama—Fukushima / Springtime in Hanamiyama—Fukushima* (2012) commissioned by local residents about the decontamination process around Fukushima Daiichi are also woven throughout the film, from footage of empty roads and destroyed structures in the exclusion zone to a promotional poster for the documentary in the background of the filmmakers' workspace. *The Heart of the Conflict* also includes an excerpt from Hashimoto Isao's multimedia work "A Time-Lapse Map of Every Nuclear Explosion since 1945" (2003) in a demonstration of the vast environmental damage caused by nuclear testing worldwide.[11] Finally, there is the dramatization of the film within the film as Judith and Masa prepare for scenes and discuss what is and is not working in the film that they are in the process of making.

The Heart of the Conflict opens with the sound of waves and a patch of grass over dry earth, an image that recalls the abstract scar in the opening credits of *Hiroshima mon amour*. The opening shot of the ground is followed by photographic stills of Masa and Judith in a field with a camera and nuclear reactors in the background. After another shot of the ground and a slow tilt to the two reactors, which become the central subject of the frame, white text appears at the horizon in Japanese and then in French asking "Est-ce que vous semez demain si le monde vient à sa fin?" (Do you sow tomorrow if the world is coming to an end?) As the film orients itself toward the future, a clock can be heard ticking, and the screen fades to white.

A fade in reveals the backs of Masa and Judith, who sit naked on a bed facing a skylight on a slanted ceiling in front of them in a scene that recalls the opening hotel room scene of *Hiroshima mon amour*. Bilingual titles identify them as "une française / フランス人" (a French woman) and "un japonais / 日本人" (a Japanese man). Masa stands up to look out the window and touches the radiator on the wall in front of him. His face is washed out by the sun from the skylight. In these opening images evoking the earth, the sun, and energy, the film constructs an alternative elemental iconography of nuclear disaster and establishes its material foundation in what will become a complex work of multiple conflicts and centers.

The multiple conflicts in *The Heart of the Conflict* include an interpersonal conflict about reproduction, an intercultural conflict about remembrance, a philosophical conflict around comparison, and the broader societal conflict around nuclear energy. Conflict structures the film as indicated in an early conversation between Masa and Judith. He tells her that she wants to be complicated, and she insists, "Je *veux* pas être compliquée. Je constate que dans ma tête ça se passe de manière compliquée, et j'ai envie d'être honnête avec ma tête." (I don't *want* to be complicated. I observe that things happen in a complicated way in my mind, and I want to be honest with my mind.) Shostakovich's Symphony no. 5 in D Minor serves as a sound bridge connecting this discussion filmed in a car to a shot of Judith meditating in their workspace, then an intertitle about montage, a white screen with the film title and subtitle in Japanese and French, and the following scene of the filmmakers walking along overgrown train tracks in a wooded area.

The intertitle frame articulates the working method for the film. The frame includes a black-and-white photograph of Sergei Eisenstein, for whom conflict is the essence of a work of art (fig 6.3). Eisenstein leans diagonally and looks up at a strip of film that cuts the other way diagonally across the frame. His suspenders are perpendicular to the film strip while the stripes on his tie parallel it, illustrating graphic conflict within the frame, between the filmmaker and his work. Bilingual text, Japanese above French, fades in over the photograph of Eisenstein: "Le montage, c'est le dépassement du conflit (lisez: contradiction) à l'intérieur du cadre, tout d'abord vers le conflit de deux fragments placés l'un à côté de l'autre . . ." (Montage is the surpassing of conflict [read: contradiction] inside the frame, first toward the conflict of two fragments placed next to each other). For Eisenstein, conflict arises from the juxtaposition or superimposition of

Figure 6.3. Intertitle with quotation in Japanese and French superimposed on image of Sergei Eisenstein in *The Heart of the Conflict*. *Source*: Cahen, Judith and Masayasu Eguchi, dirs. *Le cœur du conflit / Kokoro no katto / The Heart of the Conflict*. 2017; Vimeo.

elements within and between frames. The dialectic conflict between elements creates a greater meaning than the mere sum of elements as meaning is not inherent in individual images but rather constructed through their combinations. The frame within a frame and the text superimposed over crisscrossing diagonals illustrate the method of this film, of complex meaning created within and between frames and through combinations of text and image and of French and Japanese. Multilingualism in the film is itself evidence of the evolution of the Franco-Japanese transnational relationship, from its earlier orientation around visual art and the aestheticization of language, and from the predominantly monolingual relationship in the French-language film *Hiroshima mon amour*.[12]

 The Heart of the Conflict is structured around such juxtapositions. The dynamic process of montage is in tension with a search for a stable, identifiable center of the film, as suggested in its title. The various elements of the film orbit around its nucleus or its elusive heart. The polysemic heart—at once a symbol of love, an essential life-sustaining organ, and an evocation of the reactor core—is vulnerable in its power. As a Deleuzian "amorous organ of repetition,"[13] the heart is also the driving force of the film's many repetitions: of elements from *Hiroshima mon amour*, of the interview scene with Duras, and of the self through procreation. The film's subtitle "intime et politique" (personal and political) itself echoes the title with a key difference in the relationship between the elements. Whereas the title locates the heart as a symbol of the intimate realm within or *of* the conflict (in reference to the political realm), the subtitle sets up the terms *personal* and *political* as coequals. The working out of this relationship in the film echoes Eisenstein's own working out of the relationship between successive shots as building blocks (an outmoded idea of montage in his view) and as acts of collision, as seen for example when Japanese "ideographic characters ('shots') are juxtaposed and *explode* into a concept."[14]

If much of *The Heart of the Conflict* focuses on the interpersonal realm through interactions with the filmmakers' parents and real and imagined offspring, Judith locates the titular heart of the film in the political arena when she explains that "les déchets nucléaires, c'est le cœur du problème, même quand il n'y a pas d'accident" (nuclear waste is the heart of the problem, even when there is no accident). The act of identifying nuclear waste as the problem with little further analysis mirrors media reporting that ignores or minimizes the invisible problem of nuclear waste. In *The Heart of the Conflict*, however, the problem of invisible waste is magnified by a sustained interest in the question of contamination and its relationship to elements such as water, air, and earth as well as the question of contamination of the present and future by the past.

The contamination of temporalities is evoked most notably in contrasting footage from the 2011 Fukushima nuclear disaster and the 1959 film *Hiroshima mon amour*. Judith's desire to compare the incomparable or to close this temporal gap births a new conflict arising from the difference between these events. The opening act of *The Heart of the Conflict* also includes juxtapositions of present-day Hiroshima with Fukushima. Among the first scenes of *The Heart of the Conflict* is silent footage of the 2011 tsunami that preceded the nuclear disaster in Japan followed by grainy color footage and sound of the explosion.[15] The explosion serves as a sound bridge to black and white footage of the aftermath of the atomic bomb in Hiroshima and is overtaken by the sound of a clock ticking. The pan across the desolate Hiroshima landscape is familiar from Itō Sueo's *The Effects of the Atomic Bomb on Hiroshima and Nagasaki* cited in *Hiroshima mon amour*. The juxtaposition of these two nuclear disasters is commented upon in the following shot of a sheet of metal with a punchout of the word ECHO. Judith, wearing a black jacket, hoodie, hat, and scarf, walks out from behind this art installation outside the Hiroshima City Museum of Contemporary Art. Although the scene is in color, the museum building, the metal installation, the gravel on the ground, Judith's dark clothing, and the winter sky appear in shades of gray, creating a more complicated distinction between past and present.

Judith's trip to the museum recalls Elle's visits to the Peace Memorial Museum in *Hiroshima mon amour* and even more explicitly the couple's visit to the Museum of Contemporary Art in *H Story*. Judith, however, does not enter the museum but takes a picture of herself sitting on the ground outside in one of forty bronze casts around the ECHO installation.[16] In the following scene, again echoing Elle's recollection of her trips to the museum in *Hiroshima mon amour*, Judith sits alone in a room in the Astor Plaza Hotel, her dark reflection visible in the window, which also looks out on the Hiroshima night skyline, a superimposition of interior and exterior. She reflects on her own position in Hiroshima in narration: "À la vérité, aujourd'hui, j'étais mal. Je ne savais plus pourquoi j'étais à Hiroshima. Je me disais c'est pas mon histoire. Ou plutôt ce en quoi c'est mon histoire, ça le serait plus ailleurs." (Today, I felt bad. I no longer knew why I was in Hiroshima. I told myself it's not my history. Or rather that which is my history is elsewhere.) The personal conflict for Judith, who is trying to understand her own position in the film and in the history of the atomic bombing, arises from the juxtaposition of nuclear disasters in Japan and from the tension produced by the concurrent echo and incommensurability of these disasters. Judith's role in the film recalls that of Elle in *Hiroshima mon amour* with the repetition of the French woman's unease in Hiroshima. Significantly, though, Judith holds herself apart from the history of Hiroshima. She does not claim, as Elle does, to have seen everything or, implicitly, to understand it. This difference creates a distinct conflict between personal and collective trauma in *The Heart of the Conflict*. For Judith, the conflict is based on distance between rather than conflation of the personal and the collective.

If conflation renders comparison impossible, distance allows for at least light comparison, which may be "unbalanced, unequal, partial, even reduced to 'asides' or parenthetical comments."[17] *The Heart of the Conflict* approaches the problem of the incommensurability of personal and collective trauma in more explicit ways than does *Hiroshima mon amour*. For example, Masa recounts how his father passed away on March 11, 2011, eleven minutes before the earthquake that triggered the tsunami that flooded the reactors and led to the nuclear melt-downs at Fukushima Daiichi. A year later, he made a documentary about the triple disaster in which he never mentioned the death of his father. Judith asks Masa about this and about the relationship between the death of one man and the thousands killed that day in the tsunami. In voiceover, Masa wonders why she asks this question and how she would respond. "Deuil," (Grief) he says aloud in French, "On ne peut pas comparer" (cannot be compared). Judith nevertheless wants to compare the personal and collective traumas. Conflict arises from Judith's geographic, cultural, and emotional distance from the death of Masa's father and from her and Masa's different orientations toward comparison.

Judith also wants to compare the idea of an "artistic child" (the film they are making) with a human child, which she neither has nor wants to have. Masa, who does have children and would like another, repeats, "On ne peut pas comparer" (We can't compare). Masa's refrain to Judith recalls that of Lui to Elle in *Hiroshima mon amour*, "Tu n'as rien vu à Hiroshima" (You saw nothing in Hiroshima). Masa, who has had greater proximity to the things Judith would like to com-pare—his father's death, the March 2011 triple disaster, children of his own—refuses comparison, whereas Judith, who has more distance from these things and who senses their echoes, wants to try to com-pare them. In interrogating the commensurability of two large-scale nuclear disasters in Japan—one an intentional military attack, the other an unintentional result of a natural disaster—*The Heart of the Conflict* problematizes comparison while still finding echoes between the objects compared.

Despite the film's focus on Japan and a few scenes in or footage from Fukushima and Hiroshima, the majority of *The Heart of the Con-flict* takes place in France. The filmmakers drive through Paris taking measurements with a Geiger counter along the Seine, in front of a Japanese restaurant named "Fukushima," and under the Eiffel Tower. The song "La vie en rose" plays in the background with lyrics in Japanese, another instance of cross-cultural exchange. Judith remarks that France and Japan are among the most nuclearized countries in the world and mentions the pronuclear pact between France and Japan to reprocess plutonium waste into MOX (mixed oxide) fuel, which creates a link between Hiroshima (or rather the plutonium bomb dropped on Nagasaki) and Fukushima (where reactor three at Fukushima Daiichi used MOX fuel). They drive to the Saint-Laurent-des-Eaux Nuclear Power Plant and Judith recalls childhood trips driving by the reactors, which her parents pointed out as "modern" and "the electricity of the future."[18] In a hotel room, Judith and Masa watch *Hiroshima mon amour* on a laptop in front of a window with the nuclear reactors in the background (fig. 6.4). The juxtaposition of nuclearities within this shot bridges distant nuclear geographies and temporalities and reveals repetition with difference.[19] The eternal nuclear present of the atomic bombing of Hiroshima is renewed through a match of the tracking shot in the hospital in *Hiroshima mon amour* playing on the laptop to a shot from a car driving through wreckage in the exclusion zone around Fukushima after the 2011 triple disaster. Elle's voiceover "Comment aurais-je pu éviter de voir" (How could I have avoided seeing) provides a sound bridge between Saint-Laurent-des-Eaux (and a virtual Hiroshima from the laptop) and the exclusion zone around

Figure 6.4. *Hiroshima mon amour* plays on a laptop with Saint-Laurent-des-Eaux Nuclear Power Plant in the background in *The Heart of the Conflict*. *Source*: Cahen, Judith and Masayasu Eguchi, dirs. *Le cœur du conflit / Kokoro no katto / The Heart of the Conflict.* 2017; Vimeo.

Fukushima. The parallel tracking shots in Hiroshima and Fukushima connect past and present confrontations with images of the aftermaths of disaster. Watching *Hiroshima mon amour* in front of the aging reactors at Saint-Laurent-des-Eaux forces a confrontation with current French investments in nuclear power and the risk of future disaster.

The eternal nuclear present in *Hiroshima mon amour* becomes unmoored in *The Heart of the Conflict* as the film projects into the future. During the lengthy tracking shot through the Fukushima exclusion zone, Judith and Masa narrate alternately in French and Japanese an imagined future sixty years after Fukushima when civil applications of nuclear power will have created more damage than military ones. The story begins in the speculative mode of the fairy tale or allegory with the phrase "Il était une fois" (Once upon a time) suggesting a temporality that is neither past, present, nor future. In this speculation, Judith and Masa's imagined doubles—a younger French woman played by Mélissa Barbaud and a Japanese man played by Suzuki Kazuhiko who are dressed like Judith and Masa—walk across a white screen toward each other and kiss through the masks they wear to protect themselves from contamination. Next, Judith and Masa reenact the kiss through masks, and the color image fades to black and white. The following shot is a black-and-white freeze frame of the two couples kissing through masks, establishing continuity between the present and possible future. The chronotope of nuclear can be seen in the renewal of the fading eternal nuclear present of *Hiroshima mon amour* in which Elle and Lui are stuck in the present and in Judith and Masa's projection into the nuclear future in which contamination is ubiquitous, as suggested by the masked couple and the steady background chirp of a Geiger counter.

If nuclear waste is the heart of the conflict, the question at the heart of the film is not a technical one about how to deal with it but a broader philosophical question about how to live with ongoing nuclear disasters and whether or not to reproduce in such a world.[20] The film's opening provocation, "Do you sow tomorrow if the world is coming to an end?" brings up the ethics of procreation in such an uncertain world. Is the prospect of the end of the world reason enough not to make a film or to have a child? Or is it a pretext when the deeper reason is less clear or too complicated to put into words?

The question of reproduction for Judith is connected to the question of motherhood. The film extends its engagement with *Hiroshima mon amour* in turning to Marguerite Duras to explore this question.[21] In a filmed interview with her son Jean Mascolo, Duras, who had a complicated relationship with her own mother, shares her thoughts on maternal love, a subject about which she was never able to write. However, *The Heart of the Conflict* does not show the interview with Duras straightaway but begins with reenactments of it, just as *Hiroshima mon amour* began with reenactments of the aftermath of the atomic bomb before getting to the heart of the matter.[22] First, Masa (wearing large glasses like those worn by Duras) plays the role in a short exchange with Judith as the interviewer. "Parlons de l'amour" (Let's talk about love), she prompts him, and he responds, "Et alors" (So what). Next, in a slightly longer scene, a pregnant woman played by Olga Grumberg in a curly wig and the same large glasses takes on the role of Duras as Judith asks about maternal love. This second exchange is followed by the original footage of Duras speaking with her son about why she wrote about so many forms of love but never about maternal love (fig. 6.5). This time Duras responds, "C'est celui qui ne cesse jamais, qui est à l'abri de toutes les intempéries . . . et à la fin c'est une calamité. C'est la seule calamité du monde, c'est

Figure 6.5. Marguerite Duras and Jean Mascolo, from *Marguerite tel qu'en elle-même / Marguerite as She Was* in *The Heart of the Conflict. Source:* Cahen, Judith and Masayasu Eguchi, dirs. *Le cœur du conflit / Kokoro no katto / The Heart of the Conflict.* 2017; Vimeo.

l'amour maternel. Ça ne cesse jamais." (It's that which never stops, which is sheltered from all storms . . . and in the end it's a calamity. It's the only calamity in the world, maternal love. It never stops.) This original interview, preceded by two reenactments and followed by two more, is structurally the heart of a series of repetitions and suggests that the personal heart of the film is a question about maternal love.

Following another reenactment with the French actress Sarah Chaumette, who questions Judith's preoccupation with maternal love, Judith and Masa reenact the scene one final time, with Judith playing the role of Duras and Masa playing the role of Judith (with her glasses) playing Duras (fig. 6.6). This final reenactment occurs against a faint background of nuclear reactors on a white screen. When Masa asks her about love, she says, "Et les centrales nucléaires. Parlons des choses sérieuses" (And nuclear reactors. Let's talk about serious things) to which he responds, "On ne peut pas comparer" (We can't compare). This final reenactment by Judith and Masa returns to the recurring problem of comparison or of the comparison implied by the film's conflicting centers. That this series of interviews centers on the figure of Duras is all the more significant for her role as scenarist for *Hiroshima mon amour*, a film that was structured around and critiqued

Figure 6.6. Judith and Masa as repetitions of Duras in *The Heart of the Conflict*. *Source*: Cahen, Judith and Masayasu Eguchi, dirs. *Le cœur du conflit / Kokoro no katto / The Heart of the Conflict*. 2017; Vimeo.

for the same kind of implicit comparison of personal and collective traumas. This series of interviews shows how *The Heart of the Conflict* does more than just reference and reframe *Hiroshima mon amour* but in fact repeats it with a different set of disasters and a different set of personal and collective traumas while underscoring the significance of the nuclear background.

The Duras repetitions are preceded by a similar conversation that Judith has with her own mother. The sequence begins with Judith visiting her mother Françoise, who is in the hospital and unable to speak. An intertitle announces the next scene, three months before the accident, in which Judith interviews her mother when she is well. They sit at her dining table, and Judith begins the interview, "Maman," using the same tone and address that will be used by Mascolo to Duras in the following sequence. Judith wants to know if her mother sees a connection between maternal love and nuclear reactors. Françoise laughs and responds, "Les deux te préoccupent" (Both preoccupy you). She thinks a bit more and adds, "C'est peut-être dans le pouvoir plus ou moins destructeur d'une mère et le pouvoir plus ou moins destructeur du nucléaire. Parce que je pense que les mères sont très destructrices . . . dans ce désir du pouvoir" (Maybe it's in the more or less destructive power of a mother and in the more or less destructive power of nuclear energy. Because I think that mothers are very destructive . . . in this desire for power).

This conversation introduces an explicit comparison of the personal and the political at a fragile moment in Judith's own personal life. A set of sand timers sits on the table before them evoking the limits of human time and contrasting with the deep future of nuclear waste. The question of maternal love is a personal one about Judith's relationship with her mother and her mother's changing health as well as a broader political question about reproduction in the face of an increasingly uncertain future. During a long take of Judith and Françoise sitting at the table alternately looking at each other and looking away but never holding eye contact, Masa in voiceover asks Judith what maternal love means to her. Judith responds, "Écoute, c'est une forme d'amour qui m'a toujours à la fois manquée et étouffée. Comment ne pas fuir ce qui t'étouffe et comment ne pas chercher ailleurs ce qui manque?" (Listen, it's a form of love that always at once eluded me and smothered me. How can you not flee that which smothers you and look elsewhere for that which is missing?) Judith's interactions with her mother are presented not only as a repetition of the Duras interview but also as a repetition of the scene of Masa's father in the hospital as both filmmakers deal with their parents' mortality. It is also a response to Masa when he reflects back to Judith her question about comparing the death of his father with the death of thousands of people on the same day. Judith, too, finds herself speechless at certain moments with her mother. Her visit to the hospital as a forced confrontation with her mother's mortality and her silence in this moment suggest one possible answer to her question about comparison.

Throughout the sequence of repeated conversations between mothers and their children (or between people playing these roles), maternal love is revealed as a center of the film, one that is circled and approached in multiple ways: through Duras, through pregnant women, and through Judith's and Masa's younger doubles and their discussions about reproduction. However, it is this sequence with Judith's mother—and not the original footage of the Duras interview that follows—that becomes the heart of the film, a Deleuzian organ that sets in motion a series of repetitions. The juxtaposition of this sequence with the Duras repetitions shows a working out of the relationships between the incommensurable intimate and public, between maternal love and nuclear power, and implicitly between the incommensurable nuclear disasters at Hiroshima and Fukushima. Repetition in *The Heart of the Conflict* is revealed as a method for identifying the heart of the problem. At the heart of things, as Judith discovers, comparison may not be possible. And yet, she wants to compare, an impulse that introduces conflict.

If nuclear waste is not the intimate heart of *The Heart of the Conflict*, it nevertheless structures the filmmakers' conceptions of space and time. The spatial boundaries of nuclear waste—how to detect it, where to keep it, and how to contain it—are uncertain, particularly with the long half-lives of many radioactive elements. An imagined future sixty years after the nuclear disaster at Fukushima Daiichi is a world in which civil applications of nuclear technologies have produced more damage than military applications. The world still has no solution for nuclear waste, and concerns about contamination are widespread. In this future, the filmmakers' younger doubles hold a water tasting party, pouring bottled water into pitchers and glasses and tentatively drinking it. In voiceover narration, Judith says, "Mais le doute planait toujours sur sa contamination" (But doubt always persisted regarding its contamination). The next shot returns to the present to show Judith and Masa asking whether the food they are eating is contaminated.

The visualization of contamination concerns extends beyond that of personal contamination through ingestion. While the filmmakers draw on familiar strategies such as Geiger counters, they also work toward establishing a new elemental iconography of nuclear disaster, from the opening shot of the dry earth and patch of grass outside the Saint-Laurent-des-Eaux Nuclear Power Plant and the accompanying sound of waves to a later shot of steam rising from the reactors and dispersing into the air, an image that prompts Judith to ask if the steam contains cesium or another harmful element. Earlier in the film, when Masa recalls his trip in the contaminated zone around Fukushima Daiichi, he explains over shots of crashing waves that the power plant is five kilometers away. The next shot is of a bath at his hotel. Water laps over the edges of the tub, and Masa floats into the frame (fig. 6.7). In voiceover, he wonders about his cumulative level of radioactivity exposure: "Je suis quand même allé plusieurs fois dans la zone interdite . . . Suis-je certain que mes cellules ne sont

Figure 6.7. Masa in bath at Hotel Itakura Fukushima in *The Heart of the Conflict.* *Source*: Cahen, Judith and Masayasu Eguchi, dirs. *Le cœur du conflit / Kokoro no katto / The Heart of the Conflict.* 2017; Vimeo.

pas contaminées? Et cette eau où je suis? Et mes spermatozoïdes?"
(After all, I went inside the exclusion zone several times . . . Am I
certain that my cells aren't contaminated? And this water I'm in?
And my sperm?).

This uncertainty about the world around them is echoed in the
filmmakers' studio when Judith asks about a teapot Masa bought in
Fukushima in 2012: "Je me demande s'il n'est pas un tout petit peu
radioactif" (I wonder if it's a little bit radioactive). As they discuss
small doses of radioactivity, Judith identifies them as the heart of the
contamination problem: "C'est ça presque pour moi qui est le pire
parce que c'est sournois" (For me that's almost the worst because
it's insidious). These images of objects and elements that may be
contaminated encourage a different way of looking at the world at a
more atomic level. As David Macauley writes in *Elemental Philosophy*,
elements such as earth, air, fire, and water "are less abstract than an
often elusive and elastic notion of nature. It is easier, in brief, to engage
these entities with the senses."[23] Still, the human imperceptibility
of radioactivity suggests the insufficiency of sensory perception and
underscores the uncertainty that remains. Lacking the innate senses
and reliable tools to perceive the manufactured and enduring radioactive elements around them, what Joseph Masco terms "ubiquitous
elements" that "colonize a deep planetary future," Judith and Masa
grow increasingly uncertain and as they question their own exposure
and what it means for their future.[24]

The alternative nuclear iconography in this film and in *The Age
of Guilt and Forgiveness* also includes images of a different future for
energy. *The Heart of the Conflict* ends on a mountaintop with a long
take of a field of solar panels. A pan reveals more panels covering
rolling hills and mountains in the distance.[25] The opening quotation
"Do you sow tomorrow if the world is coming to an end?" appears
in Japanese and in French. This repetition is accompanied by a significant difference, too. This time the quotation is attributed to the
avant-garde writer and filmmaker Terayama Shuji in 1968 (fig. 6.8).
The additional context allows for a diachronic comparison of this
question asked in 1968 and again in the present. While the environmental harm of the intervening decades makes this question about
future even more urgent, the mountains "sown" with solar panels
offer an alternative vision of energy.

だちえ世界の終わりが明日だとしても
穎をまくことができるか？
　　　- 1968年　寺山修司

Est-ce que vous semez demain
si le monde vient à sa fin ?
　- 1968 Shuji Terayama -

Figure 6.8. "Do you sow tomorrow if the world is coming to an end?" Judith filming solar panel mountains at the end of *The Heart of the Conflict. Source*: Cahen, Judith and Masayasu Eguchi, dirs. *Le cœur du conflit / Kokoro no katto / The Heart of the Conflict*. 2017; Vimeo.

The possibility of this alternative energy future is accompanied by another more complicated question about art and interpretation. In a final scene in the film projecting into in the future, the imagined son (played by Nishimura Yuichiro) of Judith's young double explains that his mother hoped that he would work to deal with the problem of nuclear waste, but instead he became a film critic. He nevertheless uses his invitations on television to speak against nuclear power. A news report shows him criticizing the decision to restart the Genkai nuclear reactor in Saga Prefecture when the Fukushima problem still has not been resolved. He asks how the state can approve fifty-four reactors in such a seismic country. Finally, the self-reflexive film *The Heart of the Conflict* is not only about investigating its own core but also about how cinema reflects on issues that are too invisible or unspectacular to make headlines.

Both *The Age of Guilt and Forgiveness* and *The Heart of the Conflict* begin with the sound of waves and end with images of the sky that evoke the sun as another form of radiation and source of energy. The interest in elements and attention to water in these two relatively recent films point to ongoing concerns around the release of contaminated water stored on site at Fukushima Daiichi into the Pacific Ocean amid governmental assurances of safety. But the protagonist's trip to the Jantar Mantar Observatory at the end of *The Age of Guilt and Forgiveness* and the filmmakers' trip to the mountains covered in solar panels at the end of *The Heart of the Conflict* also suggest an orientation toward the future, a temporality that is less salient in the previous films analyzed in this book.

That both of these films reference *Hiroshima mon amour*, the prototypical French vision of Japan through a nuclear lens, in exploring the repetition and echoes of nuclear disaster in Japan; that both films feature couples who recall the Japanese man and French woman in *Hiroshima mon amour*; and that both films seek to compare nuclear disasters that took place over sixty-five years apart and over one thousand kilometers away from each other says little about the divergent paths these films take from the opening sounds of waves to the closing images of the sun. Such are the vast possibilities born from repetition. Following the move in both films from the Hiroshima Peace Memorial Museum in *Hiroshima mon amour* to the Hiroshima City Museum of Contemporary Art, cinema becomes another a way forward, a way to reflect and memorialize, a way to interpret and act, seed for fallow ground.

Conclusion

The focus in this book has been on Franco-Japanese nuclear films and on the transnational film cycle that emerged from one of the first Franco-Japanese coproductions, *Hiroshima mon amour*. In film studies, this dialogic genealogy is significant as it follows the legacy of one of the most important films for global art cinema through a nuclear lens. In comparative cultural studies, this film cycle oriented around nuclear concerns shows the possibilities and limitations of distance, repetition, and comparison in cross-cultural engagement. Cross-cultural engagement between France and Japan in cinema is also distinctive for its dialogic nature. For the environmental humanities and more specifically for nuclear studies, the film cycle studied here presents an alternative nuclear iconography that resists spectacle in favor of the nuclear mundane.

In Japan, many other films have been made about nuclear disaster and its effects, from Shindō Kaneto's *Genbaku no ko / Children of Hiroshima* (1952), the original *Gojira / Godzilla* (Honda Ishirō, 1954), and Imamura Shōhei's retrospective *Kuroi ame / Black Rain* (1989), to a stream of documentaries about the 2011 disaster at Fukushima Daiichi by new and established filmmakers such as Hamaguchi Ryūsuke.[1] Japanese films about the Fukushima disaster tend to approach the subject with greater precision. As one of the participants in Jean-Luc Vilmouth's documentary *Lunch Time* (2011/2014/2018) explains, people in Japan think that the Tōhoku region is contaminated, and people beyond Japan think that all of Japan is contaminated. However, those living in the Tōhoku region, such as the residents of the town of Yamamoto who take part in the potluck lunch in Vilmouth's film, have a much more granular understanding of fluctuating local levels of radioactivity. On the other hand, as Suwa Nobuhiro said of *Hiroshima mon amour*, a distant view can allow for greater comprehension of the tragedy.[2]

Several Japanese documentaries about the 2011 nuclear disaster center women's voices. Films such as *Ganbappe fura gāruzu! Fukushima ni ikiru kanojotachi no ima / Fukushima Hula Girls* (Kobayashi Masaki, 2011), *Chiisaki koe no kanon: Sentakusuru hitobito / Little Voices from Fukushima* (Kamanaka Hitomi, 2015), *Iitatemura no kaachantachi: Tsuchi to tomo ni / Mothers of Fukushima: Eiko & Yoshiko* (Furui Mizue, 2016), and *Atomic Refugee Moms* (Nakagawa Ayumi, 2018), among others, show women engaging in everyday domestic labor such as food preparation, child-rearing, and housekeeping while also leading public advocacy work for recognition of the harms their communities face from contamination. Such women, who also have a more local understanding of radioactivity levels in their homes, neighborhoods, and schools, are sometimes accused of radiophobia, the irrational fear of radiation, by authorities who themselves seem to fear the women's collective power. Documentary films featuring these women's voices contribute to a growing archive in the global fight for recognition of women's health and bodily autonomy.

This study has shown how French filmmakers with ties to Japan such as Keiko Courdy and Judith Cahen bring attention to women's voices as well, including interviews in their films with mothers and discussions of maternal love and its relationship to nuclear power. If Japonisme as a nineteenth-century tradition was primarily a masculine affair in the West, French engagement with Japan in the nuclear era has broadened to include women's voices, beginning with Marguerite Duras's scenario for *Hiroshima mon amour*.

The 2022 French film *L'été nucléaire / Atomic Summer* (Gaël Lépingle) imagines a major accident at the Nogent-sur-Seine Nuclear Power Plant, the closest reactor site to Paris. The film's protagonists are stuck inside the exclusion zone after what they are told is a level 5 accident but may be even more serious. They take half measures—wearing loose-fitting masks and mostly staying indoors—to protect themselves. The more abstract problem they face is one of information about the accident: it is difficult to access, or it is contradictory or untrustworthy. As they discuss whether or not to trust what government officials say about the accident on television, one of them asks whether people were told what was happening in Fukushima.

While there still seems to be significant support for nuclear power in France, recent higher budget films such as *Atomic Summer* and Rebecca Zlotowski's *Grand Central* (2013) aim at wider audiences and suggest cracks in a pro-nuclear foundation. The 2019 HBO mini-series *Chernobyl* was received in France with a bit more trepidation by those who lived under the cloud of the 1986 disaster and the hollow assurances of safety and protection that national borders would provide. The miniseries is celebrated for its particularly realistic portrayal of the disaster and of Soviet material culture during that era. A review in the French weekly *Télérama* describes *Chernobyl* as eschewing the codes of the catastrophe film, which suggests the power of realism.[3]

If *Chernobyl* comes closer to French and Japanese cinematic visions of mundane nuclear disaster, it also introduces a glaring cross-cultural issue: an English-speaking and almost entirely British cast playing Soviets. While the language barrier is acknowledged and often insisted upon in French films about Japan, the Soviet characters speaking English in *Chernobyl* suggest a certain refusal of the Cold War context in the interest of easing the viewing experience for the target audiences of a British and American coproduction in 2019. This might lead one to ask if HBO's *Chernobyl* is so different from Hollywood nuclear movies that came before it and for which profit took precedence over realism in all of its mundane expressions. English-speaking Soviets aside, the series is perhaps most appealing for its implicit reassurance that Chernobyl remains if not perfectly contained in space then at least circumscribed in time. Notably, the 2023 Netflix series *The Days* about the 2011 disaster at Fukushima Daiichi was made by Japanese directors with a Japanese cast and shot in Japanese. The trailer asks, "What was the meaning of those days for the country of Japan?"

The 2022 Russian invasion of Ukraine has brought attention anew to the vulnerability of Ukrainian nuclear sites including Chernobyl. But even in the years leading up to the invasion, as Kate Brown has documented, radioactive blueberries from Chernobyl have been mixed with less radioactive berries and shipped around the world to satisfy the demands of global consumers.[4] Those living outside of officially designated radioactive zones do not test every meal with a Geiger counter. There is little research on the dangers of low-dose and long-term exposures to radioactivity.

The nuclear lens in this book is not a substitute for a dosimeter but a tool in a search for other forms of knowledge of the radioactivity around us. Small moments in these films register the legacy of nuclear explosions and the precarious containment of waste. Scaling down to the atomic level allows for a magnification of nuclear effects that evade sensory detection and reveals new spaces for action. If we do not have all of the data, we do have these films and the sensory and affective experiences they offer to help us think through our ongoing nuclear entanglements while we work toward another possible future.

Notes

Introduction

1. "La fission brisait l'atome: la rupture de l'espace-temps historique était inséparable de cette rupture des composants de la matière même." Author's translation. Unless otherwise noted, all translations from French are the author's own. Gabrielle Hecht, "L'Empire nucléaire: les silences des 'Trente Glorieuses,'" in *Une autre histoire des "Trente Glorieuses": modernisation, contestations et pollutions dans la France d'après-guerre* (Paris: La Découverte, 2013), 161; Sean Cubitt, *Eco Media* (Amsterdam: Rodopi, 2005), 2.

2. The English title of Nothomb's novel is also *Tokyo Fiancée*. Amélie Nothomb, *Ni d'Ève ni d'Adam* (Paris: Albin Michel, 2007), a follow-up companion novel of sorts to Amélie Nothomb, *Stupeur et tremblements* (Paris: Albin Michel, 1999); Stefan Liberski, *Tokyo fiancée* (Les Films du Worso, 2014).

3. Marie-Noëlle Tranchant, "Tokyo fiancée: à la découverte du Japon," *Le Figaro*, March 3, 2015, sec. Cinéma, accessed June 14, 2023, http://www.lefigaro.fr/cinema/2015/03/03/03002-20150303ARTFIG00298—tokyo-fiancee-pauline-a-la-page.php.

4. On the significance of the documentary footage of the first nuclear tests and their relationship to time, see Jennifer Fay, "Cinema's Hot Chronology (5:29:21 Mountain War Time, July 16, 1945)," *JCMS: Journal of Cinema and Media Studies* 58, no. 2 (2019): 146–52.

5. Catalogs of such films can be found in Mick Broderick, *Nuclear Movies: A Critical Analysis and Filmography of International Feature Length Films Dealing with Experimentation, Aliens, Terrorism, Holocaust and Other Disaster Scenarios, 1914–1989* (Jefferson, NC: McFarland & Company, 1991); Hélène Puiseux, *L'apocalypse nucléaire et son cinéma* (Paris: Les Éditions du Cerf, 1987); Spencer R. Weart, *Nuclear Fear: A History of Images* (Cambridge: Harvard University Press, 1988); Toni A. Perrine, *Film and the Nuclear Age:*

Representing Cultural Anxiety, (New York: Routledge 2018); Kim Newman, *Apocalypse Movies: End of the World Cinema* (New York: St. Martin's Griffin, 2000); Jerome F. Shapiro, *Atomic Bomb Cinema: The Apocalyptic Imagination on Film* (New York: Routledge, 2002).

6. I echo Jessica Hurley's use of the *nuclear mundane* to refer to the nuclear "both in its extent and reach into every aspect of everyday life and in its contestability, as something that can be named and challenged." Jessica Hurley, *Infrastructures of Apocalypse: American Literature and the Nuclear Complex* (Minneapolis: University of Minnesota Press, 2020), 9.

7. Consider, for example, constraints imposed by US government agencies on depictions of thermonuclear war in Stanley Kramer's *On the Beach* as detailed in Mick Broderick, "Fallout *On the Beach*," *Screening the Past: An International, Refereed, Electronic Journal of Visual Media & History*, no. 36 (June 17, 2013).

8. Gabriel P. Weisberg, "Reflecting on Japonisme: The State of the Discipline in the Visual Arts," *Journal of Japonisme* 1, no. 1 (2016): 3–16.

9. Survivors of the nuclear attacks on Hiroshima and Nagasaki are referred to as *hibakusha*. This term has been updated as *global hibakusha* to include "all who have suffered the radiological effects of nuclear technologies since 1945." Robert Jacobs, *Nuclear Bodies: The Global Hibakusha* (New Haven: Yale University Press, 2022), 8.

10. Jean-Luc Nancy, *After Fukushima: The Equivalence of Catastrophes*, trans. Charlotte Mandell (New York: Fordham University Press, 2014), 13.

11. Nancy, 14.

12. Barbara Geilhorn and Kristina Iwata-Weickgenannt, "Negotiating Nuclear Disaster: An Introduction," in *Fukushima and the Arts: Negotiating Nuclear Disaster*, ed. Geilhorn and Iwata-Weickgenannt (London, New York: Routledge, 2017), 20.

13. Christian Doumet and Michaël Ferrier, eds., *Penser avec Fukushima* (Lormont: Éditions Cécile Defaut, 2016), 20; Other writing on 3.11: Michaël Ferrier, *Fukushima, Récit d'un désastre*, (Paris: Gallimard, 2012); Michaël Ferrier, "Fukushima ou la traversée du temps: une catastrophe sans fin," *Esprit*, June 2014, 33–43; Michaël Ferrier, ed., *Dans l'œil du désastre: Créer avec Fukushima* (Vincennes: Marchaisse, 2021).

14. "Proposal for a Diacritics Colloquium on Nuclear Criticism," *Diacritics* 14, no. 2, Nuclear Criticism (Summer 1984): 2–3.

15. Jacques Derrida, "No Apocalypse, Not Now (Full Speed Ahead, Seven Missiles, Seven Missives)," trans. Catherine Porter and Philip Lewis, *Diacritics* 14, no. 2, Nuclear Criticism (Summer 1984): 20–22.

16. Derrida, 28.

17. Derrida, 23.

18. Derrida, 27.

19. Hurley, *Infrastructures of Apocalypse*, 4.

20. Drew Milne and John Kinsella, "Introduction: Nuclear Theory Degree Zero, with Two Cheers for Derrida," *Angelaki* 22, no. 3 (September 2017): 2.

21. See for example Joseph Masco, *The Nuclear Borderlands: The Manhattan Project in Post-Cold War New Mexico* (Princeton: Princeton University Press, 2006); Ele Carpenter, ed., *The Nuclear Culture Source Book* (London: Black Dog Publishing, 2016); Daniel Cordle, "The Futures of Nuclear Criticism," *Alluvium* 5, no. 4 (July 29, 2016): https://alluvium.bacls.org/2016/07/29/the-futures-of-nuclear-criticism/; Molly Wallace, *Risk Criticism: Precautionary Reading in an Age of Environmental Uncertainty* (Ann Arbor: University of Michigan Press, 2016); Elizabeth M. DeLoughrey, *Allegories of the Anthropocene* (Durham: Duke University Press Books, 2019); John Kinsella and Drew Milne, *Nuclear Theory Degree Zero: Essays against the Nuclear Android* (New York: Routledge, 2021), Livia Monnet, ed., *Toxic Immanence: Decolonizing Nuclear Legacies and Futures* (Montreal: McGill-Queen's University Press, 2022).

22. Wallace, *Risk Criticism*, 12.

23. Rob Nixon, *Slow Violence and the Environmentalism of the Poor* (Cambridge: Harvard University Press, 2013), 3.

24. Elizabeth Eaves, "Why Is America Getting a New $100 Billion Nuclear Weapon?," *Bulletin of the Atomic Scientists*, February 8, 2021; David Vergun, "U.S. Facing Increasing Nuclear, Space-Based Threats, Leaders Say," US Department of Defense, April 20, 2021; David E. Sanger, William J. Broad, and Choe Sang-Hun, "Biden Is Facing an Uneasy Truth: North Korea Isn't Giving Up Its Nuclear Arsenal," *The New York Times*, May 20, 2021, sec. US.

25. The France-based multinational Areva, a group that specialized in nuclear power, and the US-based Westinghouse Electric Company (owned by the Japanese Toshiba Corporation) went bankrupt in 2016 and 2017 respectively.

26. Gabriele Schwab, *Radioactive Ghosts* (Minneapolis: University of Minnesota Press, 2020), xi.

27. "Current Population Estimates as of October 1, 2011," Statistics Bureau of Japan, accessed May 19, 2021, http://www.stat.go.jp/english/data/jinsui/2011np/.

28. David Lochbaum et al., *Fukushima: The Story of a Nuclear Disaster* (New York: The New Press, 2015), 78.

29. "Japan to Release Fukushima Water into Sea after Treatment," Reuters, April 12, 2021, https://www.reuters.com/world/asia-pacific/japan-says-release-contaminated-fukushima-water-into-sea-2021-04-12/.

30. "Fukushima Site Still Leaking after Five Years, Research Shows," Woods Hole Oceanographic Institution, March 7, 2016, http://www.whoi.edu/news-release/fukushima-site-still-leaking.

31. This follows Akira Mizuta Lippit's connection of cinema and X-ray photography as contemporaneous "phenomenologies of the inside" using "a new form of light that yielded a new visuality." Akira Mizuta Lippit, *Atomic Light (Shadow Optics)* (Minneapolis: University of Minnesota Press, 2005), 5.

32. Nuclear weapons, too, have explosive lenses, which refract and focus energy as a part of the detonation process.

33. Eva Horn, *The Future as Catastrophe: Imagining Disaster in the Modern Age*, trans. Valentine Pakis (New York: Columbia University Press, 2018), 14.

34. Carpenter, *The Nuclear Culture Source Book*, 9.

35. Joseph Masco, *The Nuclear Borderlands: The Manhattan Project in Post-Cold War New Mexico* (Princeton: Princeton University Press, 2006), 26–28.

36. Spencer R. Weart, *Nuclear Fear: A History of Images* (Cambridge: Harvard University Press, 1988), 244.

37. See Jacobson, "French Cinema vs the Bomb" for a close analysis of two such films (René Clair's *La beauté du diable* [1950] and Nicole Védrès's *La vie commence demain* [1950]); Puiseux, *L'apocalypse nucléaire et son cinéma* includes the Franco-Norwegian *La bataille de l'eau lourde* (1947); Clair's *La beauté du diable*; the short documentary *La bombe atomique en action* (1950); Henri-Georges Clouzot's *Les espions* (1957); Alain Resnais's *Hiroshima mon amour* (1959); Henri Decoin's *Nathalie agent secret* (1959); two short documentaries about the French atomic tests at Reggane: *De Valmy à Reggane* (1960) and *Reggane à l'heure* (1960); the Franco-Italian *L'Atlantide* (1961), Chris Marker's *La Jetée* (1962), Jean-Luc Godard's contribution "Le Nouveau Monde" to the Franco-Italian anthology film *Ro.Go.Pa.G* (1962); the short documentaries *Atolls à l'heure nucléaire* (1966) and *Marine, atome, Tahiti* (1967); the archival documentary *La bataille du Pacifique* (1971) and the documentary television film *La bombe de A à H* (1971); the short documentaries *L'explosion nucléaire* (1973), *La défense contre les armes nucléaires* (1975), and *Les engins balistiques* (1975); the feature film *Demain les mômes* (1976); the documentaries *Les abris antisouffle improvisés* (1977), *Ce monde est dangereux* (1977), and *Les engins à charge nucléaire* (1979); the comedy *Cherchez l'erreur* (1980); the above-mentioned science fiction film *Malevil* (1981); the documentaries *Dossier Plogoff* (1980), *Plogoff, des pierres contre des fusils* (1980), *Les forces nucléaires françaises* (1981), and *Supplément au voyage de Bougainville: les armées françaises en Polynésie* (1981); Luc Besson's *Le dernier combat* (1983); the Franco-Italian *2019 après la chute de New York* (1984); and the documentaries *La défense de la France* (1984), *Edition spéciale: comment vivre avec la menace de la guerre nucléaire* (1984), and *La guerre en face* (1985).

38. Recent commercial films include Rebecca Zlotowski's *Grand Central* (2013) about a love affair at a nuclear power plant in France; Marjane Satrapi's *Radioactive* (2019), a transnational coproduction and adaptation of

Lauren Redniss's graphic novel *Radioactive: Marie & Pierre Curie, A Tale of Love and Fallout* (2015); Olivier Peyron's *Tokyo Shaking* (2021), a Franco-Belgian fiction film about the 2011 triple disaster in Japan; and *L'été nucleaire* (2022), about a group of teenagers taking shelter in the French countryside during an accident at a nearby nuclear power plant.

39. Two noteworthy French documentaries dealing with the Pacific region more broadly are René Vautier's *Mission pacifique* (1989) on the effects of nuclear testing on the Pacific Islands, and *Hirochirac 1995* (1995), filmed at the time of the fiftieth anniversary of Hiroshima and documenting the announcement made by President Jacques Chirac that France would reengage in nuclear testing in the Pacific.

40. Nicolas Bancel, Pascal Blanchard, and Sandrine Lemaire, "Introduction. La fracture coloniale: Une crise française," in *La fracture coloniale: La société française au prisme de l'héritage colonial* (Paris: La Découverte, 2006), 15. The colonial legacy in Japan and competing narratives centering on heroes, victims, and perpetrators complicate Western understandings of Japanese denial, as examined in Akiko Hashimoto, *The Long Defeat: Cultural Trauma, Memory, and Identity in Japan*, (New York: Oxford University Press, 2015), 6.

41. M. M. Bakhtin, *The Dialogic Imagination: Four Essays*, trans. Caryl Emerson and Michael Holquist (Austin: University of Texas Press, 1981), 84.

42. Bakhtin, 425–26.

43. Mary Louise Pratt, "Coda: Concept and Chronotope," in *Arts of Living on a Damaged Planet*, ed. Anna Tsing et al. (Minneapolis, London: University of Minnesota Press, 2017), 171.

44. Doumet and Ferrier, *Penser* avec *Fukushima*.

45. Robert Stam, *Film Theory: An Introduction* (Oxford: Blackwell Publishers, 2000).

46. Michael V. Montgomery, *Carnivals and Commonplaces: Bakhtin's Chronotope, Cultural Studies, and Film*, (New York: Peter Lang Publishing, 1994), 2.

47. Vivian Sobchack, "Lounge Time: Postwar Crisis and the Chronotope of Film Noir," in *Refiguring American Film Genres: History and Theory*, ed. Nick Browne (Berkeley: University of California Press, 1998), 151.

48. Sobchack, 150.

49. Bakhtin, *Dialogic Imagination*, 99.

50. Bakhtin, 100.

51. Karen Barad, "No Small Matter: Mushroom Clouds, Ecologies of Nothingness, and Strange Topologies of Spacetimemattering," in *Arts of Living on a Damaged Planet*, ed. Anna Tsing et al. (Minneapolis, London: University of Minnesota Press, 2017), 106.

52. Barad, 109.

53. Timothy Morton, *Hyperobjects: Philosophy and Ecology after the End of the World*, (Minneapolis: University of Minnesota Press, 2013), 1.

54. Gabrielle Hecht, *Being Nuclear: Africans and the Global Uranium Trade* (Cambridge, MA: MIT Press, 2012), 14.

55. Gilles Deleuze, *Cinema 2: The Time-Image*, trans. Hugh Tomlinson and Robert Galeta (Minneapolis: University of Minnesota Press, 2010), 13, 17–18.

56. Luis Rocha Antunes and Michael Grabowski, *The Multisensory Film Experience: A Cognitive Model of Experiential Film Aesthetics* (Bristol, UK: Intellect Ltd, 2016); Laura U. Marks, *Touch: Sensuous Theory and Multisensory Media*, (Minneapolis: University of Minnesota Press, 2002); Vivian Sobchack, *The Address of the Eye: A Phenomenology of Film Experience* (Princeton: Princeton University Press, 1991).

57. Nixon includes in his definition those affiliated with struggles to "amplify causes marginalized by the corporate media" and those who document "socioenvironmental memory." Nixon, *Slow Violence*, 23–24.

58. Fabien Arribert-Narce, "Écrits du 11 mars en France et au Japon: écrire la catastrophe, entre fiction et témoignage," in *Penser* avec *Fukushima*, ed. Christian Doumet and Michaël Ferrier (Lormont: Editions Cécile Defaut, 2016), 57.

Chapter 1

1. "TOWERPEDIA | TokyoTower," accessed July 2, 2021, https://www.tokyotower.co.jp/en/towerpedia/.

2. Béatrice Rafoni, "Le néo-japonisme en France: de l'influence de la culture médiatique japonaise," *Compar(a)ison* 2 (2002): 113–23; "postjaponismes" in Olivier Gabet, ed., *Japonismes* (Paris: Flammarion, 2014), 299; "Japonisme: 'A Never-Ending Story'" in Pamela A. Genova, *Writing Japonisme: Aesthetic Translation in Nineteenth-Century French Prose* (Evanston, IL: Northwestern University Press, 2016); "second Japonisme" from Philippe Forest, *Retour à Tokyo* (Nantes: Éditions Cécile Defaut, 2014), 14; and in Susan J. Napier, *From Impressionism to Anime: Japan as Fantasy and Fan Cult in the Mind of the West* (New York: Palgrave Macmillan, 2007), 19 a "new wave" of Japonisme is implied in the following: "While I do not see anime and manga fandom as emanating directly from the earlier waves of Japonisme that swept the West, I do see it as having fascinating similarities to these earlier booms."

3. I borrow "aestheticentrism," or the "bracketing of the concerns of pedestrian Japanese, who live real lives and struggle with intellectual and ethical problems inherent in modernity" but fail to evoke wonder for the

French Japanophile, from Kojin Karatani and Sabu Kohso, "Uses of Aesthetics: After *Orientalism*," *Boundary 2* 25, no. 2 Edward W. Said (Summer 1998): 146.

4. Rey Chow, *The Age of the World Target: Self-Referentiality in War, Theory, and Comparative Work* (Durham: Duke University Press, 2006), 29.

5. Georges Louis Leclerc Buffon comte de, *Histoire naturelle, générale et particulière, tome troisième, "Variétés dans l'espèce humaine"* (Paris: Imprimerie Royale, 1749), 389–90.

6. Voltaire's writing on Japan also resembles portions of Jaucourt's entry on "Le Japon" in the *Encyclopédie*. It is unclear which text borrowed from which, or whether a third source was involved. What is now called plagiarism was not illegal at the time as copyrights did not exist. On citation or lack thereof in the *Encyclopédie*, see Dan Edelstein, Robert Morrissey, and Glenn Roe, "To Quote or Not to Quote: Citation Strategies in the *Encyclopédie*," *Journal of the History of Ideas* 74, no. 2 (April 2013): 213–36.

7. Genova, *Writing Japonisme*, 15–16.

8. Klaus Berger, *Japonisme in Western Painting from Whistler to Matisse*, trans. David Britt (Cambridge: Cambridge University Press, 1980), 17; Colta Feller Ives, *The Great Wave: The Influence of Japanese Woodcuts on French Prints* (New York: The Metropolitan Museum of Art, 1974), 7; Julie Nelson Davis debunks the wrapping paper myth in *Picturing the Floating World: Ukiyo-e in Context* (Honolulu: University of Hawai'i Press, 2021).

9. Gabriel P. Weisberg et al., *Japonisme: Japanese Influence on French Art, 1854–1910* (Cleveland: The Cleveland Museum of Art, The Rutgers University Art Gallery, The Walters Art Gallery, 1975), 143.

10. Elizabeth Emery, *Reframing Japonisme: Women and the Asian Art Market in Nineteenth-Century France, 1853–1914* (London: Bloomsbury Visual Arts, 2020), 2.

11. Philippe Burty, "Japonisme I," *La Renaissance littéraire et artistique*, May 18, 1872; "Japonisme II," June 15, 1872; "Japonisme III," July 6, 1872; "Japonisme IV," July 27, 1872; "Japonisme V," August 10, 1872; "Japonisme VI," February 8, 1873.

12. Jan Hokenson, *Japan, France, and East-West Aesthetics: French Literature, 1867–2000* (Madison, NJ: Fairleigh Dickinson University Press, 2004), 29; Gabriel P. Weisberg, "Reflecting on Japonisme: The State of the Discipline in the Visual Arts," *Journal of Japonisme* 1, no. 1 (2016): 3. Emery questions the privileging of Burty in the story of *japonisme* as he admitted he did not read Japanese and relied on those who had traveled to Japan, such as Madame Desoye, an unnamed "tea merchant on the rue de Rivoli," to confirm his intuitions about Japanese psychology and culture. Emery distinguishes between Burty's definition of the term as "the study of the art and genius of Japan" to the twentieth-century term Japonisme (with a capital "J" and not

italicized) used "to describe productions inspired by the arts and culture of Japan." Emery, *Reframing Japonisme*, 2–3.

13. Hokenson, *Japan, France*, 13.

14. Félix Régamey, *Le Japon pratique* (Paris: J. Hetzel et cie, 1891), http://catalogue.bnf.fr/ark:/12148/cb31187143k. The first section, "Le Japon vu par un artiste" (Japan seen by an artist), opens with an admonition to those who would see the Japanese and the Chinese as the same. "Il y a là une confusion regrettable qu'il importe de détruire. Car s'il est vrai que l'une des deux civilisations ait été le berceau de l'autre, elles ont entre elles beaucoup moins de rapports que cette filiation ne le laisse supposer" (1). (There is in this a regrettable confusion that is important to destroy. Because if it is true that one of the two civilizations were the cradle of the other, they have between them many fewer connections than this filiation would lead to believe.)

15. Richard R. Brettell et al., *Nineteenth- and Twentieth-Century Paintings* (Metropolitan Museum of Art, 2009), 63.

16. Weisberg et al., *Japonisme: Japanese Influence on French Art, 1854–1910*, 148.

17. Hokenson, *Japan, France*, 98; Marguerite Duras, *Un barrage contre le Pacifique*, (Paris: Gallimard, 1950), 23.

18. Roland Barthes, *L'empire des signes* (1970; repr., Paris: Seuil, 2007), 11–12.

19. Kōji Kawamoto, "French Views of the Japanese: Loti vs. Farrère," in *Selected Proceedings* (The Walls Within: Images of Westerners in Japan and Images of the Japanese Abroad, Vancouver: The Institute of Asian Research, University of British Columbia, 1988), 259.

20. See for example René Sieffert, ed., *Le Japon et la France: Images d'une découverte* (Paris: Publications Orientalistes de France, 1974); Weisberg et al., *Japonisme: Japanese Influence on French Art, 1854–1910*; Berger, *Japonisme*; Siegfried Wichmann, *Japonisme: The Japanese Influence on Western Art since 1858* (London: Thames and Hudson, 1981); Gabriel P. Weisberg and Yvonne M. L. Weisberg, *Japonisme: An Annotated Bibliography* (New Brunswick, New York, London: International Center for Japonisme, Jane Voorhees Zimmerli Art Museum, Rutgers-The State University of New Jersey; Garland Publishing, 1990); Gabriel P. Weisberg, "Rethinking Japonisme: The Popularization of a Taste," in *The Orient Expressed: Japan's Influence on Western Art 1854–1918* (Jackson, MS: Mississippi Museum of Art, 2011), 17–73.

21. Emery, *Reframing Japonisme*; Christopher Reed, *Bachelor Japanists: Japanese Aesthetics and Western Masculinities*, (New York: Columbia University Press, 2016).

22. Hokenson, *Japan, France*; Genova, *Writing Japonisme*.

23. Akane Kawakami, *Travellers' Visions: French Literary Encounters with Japan 1881–2004* (Liverpool: Liverpool University Press, 2005);

Akane Kawakami, "Walking Underground: Two Francophone Flâneurs in Twenty-First-Century Tokyo," *L'Esprit Créateur* 56, no. 3 (Fall 2016): 120–33.

24. Michaël Ferrier, *Japon: La barrière des rencontres* (Nantes: Éditions Cécile Defaut, 2009); Philippe Forest, ed., *Du Japon*, NRF (Paris: Gallimard, 2012).

25. Chinghsin Wu, "Institutionalizing Impressionism: Kuroda Seiki and Plein-Air Painting in Japan," in *Mapping Impressionist Painting in Transnational Contexts* (New York: Routledge, 2021), 134.

26. Michiaki Kawakita, *Modern Currents in Japanese Art*, trans. Charles S. Terry, vol. 24, The Heibonsha Survey of Japanese Art (New York, Tokyo: Weatherhill/Heibonsha, 1974), 59.

27. Brettell et al., *Nineteenth- and Twentieth-Century Paintings*, 61–62.

28. Musée Maillol Paris, "Foujita: Peindre dans les années folles (dossier de presse)," 2018, https://www.museemaillol.com/wp-content/uploads/2021/05/DP-Foujita-janv18-FR-avec-compression.pdf.

29. Doug Slaymaker, "Confluences: An Introduction," in *Confluences: Postwar Japan and France*, ed. Doug Slaymaker (Ann Arbor: Center for Japanese Studies, University of Michigan, 2002), 1.

30. Slaymaker, 3.

31. "Terminologie et néologie | Académie française," Académie française, accessed November 7, 2023, https://www.academie-francaise.fr/questions-de-langue#88_strong-em-terminologie-et-nologie-em-strong.

32. Daisuke Miyao, *Japonisme and the Birth of Cinema* (Durham: Duke University Press, 2020), 7.

33. Miyao, *Japonisme and the Birth of Cinema*, 12.

34. Daisuke Miyao, "Japonisme and the Birth of Cinema," *Journal of Japonisme* 1, no. 1 (2016): 79.

35. Hiroshi Komatsu, "The Lumière Cinématographe and the Production of the Cinema in Japan in the Earliest Period," *Film History* 8, no. 4 (December 1996): 438.

36. Noël Burch, *To the Distant Observer: Form and Meaning in the Japanese Cinema* (Berkeley: University of California Press, 1979), 61.

37. Donald Richie, *Japanese Cinema: An Introduction* (New York, Oxford: Oxford University Press, 1990), 2.

38. Ching Ling Foo, one of the most famous and magicians in the West at the turn of the twentieth century, inspired many American and European imitators. For more on this Orientalist tendency, see Matthew Solomon, "Up-to-Date Magic: Theatrical Conjuring and the Trick Film," *Theatre Journal* 58, no. 4 (2006): 603.

39. T. Jefferson Kline, *Unraveling French Cinema: From L'Atalante to Caché* (New York: John Wiley & Sons, 2010), 4, 9.

40. Richie, *Japanese Cinema*, 8.

41. Richie, 8–9.

42. *The Jazz Singer*, the first talking motion picture, which was projected in the United States in 1927, premiered in France in 1929, followed several months later by the first French talking motion picture *Le collier de la reine / The Queen's Necklace*.

43. Burch makes this claim in *Distant Observer*, 145–47, an important if problematic study of Japanese cinema that often aligns with Orientalist visions of Japan.

44. The 1937 publication of *Kokutai no hongi* (Fundamentals of our national polity), a government-commissioned pamphlet on national essence or Japaneseness, advocated an official national ideology on the brink of total war.

45. Colleen Kennedy-Karpat, *Rogues, Romance, and Exoticism in French Cinema of the 1930s* (Lanham, MD: Fairleigh Dickinson University Press, 2013), 154; Daisuke Miyao, *Sessue Hayakawa: Silent Cinema and Transnational Stardom* (Durham: Duke University Press, 2007), 23.

46. Miyao, *Sessue Hayakawa*, 271.

47. Kennedy-Karpat, *Rogues, Romance, and Exoticism*, 2.

48. Andrew Gordon, *A Modern History of Japan: From Tokugawa Times to the Present*, 2nd ed. (Oxford: Oxford University Press, 2009), 217.

49. Richie, *Japanese Cinema*, 39.

50. Rémi Fournier Lanzoni, *French Cinema: From Its Beginnings to the Present*, 2nd ed. (1st ed. 2002) (New York, London: Bloomsbury, 2015), 95.

51. Chow, *Age of World Target*, 29.

52. Chow, 31.

53. Hideaki Fujiki and Alastair Phillips, "Introduction: Japanese Cinema and Its Multiple Perspectives," in *The Japanese Cinema Book*, ed. Hideaki Fujiki and Alastair Phillips (London: British Film Institute, Bloomsbury, 2020), 4.

54. Ruth Benedict, *The Chrysanthemum and the Sword: Patterns of Japanese Culture* (Boston: Houghton Mifflin, 1946), 297.

55. Kyoko Hirano, "Depiction of the Atomic Bombings in Japanese Cinema during the U.S. Occupation Period," in *Hibakusha Cinema: Hiroshima, Nagasaki and the Nuclear Image in Japanese Film*, ed. Mick Broderick (London: Kegan Paul International, 1996), 104–5.

56. Kyoko Hirano, *Mr. Smith Goes to Tokyo: Japanese Cinema under the American Occupation, 1945–1952* (Washington D.C.: Smithsonian Institution Press, 1992). Hirano, "Depiction of Bombings," 115.

57. Matt Matsuda, "East of No West: The Posthistoire of Postwar France and Japan," in *Confluences: Postwar Japan and France*, ed. Doug Slaymaker (Ann Arbor: Center for Japanese Studies, University of Michigan, 2002), 16.

58. Matsuda, 17.

59. Daniel P. Aldrich, *Site Fights: Divisive Facilities and Civil Society in Japan and the West*, 2nd ed. (1st ed. 2008) (Ithaca: Cornell University Press, 2011), 154.

60. Brian R. Jacobson, "French Cinema vs. the Bomb: Atomic Science and a War of Images circa 1950," *Historical Journal of Film, Radio and Television* 42, no. 2 (2022): 196.

61. Laurent Creton and Anne Jäckel, "Business 1950–80: The End of a Golden Era for the Industry," in *The French Cinema Book*, ed. Michael Temple and Michael Witt, 2nd ed. (London: Palgrave, British Film Institute, 2018), 164.

62. Isadora Kriegel-Nicholas, "The Historical Reception of Japanese Cinema at *Cahiers du cinéma*: 1951–1961" (Dissertation, Boston, Boston University, 2016), 6–7.

63. Yoshiharu Tezuka, "A Constellation of Gazes: Europe and the Japanese Film Industry," in *The Japanese Cinema Book*, ed. Hideaki Fujiki and Alastair Phillips (London: British Film Institute, Bloomsbury, 2020), 543.

64. Tezuka, 544.

65. Tezuka, 546–47.

66. Joan Mellen, *Voices from the Japanese Cinema* (New York: Liveright, 1975), 60–61.

67. "Hommage à Madame Kawakita—La Cinémathèque française," accessed September 2, 2021, https://www.cinematheque.fr/article/927.html.

68. Creton and Jäckel, "Business 1950–80: The End of a Golden Era for the Industry," 167; Alastair Phillips, "The City: Tokyo 1958," in *The Japanese Cinema Book* (London: British Film Institute, Bloomsbury, 2020), 420.

69. Nicoleta Bazgan, "The Eiffel Tower: A Parisian Film Star," in *Paris in the Cinema: Beyond the Flâneur*, ed. Alastair Phillips and Ginette Vincendeau (London: British Film Institute, Palgrave, 2018), 17, 23.

70. Richard Roud, "The Left Bank," *Monthly Film Bulletin* 32, no. 1 (Winter 1963): 24–27.

71. Michael Bess, *The Light-Green Society: Ecology and Technological Modernity in France, 1960–2000* (Chicago: University of Chicago Press, 2003), 30.

72. Gabrielle Hecht, *The Radiance of France: Nuclear Power and National Identity after World War II*, 2nd ed. (Cambridge, MA: MIT Press, 2009), 3–4.

73. Gabrielle Hecht, "Nuclear Ontologies," *Constellations* 13, no. 3 (2006): 322.

74. Roxanne Panchasi, " 'No Hiroshima in Africa': The Algerian War and the Question of French Nuclear Tests in the Sahara," *History of the Present* 9, no. 1 (2019): 87, 105.

75. Panchasi, 94.

76. Anaïs Maurer, "Nukes and Nudes: Counter-Hegemonic Identities in the Nuclearized Pacific," *French Studies* 72, no. 3 (July 2018): 395; Sebastien Philippe and Tomas Statius, *Toxique. Enquête sur les essais nucléaires français en Polynésie* (Paris: PUF, 2021).

77. Phillips, "The City: Tokyo 1958," 430.

78. Tezuka, "A Constellation of Gazes," 545.

79. Richie, *Japanese Cinema*, 66. James Tweedie has argued that these waves were in fact part of the same phase in a longer age of new waves. James Tweedie, *The Age of New Waves: Art Cinema and the Staging of Globalization* (New York: Oxford University Press, 2013), 2.

80. David Desser, *Eros plus Massacre: An Introduction to the Japanese New Wave Cinema* (Bloomington: Indiana University Press, 1988), 4.

81. Scott Nygren, *Time Frames: Japanese Cinema and the Unfolding of History* (Minneapolis: University of Minnesota Press, 2007), 186.

82. Nygren, 189.

83. Marie-Paule Ha, *Figuring the East: Segalen, Malraux, Duras, and Barthes* (Albany: State University of New York Press, 2000), 102. Key to Barthes's experience of Japan was his friend Maurice Pinguet, to whom *L'empire des signes* is dedicated. Pinguet, a cultural anthropologist who directed the Institut franco-japonais de Tokyo from 1963–1968, had invited Barthes to visit in 1966. Pinguet, too, published an anthropological study of suicide in Japan in *La mort volontaire au Japon / Suicide in Japan* (1984). Pinguet also hosted Michel Foucault, a classmate from École normale supérieur, in Japan. Collected essays published posthumously can be found in Maurice Pinguet, *Le texte Japon*, ed. Michaël Ferrier (Paris: Seuil, 2009).

84. Other anthropological writing from the period comes from Claude Lévi-Strauss, who credits his father's interest in Japanese prints for the strong influence Japanese culture had on him as a child. His interest was renewed after the war with several visits between 1977 and 1988. His writing on Japan can be found in Claude Lévi-Strauss, *L'autre face de la lune: écrits sur le Japon* (Paris: Seuil, 2011) and Claude Lévi-Strauss, *L'anthropologie face aux problèmes du monde moderne* (Paris: Seuil, 2011), a collection of lectures delivered in 1986 at the Ishizaka Foundation in Tokyo.

85. Hannah Holtzman, "Chris Marker's Ecological Consciousness, or 36 Views of the Train in Tokyo," *French Screen Studies* 22 no. 4 (2022): 251–270.

86. Jean Fourastié, *Les trente glorieuses: ou la révolution invisible de 1946 à 1975* (Paris: Fayard, 1979); Sezin Topçu, "Atome, gloire et désenchantement: Résister à la France atomique avant 1968," in *Une autre histoire des "Trente Glorieuses": modernisation, contestations et pollutions dans la France d'après-guerre* (Paris: La Découverte, 2013), 189–209.

87. Sezin Topçu, "Les physiciens dans le mouvement antinucléaire : entre science, expertise et politique," *Cahiers d'histoire. Revue d'histoire critique*, no. 102 (October 1, 2007): 89–108.

88. Bess, *Light-Green Society*, 95.

89. Aldrich, *Site Fights*, 183.

90. Philippe Pelletier, "De la guerre totale (1941) à la guerre de Fukushima (2011)," *Outre-terre, Revue européenne de géopolitique* 35–36 (2013): 399–437.

91. The censorship code included any mention of the Battle of Oki-nawa, an event referenced in Chris Marker's film *Sans soleil* (1982) and more fully explored in *Level Five* (1996).

92. Dwight D. Eisenhower, "Address before the General Assembly of the United Nations on Peaceful Uses of Atomic Energy" (Address, 470th Plenary Meeting of the United Nations General Assembly, New York City, December 8, 1953), https://www.presidency.ucsb.edu/node/232498.

93. Matthew Penney, "Nuclear Nationalism and Fukushima," *The Asia-Pacific Journal: Japan Focus* 10, no. 11.2 (2012): 4.

94. "How the Unlucky Lucky Dragon Birthed an Era of Nuclear Fear," *Bulletin of the Atomic Scientists*, February 28, 2018.

95. Aldrich, *Site Fights*, 124.

96. Mathieu Gaulène, *Le nucléaire en Asie: Fukushima, et après?* (Arles: Editions Philippe Picquier, 2016), 143.

97. Ran Zwigenberg, "'The Coming of a Second Sun': The 1956 Atoms for Peace Exhibit in Hiroshima and Japan's Embrace of Nuclear Power," *The Asia-Pacific Journal: Japan Focus* 10, no. 6 (February 2, 2012).

98. Pelletier, "De la guerre totale," section 11.

99. Aldrich, *Site Fights*, 124.

100. Aldrich, 132–36.

101. Penney, "Nuclear Nationalism."

102. In terms of total number of reactors, France and Japan are both behind the United States, which operates ninety-three active reactors in 2022 with two new reactors under construction; however, over the past two decades the reactors in the United States have produced around 20 percent of electricity nationally compared with around 75 percent in France and 30 percent in Japan, before the 2011 disaster when all of Japan's reactors were temporarily shut down. In 2022, Japan relied on nuclear power for around 6 percent of its electricity from ten reactors in operation. "PRIS—Home," accessed June 14, 2023, https://pris.iaea.org/PRIS/home.aspx.

103. Aldrich, *Site Fights*, 161.

104. Aldrich, 182.

105. Henry Chevallier, *Histoire des luttes antinucléaires en France 1958–2008* (Fustérouau, France: La Bertrande, 2009); Aldrich, *Site Fights*, 173. "331 Parliament members voted to approve the national energy program, with only 67 opposing."

106. Lorenz Gonschor, "Mai Te Hau Roma Ra Te Huru: The Illusion of 'Autonomy' and the Ongoing Struggle for Decolonization in French Polynesia," *The Contemporary Pacific* 25, no. 2 (2013): 281.

107. Gonschor, 285.

108. Maite Mompo and Chris Brazier, *Rainbow Warriors* (Oxford: New Internationalist, 2014), 26.

109. Dieter Rucht, "The Anti-Nuclear Power Movement and the State in France," in *States and Anti-Nuclear Movements*, ed. Helena Flam (Edinburgh: Edinburgh University Press, 1994), 146.

110. For more comparison of the work and styles of Marker and Vautier, see Nicole Brenez, "Forms of Resistance and Revolt: 'We Are in Agreement with All That Has Struggled, and Is Struggling Still, since the World Began,'" in *The French Cinema Book*, ed. Michael Temple and Michael Witt, 2nd ed. (London: British Film Institute, Palgrave, 2018), 192–93.

111. Claude Simon, "Cher Kenzaburo Ōe," *Le Monde*, September 21, 1995; Kenzaburo Ōe, "Cher Claude Simon," *Le Monde*, September 28, 1995.

112. Hecht, *Radiance of France*, 345.

113. A 2021 EDF publicity campaign entitled "Le nucléaire, un allié pour le climat" (Nuclear energy, an ally for the climate) promotes nuclear energy as low-carbon, recognized by the scientific and technical community, available at a large scale, and against climate change, while responding to growing energy needs. These qualities are proclaimed in titles shown over images of collapsing icebergs and a lovely Paris illuminated at twilight. https://www.youtube.com/watch?v=cHBjwHRPtPA.

114. Aldrich, *Site Fights*, 132.

115. Penney, "Nuclear Nationalism," 6–8.

116. Mick Broderick and Robert Jacobs, "Fukushima and the Shifting Conventions of Documentary: From Broadcast to Social Media Netizenship," in *Post-1990 Documentary: Reconfiguring Independence*, ed. Camille Deprez and Judith Pernin (Edinburgh: Edinburgh University Press, 2015), 220; Jeff Kingston, "Contesting Fukushima," *The Asia-Pacific Journal: Japan Focus* 20, no. 12.1 (June 15, 2022).

117. Aldrich, *Site Fights*, 22.

118. Aldrich, 23.

119. Aldrich, 181–84.

120. Penney, "Nuclear Nationalism," 8.

121. Robert A. Jacobs, *Nuclear Bodies: The Global Hibakusha* (New Haven: Yale University Press, 2022); Gabriele Schwab, *Radioactive Ghosts* (Minneapolis: University of Minnesota Press, 2020); Gabrielle Hecht, *Being Nuclear: Africans and the Global Uranium Trade* (Cambridge, MA: MIT Press, 2012); Rob Nixon, *Slow Violence and the Environmentalism of the Poor* (Cambridge, Mass: Harvard University Press, 2013).

122. Michaël Ferrier, "L'art du repiquage: présences du Japon de Léon Rosny à Dany Laferrière," in *D'après le Japon*, ed. Laurent Zimmermann (Nantes: Éditions Cécile Defaut, 2012), 75. Ferrier sees references to Japan in several of Laferrière's books and understands Japan as more than just an object of study or admiration for him but as a way of thinking and knowing.

123. See for example Ferrier, *Japon: la barrière des rencontres*; Forest, *Retour à Tokyo*; Laurent Zimmermann, ed., *D'après le Japon* (Nantes: Éditions Cécile Defaut, 2012); Yoshikichi Furui et al., *Pour un autre roman japonais*, ed. Philippe Forest and Cécile Sakai (Paris: Éditions Cécile Defaut, 2005); Christian Doumet and Michaël Ferrier, eds., *Penser* avec *Fukushima* (Lormont: Éditions Cécile Defaut, 2016); Michael Ferrier and Nobutaka Miura, eds., *La tentation de la France, la tentation du Japon: regards croisés* (Paris: Éditions Philippe Picquier, 2003); Mathieu Gaulène, *Le nucléaire en asie: Fukushima, et après?* (Arles: Éditions Philippe Picquier, 2016); Corinne Quentin and Cécile Sakai, eds., *L'archipel des séismes: écrits du Japon après le 11 mars 2011* (Arles: Éditions Philippe Picquier, 2012).

124. Olivier Assayas, "Demonlover en un mot," interview by Stephen Sarrazin, Objectif cinéma, 2001, http://www.objectif-cinema.com/interviews/093.php.

125. As a writer for *Cahiers du cinéma*, Assayas published a special issue on Hong Kong cinema in 1985. In 1996, he made the feature film *Irma Vep* with the Hong Kong actress Maggie Cheung, whom he later married. In 1997, he made the documentary *HHH* on the Taiwanese director Hou Hsiao-Hsien.

126. Edmund Lee, "Koji Fukada on Graduating from Theatre to Become a Cannes Winner," *South China Morning Post*, April 12, 2017, sec. Culture, https://www.scmp.com/culture/film-tv/article/2086961/japanese-filmmaker-koji-fukada-cannes-winner-harmonium-his-eric; "Japanese Winner of Cannes Jury Prize Directs Movies Based on Theater Experience," *Mainichi Daily News*, May 24, 2016, https://mainichi.jp/english/articles/20160524/p2a/00m/0et/019000c.

127. "Japanese Winner of Cannes Jury Prize." *Harmonium* is another Comme des Cinémas Franco-Japanese coproduction.

128. Peter C. Pugsley and Ben McCann, *The Cinematic Influence: Interaction and Exchange between the Cinemas of France and Japan* (Bloomsbury Academic, 2023).

129. Mette Hjort, "On the Plurality of Cinematic Transnationalism," in *World Cinemas, Transnational Perspectives*, ed. Nataša Durovicová and Kathleen E. Newman (New York: Routledge, 2010), 17.

130. Tezuka, "A Constellation of Gazes" 549–52.

131. Yohann, "Interview de Jill Coulon pour son film 'Tu seras sumo,'" Dosukoi, le site français du sumo, accessed October 5, 2013, http://www.dosukoi.fr/interview-de-jill-coulon-pour-son-film-tu-seras-sumo/. Coulon's documentary was also shown on Japanese television with a different ending. The French version ends with Ogushi Takuya dropping out of the training to become a sumo wrestler and a dramatic 4:00 a.m. departure from the

stable, while the Japanese ending continues to follow Takuya, who returns to the stable several weeks later to persevere with his training.

132. Stéphane du Mesnildot, "Un été avec Koumiko," *Cahiers du cinéma*, September 2012.

133. Joseph Szarka, "France, the Nuclear Revival and the Post-Fukushima Landscape," in *The Fukushima Effect: A New Geopolitical Terrain*, ed. Richard Hindmarsh and Rebecca Priestley (Routledge, 2015), 203–22.

134. Michaël Ferrier, "Introduction: Les écrivains du corail ou d'une nouvelle arborescence—possible et souhaitable—dans la réception de la culture japonaise," in *Réceptions de la culture japonaise en France depuis 1945. Paris-Tokyo-Paris: détours par le Japon*, ed. Fabien Arribert-Narce, Kohei Kuwada, and Lucy O'Meara (Paris: Honoré Champion, 2016), 37–39; Author's interview with Michaël Ferrier, June 7, 2016; Forest, *Retour à Tokyo*, 14.

135. Géraud Bournet, *FRANCKUSHIMA: Essai graphique sur la catastrophe de Fukushima et le risque nucléaire en France* (Grenoble: Lutopiquant éditions, 2016).

136. Japan has sent 353 artists to the United States, 179 to England, and 178 to Germany. Yoko Hayashi, ed., *Domani: The Art of Tomorrow 2022–23* (Agency for Cultural Affairs, 2020), 104–5.

137. "Section 2: Fashion," Collection, Modern Japan and France: adoration, encounter, and interaction (National Diet Library), accessed August 18, 2021, https://www.ndl.go.jp/france/en/column/s2_2.html.

138. "Section 1: Cuisine," Collection, Modern Japan and France: adoration, encounter, and interaction (National Diet Library), accessed August 18, 2021, https://www.ndl.go.jp/france/en/column/s2_1.html; Sieffert, *Le Japon et la France: images d'une découverte*, 52–58.

139. Michelle Bloom, *Contemporary Sino-French Cinemas: Absent Fathers, Banned Books, and Red Balloons* (Honolulu: University of Hawai'i Press, 2015), 199.

140. As seen in a comparison of data from the Observatory of Economic Complexity at the MIT Media Lab regarding exports between France and Japan in 2010, the year before the nuclear disaster and the halt of the Japanese nuclear industry. "Products That Japan Exports to France (2010)," The Observatory of Economic Complexity, accessed May 5, 2017, http://atlas.media.mit.edu/en/visualize/tree_map/hs92/export/jpn/fra/show/2010/; "Products That France Exports to Japan (2010)," The Observatory of Economic Complexity, accessed May 5, 2017, http://atlas.media.mit.edu/en/visualize/tree_map/hs92/export/fra/jpn/show/2010/.

141. Ha, *Figuring the East*, xiii, 3, 11.

142. Hokenson, *Japan, France*, 24–25.

143. Kōichi Iwabuchi, *Recentering Globalization: Popular Culture and Japanese Transnationalism* (Durham: Duke University Press, 2002), 3, 13.

144. Edward W. Said, *Orientalism*, 25th anniversary ed. (New York: Vintage Books, 2003), xvii.

145. Said, xxix.

146. Joshua Paul Dale, "Cross-Cultural Encounters through a Lateral Gaze," in *After Orientalism: Critical Engagements, Productive Looks*, ed. Inge E. Boer (Amsterdam: Rodopi, 2003), 73–75.

147. Karatani and Kohso, "Uses of Aesthetics," 146–47.

148. Exchange is not synonymous with encounter, which connotes friction and may lack reciprocity as well. See for example "imperial encounter" in Mary Louise Pratt, *Imperial Eyes: Travel Writing and Transculturation*, 2nd rev. ed. (London, New York: Routledge, 2008); French encounters with Japan in Kawakami, *Travellers' Visions*; and Japanese encounters with French art in Shūji Takashina et al., *Paris in Japan: The Japanese Encounter with European Painting* (Tokyo, St. Louis: Japan Foundation, Washington University, 1987).

Chapter 2

1. Richard Werly, "Un thème qui tétanise les cinéastes japonais: L'atomisation de Hiroshima et Nagasaki reste taboue," *Libération*, October 17, 2001.

2. Michihiko Hachiya, *Hiroshima Diary: The Journal of a Japanese Physician, August 6–September 30, 1945*, trans. Warner Wells and Neal Tsukifuji (Chapel Hill: University of North Carolina Press, 1955), 37.

3. Argos initiated the coproduction in part due to "funds stuck in Japan that could not be transferred out." Richard Neupert, *A History of the French New Wave Cinema*, 2nd ed., (Madison: University of Wisconsin Press, 2007), 304; Pathé Overseas, "Pathé Overseas to Nagata Masaichi, President of Daiei Motion Picture Co. about 'Film on the Atom Bomb,'" April 26, 1957, ARG/D178, Argos Films.

4. In 1958, the world saw a record 116 nuclear weapon test explosions, more than twice the number in any previous year. By the end of that year, the three nuclear weapon states—the United States, the Soviet Union, and the United Kingdom—observed a moratorium on nuclear testing until September 1961. Meanwhile, France was preparing to join the nuclear club. In 1959, France faced international criticism for its plans to test the French bomb. Undeterred, President Charles de Gaulle went ahead with the plan. Vitaly Fedchenko, "Nuclear Explosions, 1945–2013," in *SIPRI Yearbook 2014: Armaments, Disarmament and International Security* (Oxford: Oxford University Press, 2014), 350.

5. An illuminating discussion of the use of recycled images of the disaster in *Hiroshima mon amour* appears in Brian R. Jacobson, "French Cinema

vs. the Bomb: Atomic Science and a War of Images circa 1950," *Historical Journal of Film, Radio and Television* 42, no. 2 (2022): 191–218.

6. Marie-Claire Ropars-Wuilleumier, "How History Begets Meaning: Alain Resnais' *Hiroshima mon amour* (1959)," in *French Film: Texts and Contexts*, ed. Susan Hayward and Ginette Vincendeau (London: Routledge, 1990), 179.

7. Toshihiro Higuchi, *Political Fallout: Nuclear Weapons Testing and the Making of a Global Environmental Crisis* (Redwood City: Stanford University Press, 2020), 12.

8. Pathé Overseas, "Pathé Overseas to Nagata Masaichi, President of Daiei Motion Picture Co. about 'Film on the Atom Bomb,'" April 26, 1957, ARG/D178, Argos Films.

9. Tweedie, *The Age of New Waves*.

10. Anatole Dauman, "Anatole Dauman to Lux Films," September 25, 1958, ARG/D178, Argos Films.

11. Yuko Shibata, "Postcolonial *Hiroshima, Mon Amour*: Franco-Japanese Collaboration in the American Shadow," in *The Trans-Pacific Imagination: Rethinking Boundary, Culture and Society* (Singapore: World Scientific Publishing Company, 2012), 219.

12. Shibata, 221.

13. Karatani and Kohso, "Uses of Aesthetics," 147.

14. Raymond Ravar, *Tu n'as rien vu à Hiroshima!* (Bruxelles: Institut de Sociologie, 1962), 207.

15. Jean-Charles Tacchella, *Jean-Charles Tacchella, mémoires* (Biarritz: SEGUIER, 2017), 166.

16. In France, *Typhoon over Nagasaki* sold more than twice as many tickets as *Hiroshima mon amour* upon its initial release and was in the top ten French films in 1957. François Truffaut, "Le cinéma français crève sous les fausses légendes," *Arts, spectacles*, May 15, 1957.

17. Donald Richie, "'Mono No Aware': Hiroshima in Film," in *Hibakusha Cinema: Hiroshima, Nagasaki and the Nuclear Image in Japanese Film* (London, New York: Kegan Paul International, 1996), 30.

18. Sarah Leperchey, *Alain Resnais: une lecture topologique* (Paris: Editions L'Harmattan, 2000), 64.

19. Donald Richie and Paul Schrader, *A Hundred Years of Japanese Film: A Concise History, with a Selective Guide to DVDs and Videos*, rev. ed. (New York, NY: Kodansha USA, 2012), 40.

20. Yuko Shibata, *Producing Hiroshima and Nagasaki: Literature, Film, and Transnational Politics* (Honolulu: University of Hawai'i Press, 2018), 1–2; Mirei Seki, "La réception de *Hiroshima mon amour* au Japon," in *Orient(s) de Marguerite Duras*, ed. Florence de Chalonge, Akiko Ueda, and Yann Mével (Amsterdam: Rodopi, 2014), 229.

21. Seki, "La réception au Japon," 223.

22. Shibata, *Producing Hiroshima and Nagasaki*, 2.

23. "Modern Japan and France—Adoration, Encounter and Interaction," Collection, accessed December 1, 2019, https://www.ndl.go.jp/france/en/index.html.

24. Jean Domarchi et al., "Hiroshima, notre amour," *Cahiers du cinéma* 97 (July 1959): 1–5.

25. Roland Barthes, *L'empire des signes* (1970; repr., Paris: Seuil, 2007), 11.

26. Fournier Lanzoni, *French Cinema*, 224–25.

27. Gilles Durieux, *Jean Marais: biographie* (Paris: Flammarion, 2005), 13.

28. Miyao, *Japonisme and the Birth of Cinema*, 2020, 13–14.

29. Marguerite Duras, *Hiroshima mon amour: scénario et dialogues* (Paris: Gallimard, 1960), 151.

30. Richie, "'Mono No Aware': Hiroshima in Film," 35–36.

31. Rey Chow, "When Whiteness Feminizes . . . : Some Consequences of a Supplementary Logic," *Differences: A Journal of Feminist Cultural Studies* 11, no. 3 (October 1, 1999): 157; Seki, "La réception au Japon," 227–28.

32. Tsutomu Iwasaki, "La post-synchronisation de *Hiroshima mon amour*," in *Orient(s) de Marguerite Duras*, ed. Florence de Chalonge, Yann Mével, and Akiko Ueda (Amsterdam: Rodopi, 2014), 372.

33. Alain Resnais, "Un entretien avec Alain Resnais," interview by Michel Delahaye, Cinéma no. 38, July 1959, 9.

34. Peter Cowie, Audio Commentary, *Hiroshima mon amour*, DVD (Criterion Collection, 2003).

35. Duras, *Hiroshima mon amour*, 10.

36. Emma Wilson, *Alain Resnais* (Manchester: Manchester University Press, 2006), 6.

37. Alain Resnais, Histoire sans images: *Hiroshima mon amour*, interview by Michel Polac, INA, Argos Films, Arte Video, 2004, DVD, 1966.

38. Melissa Croteau, *Transcendence and Spirituality in Japanese Cinema: Framing Sacred Spaces* (London: Routledge, 2023), 48–49.

39. Abé Mark Nornes, *Japanese Documentary Film: The Meiji Era through Hiroshima* (Minneapolis: University of Minnesota Press, 2003), 210.

40. Wilson, *Alain Resnais*, 50.

41. Domarchi et al., "Hiroshima, notre amour," 2.

42. Alain Resnais, *Le Monde*, May 9, 1959, in *Hiroshima mon amour*, DVD booklet, Argos, 2004.

43. Bill Nichols, *Introduction to Documentary*, 2nd ed. (Bloomington: Indiana University Press, 2010), 150.

44. Alain Resnais, "Conversation avec Alain Resnais," interview by Pierre Wildenstein, Téléciné, April 1960, 6.

45. Bernard Pingaud, "À Propos d'*Hiroshima mon amour*," *Positif*, no. 35 (1960): 70.

46. Pingaud, 71.

47. Chow, *Age of World Target*, 25.

48. Resnais, Un entretien, 5.

49. Sylvette Baudrot, Hiroshima mon amour shooting script (1958), BAUDROT-GU62-B24, Fonds Sylvette Baudrot-Guilbaud.

50. Wallace, *Risk Criticism*, 12.

51. Croteau, *Transcendence and Spirituality*, 44.

52. Pingaud, "À Propos d'Hiroshima mon amour," 69.

53. Robert Benayoun, *Alain Resnais: arpenteur de l'imaginaire* (Paris: Éditions Stock, 1980), 69.

54. Ropars-Wuilleumier, "How History Begets Meaning," 179.

55. Deleuze, *Cinema 2*, 137.

56. Bakhtin, *Dialogic Imagination*, 425–26.

57. Montgomery, *Carnivals and Commonplaces: Bakhtin's Chronotope, Cultural Studies, and Film*; Sobchack, "Lounge Time."

58. Bakhtin, *Dialogic Imagination*, 248.

59. Bakhtin, 248.

60. Bakhtin, 248.

61. Domarchi et al., "Hiroshima, notre amour," 16.

62. Ropars-Wuilleumier, "How History Begets Meaning," 175–76.

63. Even in Japan, the film has been promoted more recently with the French title in katakana.

64. Hecht, *The Radiance of France*, 2.

Chapter 3

1. Shibata, *Producing Hiroshima and Nagasaki*, 1–2.

2. Maureen Cheryn Turim, *The Films of Oshima Nagisa, Images of a Japanese Iconoclast* (Berkeley: University of California Press, 1998), 14, 210.

3. Élise Domenach, "Filmer ce qu'on ne peut pas filmer: Entretien avec Suwa Nobuhiro à propos du *Téléphone du vent (Kaze no denwa*, 2020)," in *Dans l'oeil du désastre: Créer avec Fukushima*, by Michaël Ferrier, trans. Yū Shibuya (Vincennes: Éditions Thierry Marchaisse, 2021), 185, 191. Suwa's French films during this period include *Un couple parfait / A Perfect Couple* (2005), "Place des Victoires" in *Paris, je t'aime* (2006), *Yuki et Nina* (2009) co-directed with Hippolyte Girardot, and *Le lion est mort ce soir / The Lion Sleeps Tonight* (2017).

4. Serge Kaganski, "Sur le tournage de *H Story*," *Les Inrocks*, 2001, https://www.lesinrocks.com/2001/05/08/cinema/actualite-cinema/nobuhiro-suwa-sur-le-tournage-de-h-story-11218590/.

5. *Fukushima mon amour* was the title used for the premiere of Dorrie's film at the Berlin Film Festival. It was also used in France and in Japan, where it was transliterated using katakana. The film was later released in Germany as *Grüsse aus Fukushima.*

6. Deleuze, *Cinema 2*, 69.

7. The crystal approach is inspired by that of Jessica Fernanda Conejo Muñoz in "Memory and Distance: On Nobuhiro Suwa's *A Letter from Hiroshima*," *Genocide Studies and Prevention: An International Journal* 12, no. 2 (2018): 125–39. Muñoz uses the crystal in a more focused analysis of visitors' divergent gazes at the Hiroshima Peace Memorial Museum in *A Letter from Hiroshima.*

8. Charles Tesson, "Le secret derrière la cage," *Cahiers du cinéma,* June 1986, 18.

9. Serge Silberman, "Vivre le film: entretien avec Serge Silberman," *Cahiers du cinéma,* November 1986, 20.

10. René Prédal, *Jean-Claude Carrière, scénariste: L'art de raconter des histoires* (Paris: Éditions du Cerf, 1994), 366; Nagisa Oshima, "Chronique d'un eleveur," *Cahiers du cinéma,* November 1986, 18.

11. Tezuka, "A Constellation of Gazes," 549.

12. Richie, *Japanese Cinema*, 201–2.

13. Creton and Jäckel, "Business 1950–80: The End of a Golden Era for the Industry," 171.

14. Yoshiharu Tezuka, *Japanese Cinema Goes Global: Filmworkers' Journeys* (Hong Kong: Hong Kong University Press, 2012), 70–71.

15. Ōshima dismissed the comparison with Godard. When asked about their common concerns, Ōshima responded, "One is politics and the other is cinema." Mellen, *Voices from the Japanese Cinema*, 259.

16. Desser, *Eros plus Massacre*, 4.

17. *Night and Fog in Japan* was also pulled from Japanese theaters after a week. Shibata, *Producing Hiroshima and Nagasaki*, 5.

18. Nygren, *Time Frames: Japanese Cinema and the Unfolding of History*, 190. *Seishun zankoku monogatari / Cruel Tales of Youth* (1960).

19. Desser, *Eros plus Massacre*, 1.

20. In 1983, US President Ronald Reagan denounced the Soviet Union as an "evil empire" and began development of the Strategic Defense Initiative (SDI), or "Star Wars" as it was popularly known. Nuclear war was narrowly averted on September 26, 1983, when Soviet officer Stanislav Petrov judged that a report from the early warning system of an incoming missile launched from the United States was false. The Able Archer war scare in November 1983 during NATO military exercises in Europe led Soviet officials to fear imminent attack and to deploy nuclear forces, as detailed in Nate Jones, ed., *Able Archer 83: The Secret History of the NATO Exercise That Almost Triggered Nuclear War*, (New York: The New Press, 2016). The Able Archer incident

has been compared to the Cuban Missile Crisis in terms of close calls. A similar close call had been dramatized in John Badham's film *WarGames* released earlier that year.

21. *Max mon amour* was released in Japan the following year in 1987.

22. Broderick, *Nuclear Movies*, 42.

23. Tesson, "Le secret derrière la cage," 19.

24. Garry Leonard, "Technically Human: Kubrick's Monolith and Heidegger's Propriative Event," *Film Criticism* 36, no. 1 (2012): 45.

25. For Esteve Riambau, this scene recalls the ending of *In the Realm of the Senses* with the castration of the lover. Esteve Riambau, "Forbidden Loves: *Merry Christmas, Mr. Lawrence* and *Max mon amour*," in *Nagisa Oshima* (Festival Internacional de Cine de Donostia-San Sebastían S. A. Ministerio de Educacíon, Cultura y Deporte/I.C.A.A./Filmoteca Española, 2013), 274.

26. Deleuze, *Cinema 2*, 94.

27. Nagisa Oshima, " 'Max mon amour': Un film de Nagisa Oshima" (s.d.), MIZRAHI16-B4, Fonds Simon Mizrahi.

28. Suwa and Kramer first met in Paris after the Cannes Film Festival to discuss a collaboration. Kramer, who worked in France with French support for his films, might be seen as a model for Suwa, who would make several films in France after *H Story*.

29. Marine Landrot, "Les fantômes de Hiroshima, retour sur le tournage de 'H Story,' de Nobuhiro Suwa," *Télérama*, October 17, 2001, 41.

30. Charles Tesson, "Rencontre/Nobuhiro Suwa," *Cahiers du cinéma*, 2001, 70.

31. Kaganski, "Sur le tournage de *H Story*."

32. Tesson, "Rencontre/Nobuhiro Suwa," 70–71.

33. Olivier Ammour-Mayeur, "*H Story* ou l'esthétique du 'Remake relevant,'" in *Orient(s) de Marguerite Duras*, ed. Florence de Chalonge, Akiko Ueda, and Yann Mével (Amsterdam: Rodopi, 2014).

34. Gilles Deleuze, *Cinema 2: The Time-Image*, trans. Hugh Tomlinson and Robert Galeta (Minneapolis: University of Minnesota Press, 2010), 68, 76.

35. Deleuze, 82.

36. Léaud would later star in Suwa's *Le lion est mort ce soir / The Lion Sleeps Tonight* (2017).

37. Iain Robert Smith and Constantine Verevis, "Introduction: Transnational Film Remakes," in *Transnational Film Remakes*, ed. Constantine Verevis and Iain Robert Smith (Edinburgh: Edinburgh University Press, 2017), 2.

38. As Lucy Mazdon points out, this is the relationship of so many Hollywood remakes of French cinema in which the American "copy" descends from the "high art of the French 'original.'" Lucy Mazdon, *Encore Hollywood: Remaking French Cinema* (London: British Film Institute, 2000), 5.

39. Aliza Ma, "Film in Flux," *Criterion Collection DVD*, May 1, 2021.

40. Deleuze, *Cinema 2*, 86.

41. The footage was finally released for public view in 1982. Over 90,000 feet of this raw footage (81 reels) are held in National Archives in College Park, MD, #342 USAF. Lesley M. M. Blume, *Fallout: The Hiroshima Cover-Up and the Reporter Who Revealed It to the World* (New York: Simon and Schuster, 2020), 62; *Atomic Cover-Up*, 2021; Greg Mitchell, *Atomic Cover-Up: Two U.S. Soldiers, Hiroshima & Nagasaki, and The Greatest Movie Never Made* (New York: CreateSpace Independent Publishing Platform, 2012), 9–11.

42. Shibata, *Producing Hiroshima and Nagasaki*, 6.

43. Shibata, 8.

44. Greg Hainge, "A Tale of (at Least) Two Hiroshimas: Nobuhiro Suwa's *H Story* and Alain Resnais's *Hiroshima mon amour*," *Contemporary French Civilization* 32, no. 2 (2008): 152.

45. Marine Landrot, "Les fantômes de Hiroshima, retour sur le tournage de 'H Story,' de Nobuhiro Suwa," *Télérama*, October 17, 2001, 39, 41.

46. Suwa recounts this unscripted moment in Tesson, "Rencontre/ Nobuhiro Suwa," 71.

47. Deleuze, *Cinema 2*, 86.

48. In actuality, Dalle did not speak Japanese, and Machida did not speak French. Kaganski, "Sur le tournage de *H Story*."

49. Landrot, "Les fantômes de Hiroshima, retour sur le tournage de 'H Story,' de Nobuhiro Suwa," 42.

50. The two other short films that make up *After War* are *Survival Game* from the Korean director Moon Seung-Wook and *The New Year* from the Chinese filmmaker Wang Xiao-shuai.

51. *H Story* received considerable attention at Cannes, and it would not be unreasonable to expect that many viewers watching *A Letter from Hiroshima* at a smaller festival would also be familiar with *H Story*. Yet, in Japan, *H Story* was not released until a year after *A Letter from Hiroshima*'s premiere at the Jeonju International Film Festival.

52. Lisa Yoneyama, *Hiroshima Traces: Time, Space, and the Dialectics of Memory*, (Berkeley: University of California Press, 1999), 121. Into the twenty-first century, this has not significantly changed.

53. Ian Buruma, *The Wages of Guilt: Memories of War in Germany and Japan* (New York: Farrar, Straus and Giroux, 1994), 96.

54. Buruma, 96. "Monument in Memory of the Korean Victims of the A-Bomb," accessed November 8, 2023, http://www.pcf.city.hiroshima.jp/virtual/map-e/.

55. Yoneyama, *Hiroshima Traces*, 121–22.

56. Kaganski, "Sur le tournage de *H Story*."

57. Hjort, "Cinematic Transnationalism," 17.

Chapter 4

1. Colin MacCabe and Adam Bartos, *Studio: Remembering Chris Marker* (New York: OR Books, 2017), 30–31. MacCabe reports, "Marker told me that he became a filmmaker in order to travel. Travel was his passion, filmmaking simply the profession that seemed the most easy to combine with trips around the world."

2. Nora M. Alter, *Chris Marker* (Urbana: University of Illinois Press, 2006), 154.

3. Articles that focus on Marker's Japan include: Grace An, "A Par-Asian Cinematic Imaginary," *Contemporary French and Francophone Studies* 10, no. 1 (2006): 15–23; Mathieu Capel, "L'érotique Japon," *Positif*, no. 632 (2013): 108–10; Fumio Chiba, "Le Japon de Chris Marker," in *Réceptions de la culture japonaise en France depuis 1945. Paris-Tokyo-Paris: détours par le Japon*, ed. Fabien Arribert-Narce, Kohei Kuwada, and Lucy O'Meara (Paris: Honoré Champion, 2016): 249–61; Emi Koide, "Le Japon selon Chris Marker," *Appareil* 6 (2010): 1–9; Stéphane du Mesnildot, "Notes de chevet sur le Japon de Chris Marker," *Vertigo*, no. 46 (2013): 50–56.

4. Catherine Lupton, *Chris Marker: Memories of the Future* (London: Reaktion Books, 2005), 101.

5. Chris Darke, *La Jetée*, BFI Film Classics (London: Palgrave, 2016), 18.

6. An, "A Par-Asian Cinematic Imaginary," 18.

7. Hayao Shibata to Anatole Dauman, "Level Five," March 4, 1997, Vst no.9 // 09–2012 Carton 10, Argos Films.

8. Jacques Rancière, "Re-Visions: Remarks on the Love of Cinema: An Interview by Oliver Davis," *Journal of Visual Culture* 10, no. 3 (December 1, 2011): 303.

9. André Bazin, "Bazin on Marker (1958)," trans. Dave Kehr in *Essays on the Essay Film*, ed. Nora M. Alter and Timothy Corrigan (New York: Columbia University Press, 2017): 103.

10. Rancière, "Re-Visions," 295.

11. I am indebted in this approach to Sarah Cooper's detailed readings of Marker's films with attention to time. Sarah Cooper, *Chris Marker* (Manchester, UK: Manchester University Press, 2008).

12. Vivian Sobchack, *The Address of the Eye: A Phenomenology of Film Experience* (Princeton: Princeton University Press, 1991), 3–4.

13. Jenny Chamarette, *Phenomenology and the Future of Film: Rethinking Subjectivity beyond French Cinema* (New York: Palgrave Macmillan, 2012).

14. In instances of inconsistency, the dates for Marker's films mentioned here come from "Filmographie de Chris Marker," *L'Avant-Scène Cinéma*, no. 606 (October 2013): 34–35.

15. Darke, *La Jetée*, 45–46.

16. Janet Harbord, *Chris Marker, La Jetée* (London: Afterall Books, 2009), 11.

17. Bakhtin, *Dialogic Imagination*, 248.

18. Darke, *La Jetée*, 80.

19. Chip Proser, "Correspondence—La Jetée," 1981, MARKER90-B16, Fonds Chris Marker. "La Jétée" is consistently misspelled in Proser's letters until Marker, who ultimately refuses the offer, finally corrects him. The remake rights were finally granted for the film that became *12 Monkeys* (Terry Gilliam, 1995).

20. Darke, *La Jetée*, 18.

21. David Deamer, *Deleuze, Japanese Cinema, and the Atom Bomb: The Spectre of Impossibility* (New York: Bloomsbury, 2014).

22. More recently, this view of the Olympics as an opportunity for renewal was invoked by the organizers of the 2020 Tokyo Games, dubbed the "Recovery Olympics," this time asking the world to forget not war but the nuclear disaster at Fukushima Daiichi. See Muto Ruiko and Norma Field, "This Will Still Be True Tomorrow: 'Fukushima Ain't Got the Time for Olympic Games': Two Texts on Nuclear Disaster and Pandemic," *The Asia-Pacific Journal: Japan Focus* 18, no. 13 (June 25, 2020): 20.

23. Lupton, *Chris Marker*, 152.

24. Lupton, 109.

25. Chiba, "Le Japon de Chris Marker," 258.

26. Colin MacCabe, "An Interview with Chris Marker—October 2010," *Critical Quarterly* 55, no. 3 (October 1, 2013): 87.

27. David Montero, "Film Also Ages: Time and Images in Chris Marker's Sans Soleil," *Studies in French Cinema* 6, no. 2 (January 1, 2006): 109.

28. Timothy J. Craig, *Japan Pop! Inside the World of Japanese Popular Culture* (Armonk, NY: M.E. Sharpe, 2000), 295.

29. Jon Kear, *Sunless/Sans Soleil*, Cinetek (Wiltshire: Flicks Books, 1999), 7–8.

30. Lupton, *Chris Marker*, 153, 157.

31. Raymond Bellour, "Chris Marker and Level Five," accessed August 2, 2020, http://www.screeningthepast.com/2013/12/chris-marker-and-level-five/.

32. Raymond Bellour, *L'entre-images 2: Mots, images* (Paris: P.O.L., 1999), 227.

33. For more on this history, see Henry Chevallier, *Histoire des luttes antinucléaires en France 1958–2008* (Fustérouau, France: La Bertrande, 2009).

34. Yamagata International Documentary Film Festival, *Memories of the Future. Chris Marker's Travels and Trials* (Yamagata, 2013); Yu Kaneko and Chiho Higashi, *Chris Marker: cinéaste nomade et engagé* (Tokyo: Mori Shosha, 2014).

Chapter 5

1. Miyako, a coastal city devastated by the tsunami, is in Iwate prefecture, a few hundred miles north of the Fukushima Daiichi power plant.

2. The long edit version of the footage is not shown in full in Courdy's web-documentary or film but can be accessed in the JAPAN WEB-DOCUMENTARY PROJECT collection on YouTube: Keita Okamoto, *Tsunami Miyako* (Miyako City Hall, Iwate prefecture, 2011), https://www.youtube.com/watch?v=YLeSbbgnXmE.

3. As of the date of writing, this web-documentary is no longer listed on the KAMI Productions website.

4. Matsubayshi's *Fukushima: Memories of the Lost Landscape* won the Prix Anthropologique et développement durable at the 2012 Festival International Jean Rouch. Funahashi's *Nuclear Nation II* was selected for the Compétition internationale at the 2015 Cinéma du réel festival and chosen by the Commission nationale de sélection des médiathèques for distribution in French libraries.

5. See Daniel O'Neill, "Rewilding Futures: Japan's Nuclear Exclusion Zones and Post 3.11 Eco-Cinema," *Journal of Japanese and Korean Cinema* 11, no. 2 (2019): 85–100.

6. This definition came from the "Yonaoshi" page in Courdy's web-documentary.

7. A June 12, 2017, post on the "Japan Web-documentary project" Facebook page invites visitors to access the film online for free and encourages them to "partager sans modération."

8. The films are hosted on Vimeo, where they are password protected and have been viewed relatively few times.

9. Keiko Courdy, email message to the author, August 18, 2020.

10. Wallace, *Risk Criticism*, 20.

11. Lev Manovich, *The Language of New Media* (Cambridge, MA: MIT Press, 2002), 314.

12. Manovich, 316.

13. Manovich, 317.

14. Keiko Courdy, email message to the author, August 17, 2020.

15. Translation from the English version of the web-documentary.

16. Hjort, "Cinematic Transnationalism," 17.

17. Philippe Rouy, Interview with Philippe Rouy: Blindness in images, blindness of society off-camera, interview by Élise Domenach, *Fukushima en*

cinéma. Voix du cinéma japonais. Published by U of Tokyo Center for Philosophy, 2015, 121, 139.

18. Philippe Rouy, email message to the author, July 3, 2017.

19. Rouy, Interview with Philippe Rouy, 139.

20. "TEPCO : Nuclear Power Station | Fukuichi Live Camera (Images of Unit 4 Side)," accessed August 31, 2020, https://www.tepco.co.jp/en/nu/f1-np/camera/index-e.html.

21. Rouy, Interview with Philippe Rouy, 129, 146–47.

22. Edan Corkill, "Are We Pointing at the Right Guy?" *The Japan Times*, March 8, 2012, https://www.japantimes.co.jp/culture/2012/03/08/arts/are-we-pointing-at-the-right-guy-2/.

23. Anonymous, "About the Pointing a Finger toward Fukuichi Live Cam," accessed December 5, 2016, http://pointatfuku1cam.nobody.jp/e.html.

24. Anna Volkmar, *Art and Nuclear Power: The Role of Culture in the Environmental Debate* (Lanham, MD: Lexington Books, 2022), 119.

25. Morton, *Hyperobjects*, 60.

26. Philippe Rouy, ed., "Fukushima (3 Films) Textes et entretiens," n.d.

27. Non-human animals left behind in the exclusion zone and mourned by their human companions are a common motif in many films about the nuclear disaster at Fukushima Daiichi. Horses, in particular, are the subject of works such as Matsubayashi Yojyu's documentary film *Matsuri No Uma / The Horses of Fukushima* (2013); and Furukawa Hideo's novel *Umatachi Yo, Sore Demo Hikari Wa Muku De* (Tokyo: Shinchōsha, 2011), translated by Doug Slaymaker and Akiko Takenaka as *Horses, Horses, in the End the Light Remains Pure: A Tale That Begins with Fukushima* (Columbia University Press, 2016).

28. Morton, *Hyperobjects*, 66.

29. Lippit, *Atomic Light*, 30.

30. Rouy, Interview with Philippe Rouy, 137.

31. Rouy, 140.

32. Rouy, 122, 140.

33. Hjort, "Cinematic Transnationalism," 28.

34. Rouy, Interview with Philippe Rouy, 125–26, 143.

35. "Villa Kujoyama | Philippe Rouy," accessed December 31, 2022, http://www.villakujoyama.jp/resident/philippe-rouy-fr/.

Chapter 6

1. Robert Jacobs, "Not Seeing the Contaminated Forest for the Decontaminated Trees in Fukushima," *The Asia-Pacific Journal: Japan Focus* 19, no. 17 Legacies of Fukushima: 3.11 in Context (September 1, 2021).

2. Nancy, *After Fukushima*, 14.

3. Robert Jacobs, "Born Violent: The Origins of Nuclear Power," *Asian Journal of Peacebuilding* 7, no. 1 (2019): 9.

4. Nancy underscores the distinction between equivalence, designating the Marxist exchange value, and equality, designating the equal dignity of all living humans, a dignity that cannot be given a price. Nancy, *After Fukushima*, 13, 40.

5. Gilles Deleuze, *Difference and Repetition*, trans. Paul Patton (New York: Columbia University Press, 1994).

6. Linda Gordon, "A Meditation on Comparison in Historical Scholarship," in *Comparison: Theories, Approaches, Uses*, ed. Rita Felski and Susan Stanford Friedman, 315–35. (Baltimore: Johns Hopkins University Press, 2013), 320.

7. Gordon, 325.

8. "Jun Yang," accessed April 12, 2022, http://junyang.info/about/.

9. Jun Yang, *The Age of Guilt and Forgiveness*, accessed January 14, 2022, http://junyang.info/project/the-age-of/. The film has been shown as part of an installation entitled *A Maze and Observatory as a Memorial of the Past* at the Mori Art Museum in Tokyo (2016), the Hiroshima Film Festival (2016), the Kuangdu Museum in Taipei (2016), and the Art Sonje Center in Seoul (2018).

10. Jun Yang, "Paris Syndrome," Jun Yang, accessed April 6, 2022, http://junyang.info/project/paris-syndrome/. The *Paris Syndrome* works include a film, café, and hotel room at the Galerie für Zeitgenössische Kunst Leipzig (Contemporary Art Gallery Leipzig) in Germany, as well as various installations: *Paris Syndrome Café* (2007), *Paris Syndrome* (2007/2008), *Paris Syndrome @ Vitamin Creative Space* (2008), *Paris Syndrome: Cige Beijing* (2008), *Paris Syndrome Hotel* (2010). Yang describes Paris Syndrome as the psychological disorder or kind of negative culture shock afflicting Japanese visitors in Paris.

11. This multimedia work is also known as "1945–1998" and shows the 2,053 nuclear tests and explosions that took place between these years. Masa and Judith watch from 1964–67.

12. The aestheticization of kanji in a decorative and exotic border added on to Vincent van Gogh's *Flower Plum Orchard (After Hiroshige)* (1887) offers one such example in the tradition of Japonisme. "Flowering Plum Orchard (after Hiroshige) Vincent van Gogh, 1887," Van Gogh Museum, accessed April 27, 2022, https://www.vangoghmuseum.nl/en/collection/s0115V1962.

13. Deleuze, *Difference and Repetition*, 2.

14. Sergei Eisenstein, "The Dramaturgy of Film Form (The Dialectical Approach to Film Form)," in *Critical Visions in Film Theory: Classic and Contemporary Readings*, ed. Timothy Corrigan, Patricia White, and Meta Mazaj (Boston: Bedford/St. Martin's, 2010), 266.

15. The tsunami footage is credited to Kamiya Koichi.

16. *ECHO—son virtuel* (2007) by Fujimoto Yukio is an outdoor installation at the Hiroshima City Museum of Contemporary Art. The bronze casts are part of Magdalena Abakanowicz's outdoor installation *Space of Becalmed Beings* (1992–93), also at the Hiroshima City Museum of Contemporary Art commissioned by the city of Hiroshima to mark the 50th anniversary of the dropping of the atomic bomb.

17. Gordon, "A Meditation on Comparison in Historical Scholarship," 333.

18. Saint-Laurent-des-Eaux was the site of two INES level 4 accidents in 1969 and 1980, the most serious accidents in France to date. On the International Nuclear and Radiological Event Scale (INES), events at level 3 and below are classified as "incidents," and levels 4–7 are classified as accidents. The accident at Fukushima Daiichi was a level 7 major accident.

19. I borrow "nuclearity" from Hecht, *Being Nuclear*, 14. "The qualities that make a nation, a program, a technology, a material, or a workplace count as 'nuclear' remain unstable, even today. There isn't one nuclear ontology; there are many. My term for this contested terrain of being, this unsettled classificatory scheme, is nuclearity."

20. The question of waste is more thoroughly explored in Michael Madsen's documentary *Into Eternity* (2010).

21. The filmmakers had both seen *Hiroshima mon amour* several times and saw it together in a theater in Paris upon its rerelease in 2013. Cahen describes the film as more significant than just a brief allusion in *The Heart of the Conflict*. Judith Cahen in discussion with the author, June 2023.

22. The interview with Duras is extracted from the documentary *Marguerite tel qu'en elle-même / Marguerite as She Was* (Dominique Auvray, 2002).

23. David Macauley, *Elemental Philosophy: Earth, Air, Fire, and Water as Environmental Ideas* (Albany: State University of New York Press, 2010), 4.

24. Joseph Masco, "The Artificial World," in *Reactivating Elements: Chemistry, Ecology, Practice*, ed. Dimitris Papadopoulos, María Puig de la Bellacasa, and Natasha Myers (Durham: Duke University Press, 2021), 133.

25. The location of the solar panels is unidentified in the film. Cahen has said that many viewers have asked about the location of this shot, which they often guess to be Japan (the previous scene takes place at the Genkai Nuclear Power Plant in Saga, Japan) but is actually in the southern Alps in France. Email message to the author, August 8, 2019.

Conclusion

1. Hamaguchi's films co-directed with Sakai Kō include *The Sound of Waves* (2012), *Voices from the Waves: Kesennuma* (2013) and *Voices from the*

Waves: Shinchimachi (2013). See also Élise Domenach, "Fukushima au cinéma. Comment survivre à notre folie?," *Positif*, September 2013; Élise Domenach, "Catastrophe, silences et voix dans quelques films post-Fukushima : de l'aveuglement à l'éducation de notre regard," *A contrario*, no. 26 (October 15, 2018): 69–93; Stéphane du Mesnildot, "Génération Fukushima," *Cahiers du cinéma*, décembre 2019; Rachel DiNitto, "Toxic Interdependencies: 3/11 Cinema," in *The Japanese Cinema Book*, ed. Hideaki Fujiki and Alastair Phillips (London: British Film Institute, Bloomsbury, 2020), 379–93.

2. Richard Werly, "Un thème qui tétanise les cinéastes japonais: L'atomisation de Hiroshima et Nagasaki reste taboue," *Libération*, October 17, 2001. *H Story* was Suwa's last film made in Japan until *Voices in the Wind* (2020) about a nuclear refugee who relocated to Hiroshima after the 2011 triple disaster, a film he has suggested may be his final. Élise Domenach, "Filmer ce qu'on ne peut pas filmer: Entretien avec Suwa Nobuhiro à propos du *Téléphone du vent* (*Kaze no denwa*, 2020)," in *Dans l'oeil du désastre: Créer avec Fukushima*, by Michaël Ferrier, trans. Yū Shibuya (Vincennes: Éditions Thierry Marchaisse, 2021), 191.

3. Isabelle Poitte, "Chernobyl," *Télérama*, September 2, 2020, https://www.telerama.fr/chernobyl-6691485.php.

4. Kate Brown, *Manual for Survival: A Chernobyl Guide to the Future* (New York: W. W. Norton & Company, 2019), 301.

References

Filmography

1940

The Effects of the Atomic Bomb on Hiroshima and Nagasaki (Itō Sueo, 1946)
La bataille de l'eau lourde / Operation Swallow: The Battle for Heavy Water (Jean Dréville, 1947)

1950

La beauté du diable / Beauty and the Devil (René Clair, 1950)
La vie commence demain / Life Begins Tomorrow (Nicole Védrès, 1950)
Ikiru / To Live (Kurosawa Akira, 1952)
Hiroshima (Sekigawa Hideo, 1953)
Gojira / Godzilla (Honda Ishirō, 1954)
Ikimono no kiroku / I Live in Fear (Kurosawa Akira, 1955)
Nuit et brouillard / Night and Fog (Alain Resnais, 1955)
Ikiteite yokatta / It Is Good to Live (Kamei Fumio, 1956)
Les espions / The Spies (Henri-Georges Clouzot, 1957)
Typhon sur Nagasaki / Typhoon over Nagasaki (Yves Ciampi, 1957)
Tokyo 1958 (Teshigahara Hiroshi, 1958)
Ai to kibō no machi / A Town of Love and Hope (Ōshima Nagisa, 1959)
Hiroshima mon amour (Marguerite Duras, Alain Resnais, 1959)
Nathalie agent secret / Nathalie Secret Agent (Henri Decoin, 1959)
Les quatre cents coups / The 400 Blows (François Truffaut, 1959)

1960

Nihon no yoru to kiri / Night and Fog in Japan (Ōshima Nagisa, 1960)
Seishun zankoku monogatari / Cruel Tales of Youth (Ōshima Nagisa, 1960)

231

L'Atlantide / Journey beneath the Desert (Edgar G. Ulmer, 1961)

Mothra (Honda Ishirō, 1961)

L'année dernière à Marienbad / Last Year at Marienbad (Alain Resnais, 1962)

La Jetée (Chris Marker, 1962)

Ro.Go.Pa.G. (Jean-Luc Godard, Ugo Gregoretti, Pier Paolo Pasolini, Roberto Rossellini, 1962)

Dr. Strangelove (Stanley Kubrick, 1964)

Le mystère Koumiko / The Koumiko Mystery (Chris Marker, 1965)

Si j'avais quatre dromadaires / If I Had Four Dromedaries (Chris Marker, 1966)

1970

La bataille de Fessenheim / The Battle of Fessenheim (Guy Seligmann, 1971)

Kashima Paradise (Bénie Deswarte, Yann Le Masson, 1973)

Les atomes nous veulent-ils du bien? / Do Atoms Wish Us Well? (Claude Otzenberger, 1975)

Mets pas tes doigts dans ton nez, ils sont radioactifs / Don't Put Your Fingers in Your Nose, They Are Radioactive (ISKRA, 1975)

Ai no korida / L'empire des sens / In the Realm of the Senses (Ōshima Nagisa, 1976)

Condamnés à réussir / Condemned to Succeed (ISKRA, 1976)

Demain les mômes / Tomorrow's Children (Jean Pourtale, 1976)

Le fond de l'air est rouge / A Grin without a Cat (Chris Marker, 1977)

Nucléaire, danger immédiat / Nuclear Energy, an Immediate Danger (Serge Poljinsky, 1977)

Ai no bōrei / L'empire de la passion / Empire of Passion (Ōshima Nagisa, 1978)

1980

Dossier Plogoff / The Plogoff Case (ISKRA, 1980)

Plogoff, des pierres contre des fusils / Plogoff, Rocks against Rifles (Félix Le Garrec, Nicole Le Garrec, 1980)

Malevil (Christian de Chalonge, 1981)

Laissé inachevé à Tokyo / Left Unfinished in Tokyo (Olivier Assayas, 1982)

Sans soleil (Chris Marker, 1982)

The Day After (Nicholas Meyer, 1983)

Le dernier combat / The Last Battle (Luc Besson, 1983)

Furyo / Merry Christmas, Mr. Lawrence (Ōshima Nagisa, 1983)

WarGames (John Badham, 1983)

2019 après la chute de New York / 2019: After the Fall of New York (Sergio Martino, 1984)

The Terminator (James Cameron, 1984)

Threads (Mick Jackson, 1984)

A.K. (Chris Marker, 1985)
Ran (Kurosawa Akira, 1985)
Max mon amour (Ōshima Nagisa, 1986)
Bikini mon amour (Oliver Herbrich, 1987)
L'héritage de la chouette / The Owl's Legacy (Chris Marker, 1989)
Kuroi ame / Black Rain (Imamura Shōhei, 1989)
Mission pacifique / Pacific Mission (René Vautier, 1989)

1990

Yume / Dreams (Kurosawa Akira, 1990)
Tokyo Days (Chris Marker, 1991)
Bullfight / Okinawa (Chris Marker, 1992)
3 Video Haikus ("Petite ceinture," "Tchaïka," and "Owl Gets in Your Eyes,")
    (Chris Marker, 1994)
12 Monkeys (Terry Gilliam, 1995)
Hirochirac 1995 (René Vautier, 1995)
Irma Vep (Olivier Assayas, 1996)
Level Five (Chris Marker, 1996)
Immemory (Chris Marker, 1997)

2000

H Story (Suwa Nobuiro, 2001)
Wasabi (Gérard Krawczyk, Luc Besson, 2001)
Demonlover (Olivier Assayas, 2002)
Jeonjaeng geu ihu / After War (*A Letter from Hiroshima* segment, Suwa
    Nobuhiro, 2002)
Kagami no onnatachi / Femmes en miroir / Women in the Mirror (Yoshida
    Yoshishige, 2002)
Marguerite tel qu'en elle-même / Marguerite as She Was (Dominique Auvray,
    2002).
A Time-Lapse Map of Every Nuclear Explosion since 1945 (Hashimoto Isao, 2003)
Un couple parfait / A Perfect Couple (Suwa Nobuhiro, 2005)
Blessures atomiques / Atomic Wounds (Marc Petitjean, 2006)
Paris, je t'aime (Collective, 2006)
Zakuro yashiki / La grenadière (Fukada Kōji, 2006)
Tokyo! (Michel Gondry, Leos Carax, Joon-ho Bong, 2008)
Enter the Void (Gaspar Noé, 2009)
R.A.S. nucléaire, rien à signaler / Nuclear Energy, Nothing to Report (Alain de
    Halleux, 2009)
Yuki et Nina / Yuki and Nina (Suwa Nobuhiro, 2009)

2010

Into Eternity (Michael Madsen, 2010)
Atomic Bombs on Planet Earth (Peter Greenaway, 2011)
Ganbappe fura gāruzu! Fukushima ni ikiru kanojotachi no ima / Fukushima Hula Girls (Kobayashi Masaki, 2011)
Kurosawa: la voie / Kurosawa's Way (Catherine Cadou, 2011)
Lunch Time (Jean-Luc Vilmouth, 2011/2014/2018)
Soma kanka / Fukushima: Memories of the Lost Landscape (Matsubayashi Yojyu, 2011)
4 bâtiments, face à la mer / 4 Buildings, Facing the Sea (Philippe Rouy, 2012)
Futuba kara tōku hanarete / Nuclear Nation: The Fukushima Refugees Story (Funahashi Atsushi, 2012)
L'incommensurable : une recherche audio-visuelle après Fukushima / The Incommensurable: An Audiovisual Study after Fukushima (Angela Melitopoulos, Maurizio Lazzarato, 2012)
Le monde après Fukushima / The World after Fukushima (Kenichi Watanabe, 2012)
Mujin chitai / No Man's Zone (Fujiwara Toshi, 2012)
Le printemps de Hanamiyama—Fukushima / Springtime in Hanamiyama—Fukushima (Masayasu Eguchi, 2012)
Tous cobayes? / All of Us Guinea-Pigs Now? (Jean-Paul Jaud, 2012)
Welcome to Fukushima (Alain de Halleux, 2012)
Au de-là du nuage °Yonaoshi 3.11 / Beyond the Cloud (Keiko Courdy, 2013)
Grand Central (Rebecca Zlotowski, 2013)
Hotori no Sakuko / Au revoir l'été (Fukada Kōji, 2013)
Machine to Machine (Philippe Rouy, 2013)
Matsuri no uma / The Horses of Fukushima (Matsubayashi Yojyu, 2013)
Tu seras sumo / A Normal Life. Chronicle of a Sumo Wrestler (Jill Coulon, 2013)
Fovea centralis (Philippe Rouy, 2014)
Fukushima, des particules et des hommes / Fukushima, Particles and Men (Claude-Julie Parisot, Gil Rabier, 2014)
Futaba kara toku hanarete dainibu / Nuclear Nation II (Funahashi Atsushi, 2014)
Gambarō / Courage! / Stay Strong! (Thierry Ribault, Alain Saulière, 2014)
Irak mon amour (Véronique Bréchot, 2014)
Sans titre (masque humain) / Untitled (Human Mask) (Pierre Huyghe, 2014)
Tokyo fiancée (Stefan Liberski, 2014)
Cendres / Ashes (Idrissa Guiro, Mélanie Pavy, 2015)
Chiisaki koe no kanon: Sentakusuru hitobito / Little Voices from Fukushima (Kamanaka Hitomi, 2015)
Chris Marker: Never Explain, Never Complain (Arnaud Lambert, Jean-Marie Barbe, 2015)

De Hiroshima à Fukushima / From Hiroshima to Fukushima (Marc Petitjean, 2015)

Libres! / Free! (Jean-Paul Jaud, 2015)

Sayonara (Fukada Kōji, 2015)

Terres nucléaires: une histoire du plutonium / Nuclear Lands: A History of Pluto-nium (Kenichi Watanabe, 2015)

Tsunami (Jacques Deschamps, 2015)

The Age of Guilt and Forgiveness (Jun Yang, 2016)

Demi-vie à Fukushima / Half-Life in Fukushima (Mark Olexa, Francesca Scalisi, 2016)

Grüße aus Fukushima / Fukushima mon amour (Doris Dörrie, 2016)

Dagereotaipu no onna / Le secret de la chambre noir / Daguerreotype (Kurosawa Kiyoshi, 2017)

Iitatemura no kaachantachi: Tsuchi to tomo ni / Mothers of Fukushima: Eiko & Yoshiko (Furui Mizue, 2016)

A Safe Place (Keiko Courdy, 2017)

Le cœur du conflit / Kokoro no katto / The Heart of the Conflict (Judith Cahen, Masayasu Eguchi, 2017)

Le lion est mort ce soir / The Lion Sleeps Tonight (Suwa Nobuhiro, 2017)

Revenir à Fukushima / Return to Fukushima (Marie Linton, 2017)

Atomic Refugee Moms (Nakagawa Ayumi, 2018)

Beyond the Waves (Alain de Halleux, Tanaka Aya, 2018)

La grande muraille du Japon / The Great Wall of Japan (Maris Linton, 2018)

Chernobyl (Craig Mazin, 2019)

La vérité / The Truth (Kore-eda Hirokazu, 2019)

Radioactive (Marjane Satrapi, 2019)

2020

Kaze no denwa / Voices in the Wind (Suwa Nobuhiro, 2020)

Notre ami, l'atome: Un siècle de radioactivité / Our Friend the Atom: A Century of Radioactivity (Kenichi Watanabe, 2020)

Atomic Cover-Up (Greg Mitchell, Suzanne Mitchell, 2021)

L'île invisible / The Invisible Island (Keiko Courdy, 2021)

Tokyo Shaking (Olivier Peyron, 2021)

L'été nucléaire / Atomic Summer (Gaël Lépingle, 2022)

The Days (Nakata Hideo, Nishiura Masaki, 2023)

Archival Sources

Bibliothèque du film (Cinémathèque française), Paris

Collection des Scénarios
Collection Jaune
Fonds Chris Marker
Fonds Simon Mizrahi
Fonds Sylvette Baudrot-Guilbaud
Fonds Yves Kovacs
Bibliothèque Raymond Chirat (Institut Lumière), Lyon
Fonds Argos

Bibliography

Académie française. "Terminologie et néologie | Académie Française."
    Accessed November 7, 2023. https://www.academie-francaise.fr/
    questions-de-langue#88_strong-em-terminologie-et-nologie-em-strong.
Aldrich, Daniel P. *Site Fights: Divisive Facilities and Civil Society in Japan and
    the West*. 2nd ed. Ithaca: Cornell University Press, 2011.
Alter, Nora M. *Chris Marker*. Urbana: University of Illinois Press, 2006.
Ammour-Mayeur, Olivier. "*H Story* ou l'esthétique du 'remake relevant.'" In
    Orient(s) de Marguerite Duras, edited by Florence de Chalonge, Akiko
    Ueda, and Yann Mével, 237–50. Amsterdam: Rodopi, 2014.
An, Grace. "A Par-Asian Cinematic Imaginary." *Contemporary French and
    Francophone Studies* 10, no. 1 (2006): 15–23.
Anonymous. "About the Pointing a Finger toward Fukuichi Live Cam."
    Accessed December 5, 2016. http://pointatfuku1cam.nobody.jp/e.html.
Antunes, Luis Rocha, and Michael Grabowski. *The Multisensory Film Expe-
    rience: A Cognitive Model of Experiential Film Aesthetics*. Bristol, UK:
    Intellect Ltd., 2016.
Arribert-Narce, Fabien. "Écrits du 11 mars en France et au Japon: Écrire
    la catastrophe, entre fiction et témoignage." In *Penser* avec *Fukushima*,
    edited by Christian Doumet and Michaël Ferrier, 57–96. Lormont:
    Editions Cécile Defaut, 2016.
Assayas, Olivier. "Demonlover en un mot." Interview by Stephen Sarrazin.
    Objectif cinéma, 2001. http://www.objectif-cinema.com/interviews/093.
    php.
Bakhtin, M. M. *The Dialogic Imagination: Four Essays*. Translated by Caryl
    Emerson and Michael Holquist. Austin: University of Texas Press, 1981.
Bancel, Nicolas, Pascal Blanchard, and Sandrine Lemaire. "Introduction. La
    fracture coloniale: une crise française." In *La fracture coloniale: La société
    française au prisme de l'héritage colonial*, edited by Pascal Blanchard, Nico-
    las Bancel, and Sandrine Lemaire, 9–31. Paris: La Découverte, 2006.
Barad, Karen. "No Small Matter: Mushroom Clouds, Ecologies of Noth-
    ingness, and Strange Topologies of Spacetimemattering." In *Arts of*

Living on a Damaged Planet, edited by Anna Tsing, Heather Swanson, Elaine Gan, and Nils Bubandt, 103–20. Minneapolis: University of Minnesota Press, 2017.

Barthes, Roland. *L'empire des signes*. (1970; reprinted by Paris: Seuil, 2007).

Bazgan, Nicoleta. "The Eiffel Tower: A Parisian Film Star." In *Paris in the Cinema: Beyond the Flâneur*, edited by Alastair Phillips and Ginette Vincendeau, 17–25. London: British Film Institute, Palgrave, 2018.

Bazin, André. "Bazin on Marker (1958)." Translated by Dave Kehr. In *Essays on the Essay Film*, edited by Nora M. Alter and Timothy Corrigan, 102–05. New York: Columbia University Press, 2017.

Bellour, Raymond. "Chris Marker and Level Five." Accessed September 2, 2016. http://www.screeningthepast.com/2013/12/chris-marker-and-level-five/.

———. *L'entre-images 2: Mots, Images*. Paris: P.O.L., 1999.

Benayoun, Robert. *Alain Resnais: arpenteur de l'imaginaire*. Paris: Éditions Stock, 1980.

Benedict, Ruth. *The Chrysanthemum and the Sword: Patterns of Japanese Culture*. Boston: Houghton Mifflin, 1946.

Berger, Klaus. *Japonisme in Western Painting from Whistler to Matisse*. Translated by David Britt. Cambridge: Cambridge University Press, 1980.

Bess, Michael. *The Light-Green Society: Ecology and Technological Modernity in France, 1960–2000*. Chicago: University of Chicago Press, 2003.

Bloom, Michelle. *Contemporary Sino-French Cinemas: Absent Fathers, Banned Books, and Red Balloons*. Honolulu: University of Hawai'i Press, 2015.

Blume, Lesley M. M. *Fallout: The Hiroshima Cover-up and the Reporter Who Revealed It to the World*. New York: Simon and Schuster, 2020.

Bournet, Géraud. *FRANCKUSHIMA: Essai graphique sur la catastrophe de Fukushima et le risque nucléaire en France*. Grenoble: Lutopiquant éditions, 2016.

Brenez, Nicole. "Forms of Resistance and Revolt: 'We Are in Agreement with All That Has Struggled, and Is Struggling Still, since the World Began.'" In *The French Cinema Book*, edited by Michael Temple and Michael Witt, 2nd ed., 191–203. London: British Film Institute, Palgrave, 2018.

Brettell, Richard R., Paul Hayes Tucker, Natalie Henderson Lee, and Metropolitan Museum of Art (New York N.Y.). *Nineteenth- and Twentieth-Century Paintings*. New York: Metropolitan Museum of Art, 2009.

Broderick, Mick. "Fallout *On the Beach*." *Screening the Past: An International, Refereed, Electronic Journal of Visual Media & History*, no. 36 (June 17, 2013). http://www.screeningthepast.com/2013/06/fallout-on-the-beach/.

———. *Nuclear Movies: A Critical Analysis and Filmography of International Feature Length Films Dealing with Experimentation, Aliens, Terrorism, Holocaust and Other Disaster Scenarios, 1914–1989*. 2nd ed. Jefferson, NC: McFarland & Company, 1991.

Broderick, Mick, and Robert Jacobs. "Fukushima and the Shifting Conventions of Documentary: From Broadcast to Social Media Netizenship." In *Post-1990 Documentary: Reconfiguring Independence*, edited by Camille Deprez and Judith Pernin, 217–32. Edinburgh: Edinburgh University Press, 2015.

Brown, Kate. *Manual for Survival: A Chernobyl Guide to the Future*. New York: W. W. Norton & Company, 2019.

Buffon, Georges Louis Leclerc, comte de. *Histoire naturelle, générale et particulière, tome troisième, "Variétés dans l'espèce humaine."* Paris: Imprimerie Royale, 1749.

Burch, Noël. *To the Distant Observer: Form and Meaning in the Japanese Cinema*. Berkeley: University of California Press, 1979.

Burty, Philippe. "Japonisme I." *La renaissance littéraire et artistique*, May 18, 1872.

———. "Japonisme II." *La renaissance littéraire et artistique*, June 15, 1872.

———. "Japonisme III." *La renaissance littéraire et artistique*, July 6, 1872.

———. "Japonisme IV." *La renaissance littéraire et artistique*, July 27, 1872.

———. "Japonisme V." *La renaissance littéraire et artistique*, August 10, 1872.

———. "Japonisme VI." *La renaissance littéraire et artistique*, February 8, 1873.

Buruma, Ian. *The Wages of Guilt: Memories of War in Germany and Japan*. New York: Farrar, Straus and Giroux, 1994.

Capel, Mathieu. "L'érotique Japon." *Positif*, no. 632 (2013): 108–10.

Carpenter, Ele, ed. *The Nuclear Culture Source Book*. London: Black Dog Publishing, 2016.

Chamarette, Jenny. *Phenomenology and the Future of Film: Rethinking Subjectivity beyond French Cinema*. New York: Palgrave Macmillan, 2012.

Chevallier, Henry. *Histoire des luttes antinucléaires en France 1958–2008*. Fustérouau, France: La Bertrande, 2009.

Chiba, Fumio. "Le Japon de Chris Marker." In *Réceptions de la culture japonaise en France depuis 1945. Paris-Tokyo-Paris: détours par le Japon*, edited by Fabien Arribert-Narce, Kohei Kuwada, and Lucy O'Meara, 249–61. Paris: Honoré Champion, 2016.

Chow, Rey. *The Age of the World Target: Self-Referentiality in War, Theory, and Comparative Work*. Durham: Duke University Press, 2006.

———. "When Whiteness Feminizes . . . : Some Consequences of a Supplementary Logic." *Differences: A Journal of Feminist Cultural Studies* 11, no. 3 (October 1, 1999): 137–68.

Conejo Muñoz, Jessica Fernanda. "Memory and Distance: On Nobuhiro Suwa's *A Letter from Hiroshima*." *Genocide Studies and Prevention: An International Journal* 12, no. 2 (2018): 125–39.

Cooper, Sarah. *Chris Marker*. Manchester, UK: Manchester University Press, 2008.

Cordle, Daniel. "The Futures of Nuclear Criticism." *Alluvium* 5, no. 4 (July 29, 2016). https://alluvium.bacls.org/2016/07/29/the-futures-of-nuclear-criticism/.

Corkill, Edan. "Are We Pointing At the Right Guy?" *The Japan Times*, March 8, 2012. https://www.japantimes.co.jp/culture/2012/03/08/arts/are-we-pointing-at-the-right-guy-2/.

Craig, Timothy J. *Japan Pop! Inside the World of Japanese Popular Culture*. Armonk, NY: M.E. Sharpe, 2000.

Creton, Laurent, and Anne Jäckel. "Business 1950–80: The End of a Golden Era for the Industry." In *The French Cinema Book*, edited by Michael Temple and Michael Witt, 2nd ed., 164–79. London: British Film Institute, Palgrave, 2018.

Croteau, Melissa. *Transcendence and Spirituality in Japanese Cinema: Framing Sacred Spaces*. London: Routledge, 2023.

Cubitt, Sean. *Eco Media*. Amsterdam: Rodopi, 2005.

Dale, Joshua Paul. "Cross-Cultural Encounters through a Lateral Gaze." In *After Orientalism: Critical Engagements, Productive Looks*, edited by Inge E. Boer, 63–79. Amsterdam: Rodopi, 2003.

Darke, Chris. *La Jetée*. BFI Film Classics. London: Palgrave, 2016.

Davis, Julie Nelson. *Picturing the Floating World: Ukiyo-e in Context*. Honolulu: University of Hawai'i Press, 2021.

Deamer, David. *Deleuze, Japanese Cinema, and the Atom Bomb: The Spectre of Impossibility*. New York: Bloomsbury, 2014.

Deleuze, Gilles. *Cinema 2: The Time-Image*. Translated by Hugh Tomlinson and Robert Galeta. Minneapolis: University of Minnesota Press, 2010.

———. *Difference and Repetition*. Translated by Paul Patton. New York: Columbia University Press, 1994.

DeLoughrey, Elizabeth M. *Allegories of the Anthropocene*. Durham: Duke University Press Books, 2019.

Derrida, Jacques. "No Apocalypse, Not Now (Full Speed Ahead, Seven Missiles, Seven Missives)." Translated by Catherine Porter and Philip Lewis. *Diacritics* 14, no. 2, Nuclear Criticism (Summer 1984): 20–31.

Desser, David. *Eros plus Massacre: An Introduction to the Japanese New Wave Cinema*. Bloomington: Indiana University Press, 1988.

DiNitto, Rachel. "Toxic Interdependencies: 3/11 Cinema." In *The Japanese Cinema Book*, edited by Hideaki Fujiki and Alastair Phillips, 379–93. London: British Film Institute, Bloomsbury, 2020.

Domarchi, Jean, Jacques Donio-Valcroze, Jean-Luc Godard, Pierre Kast, Jacques Rivette, and Eric Rohmer. "Hiroshima, notre amour." *Cahiers du cinéma* 97 (July 1959): 1–18.

Domenach, Élise. "Catastrophe, silences et voix dans quelques films post-Fukushima: de l'aveuglement à l'éducation de notre regard." *A contrario*, no. 26 (October 15, 2018): 69–93.

———. "Filmer ce qu'on ne peut pas filmer: entretien avec Suwa Nobuhiro à propos du *Téléphone du vent* (*Kaze no denwa*, 2020)." In *Dans l'oeil du désastre: Créer avec Fukushima*, by Michaël Ferrier, translated by Yū Shibuya. Vincennes: Éditions Thierry Marchaisse, 2021.

———. "Fukushima au cinéma. Comment survivre à notre folie?" *Positif*, September 2013.

Doumet, Christian, and Michaël Ferrier, eds. *Penser* avec *Fukushima*. Lormont: Éditions Cécile Defaut, 2016.

Duras, Marguerite. *Hiroshima mon amour: scénario et dialogues*. Paris: Gallimard, 1960.

———. *Un barrage contre le Pacifique*. Paris: Gallimard, 1950.

Durieux, Gilles. *Jean Marais: biographie*. Paris: Flammarion, 2005.

Eaves, Elizabeth. "Why Is America Getting a New $100 Billion Nuclear Weapon?" *Bulletin of the Atomic Scientists* (blog), February 8, 2021. https://thebulletin.org/2021/02/why-is-america-getting-a-new-100-billion-nuclear-weapon/.

Edelstein, Dan, Robert Morrissey, and Glenn Roe. "To Quote or Not to Quote: Citation Strategies in the *Encyclopédie*." *Journal of the History of Ideas* 74, no. 2 (April 2013): 213–36.

Eisenhower, Dwight D. "Address before the General Assembly of the United Nations on Peaceful Uses of Atomic Energy." Address presented at the 470th Plenary Meeting of the United Nations General Assembly, New York City, December 8, 1953.

Eisenstein, Sergei. "The Dramaturgy of Film Form (The Dialectical Approach to Film Form)." In *Critical Visions in Film Theory: Classic and Contemporary Readings*, edited by Timothy Corrigan, Patricia White, and Meta Mazaj, 262–79. Boston: Bedford/St. Martin's, 2010.

Emery, Elizabeth. *Reframing Japonisme: Women and the Asian Art Market in Nineteenth-Century France, 1853–1914*. London: Bloomsbury Visual Arts, 2020.

Fay, Jennifer. "Cinema's Hot Chronology (5:29:21 Mountain War Time, July 16, 1945)." *JCMS: Journal of Cinema and Media Studies* 58, no. 2 (2019): 146–52.

Fedchenko, Vitaly. "Nuclear Explosions, 1945–2013." In *SIPRI Yearbook 2014: Armaments, Disarmament and International Security*, 346–51. Oxford: Oxford University Press, 2014.

Ferrier, Michaël, ed. *Dans l'œil du désastre: Créer avec Fukushima*. Vincennes: Marchaisse, 2021.

———. "Fukushima ou la traversée du temps: une catastrophe sans fin." *Esprit*, June 2014, 33–43.

————. "Introduction: Les écrivains du corail ou d'une nouvelle arborescence—possible et souhaitable—dans la réception de la culture japonaise." In *Réceptions de la culture japonaise en France depuis 1945. Paris-Tokyo-Paris: détours par le Japon*, edited by Fabien Arribert-Narce, Kohei Kuwada, and Lucy O'Meara, 27–47. Paris: Honoré Champion, 2016.

————. *Japon: La barrière des rencontres*. Nantes: Editions Cécile Defaut, 2009.

————. "L'art du repiquage: présences du Japon de Léon Rosny à Dany Laferrière." In *D'après le Japon*, edited by Laurent Zimmermann. Nantes: Editions Cécile Defaut, 2012.

————. *Fukushima, Récit d'un désastre*. Paris: Gallimard, 2012.

Ferrier, Michaël, and Nobutaka Miura, eds. *La tentation de la France, la tentation du Japon: regards croisés*. Paris: Éditions Philippe Picquier, 2003.

"Filmographie de Chris Marker." *L'Avant-Scène Cinéma*, no. 606 (October 2013): 34–35.

Forest, Philippe, ed. *Du Japon*. Paris: Gallimard, 2012.

————. *Retour à Tokyo*. Nantes: Éditions Cécile Defaut, 2014.

Fourastié, Jean. *Les trente glorieuses: ou la révolution invisible de 1946 à 1975*. Paris: Fayard, 1979.

Fournier Lanzoni, Rémi. *French Cinema: From Its Beginnings to the Present*. 2nd ed. London: Bloomsbury, 2015.

Fujiki, Hideaki, and Alastair Phillips. "Introduction: Japanese Cinema and Its Multiple Perspectives." In *The Japanese Cinema Book*, edited by Hideaki Fujiki and Alastair Phillips, 1–22. London: British Film Institute, Bloomsbury, 2020.

Furui, Yoshikichi, Yūko Tsushima, Natsuki Ikezawa, and Toshiyuki Horie. *Pour un autre roman japonais*. Edited by Philippe Forest and Cécile Sakai. Paris: Editions Cécile Defaut, 2005.

Gabet, Olivier, ed. *Japonismes*. Paris: Flammarion, 2014.

Gaulène, Mathieu. *Le nucléaire en Asie: Fukushima, et après?* Arles: Editions Philippe Picquier, 2016.

Geilhorn, Barbara, and Kristina Iwata-Weickgenannt. "Negotiating Nuclear Disaster: An Introduction." In *Fukushima and the Arts: Negotiating Nuclear Disaster*, edited by Barbara Geilhorn and Kristina Iwata-Weickgenannt, 1–20. New York: Routledge, 2017.

Genova, Pamela A. *Writing Japonisme: Aesthetic Translation in Nineteenth-Century French Prose*. Evanston: Northwestern University Press, 2016.

Gonschor, Lorenz. "Mai Te Hau Roma Ra Te Huru: The Illusion of 'Autonomy' and the Ongoing Struggle for Decolonization in French Polynesia." *The Contemporary Pacific* 25, no. 2 (2013): 259–96.

Gordon, Andrew. *A Modern History of Japan: From Tokugawa Times to the Present*. 2nd ed. Oxford: Oxford University Press, 2009.

Gordon, Linda. "A Meditation on Comparison in Historical Scholarship." In *Comparison: Theories, Approaches, Uses*, edited by Rita Felski and Susan Stanford Friedman, 315–35. Baltimore: Johns Hopkins University Press, 2013.

Ha, Marie-Paule. *Figuring the East: Segalen, Malraux, Duras, and Barthes*. Albany: State University of New York Press, 2000.

Hachiya, Michihiko. *Hiroshima Diary: The Journal of a Japanese Physician, August 6–September 30, 1945*. Translated by Warner Wells and Neal Tsukifuji. Chapel Hill: University of North Carolina Press, 1955.

Hainge, Greg. "A Tale of (at Least) Two Hiroshimas: Nobuhiro Suwa's *H Story* and Alain Resnais's *Hiroshima mon amour*." *Contemporary French Civilization* 32, no. 2 (2008): 147–73.

Harbord, Janet. *Chris Marker, La Jetée*. London: Afterall Books, 2009.

Hashimoto, Akiko. *The Long Defeat: Cultural Trauma, Memory, and Identity in Japan*. 1st edition. New York: Oxford University Press, 2015.

Hayashi, Yoko, ed. *Domani: The Art of Tomorrow 2022–23*. Tokyo: Agency for Cultural Affairs, 2020.

Hecht, Gabrielle. *Being Nuclear: Africans and the Global Uranium Trade*. Cambridge, MA: MIT Press, 2012.

———. "L'Empire nucléaire: les silences des 'Trente Glorieuses.'" In *Une autre histoire des "Trente Glorieuses": modernisation, contestations et pollutions dans la France d'après-guerre*, 159–78. Paris: La Découverte, 2013.

———. *The Radiance of France: Nuclear Power and National Identity after World War II*. 2nd ed. Cambridge, MA: MIT Press, 2009.

Higuchi, Toshihiro. *Political Fallout: Nuclear Weapons Testing and the Making of a Global Environmental Crisis*. Redwood City: Stanford University Press, 2020.

Hirano, Kyoko. "Depiction of the Atomic Bombings in Japanese Cinema during the U.S. Occupation Period." In *Hibakusha Cinema: Hiroshima, Nagasaki and the Nuclear Image in Japanese Film*, edited by Mick Broderick, 103–19. London: Kegan Paul International, 1996.

———. *Mr. Smith Goes to Tokyo: Japanese Cinema Under the American Occupation, 1945–1952*. Washington D.C.: Smithsonian Institution Press, 1992.

Hjort, Mette. "On the Plurality of Cinematic Transnationalism." In *World Cinemas, Transnational Perspectives*, edited by Nataša Ďurovičová and Kathleen E. Newman, 12–33. New York: Routledge, 2010.

Hokenson, Jan. *Japan, France, and East-West Aesthetics: French Literature, 1867–2000*. Madison, NJ: Fairleigh Dickinson University Press, 2004.

Holtzman, Hannah. "Chris Marker's Ecological Consciousness, or 36 Views of the Train in Tokyo." *French Screen Studies* 22, no. 4 (2022): 251–70.

"Hommage à Madame Kawakita—La Cinémathèque française." Accessed September 2, 2021. https://www.cinematheque.fr/article/927.html.

Horn, Eva. *The Future as Catastrophe: Imagining Disaster in the Modern Age.* Translated by Valentine Pakis. New York: Columbia University Press, 2018.

Hurley, Jessica. *Infrastructures of Apocalypse: American Literature and the Nuclear Complex.* Minneapolis: University of Minnesota Press, 2020.

Ives, Colta Feller. *The Great Wave: The Influence of Japanese Woodcuts on French Prints.* New York: The Metropolitan Museum of Art, 1974.

Iwabuchi, Kōichi. *Recentering Globalization: Popular Culture and Japanese Transnationalism.* Durham: Duke University Press, 2002.

Iwasaki, Tsutomu. "La post-synchronisation de *Hiroshima mon amour.*" In *Orient(s) de Marguerite Duras*, edited by Florence de Chalonge, Yann Mével, and Akiko Ueda, 369–75. Amsterdam: Rodopi, 2014.

Jacobs, Robert. "Born Violent: The Origins of Nuclear Power." *Asian Journal of Peacebuilding* 7, no. 1 (2019): 9–29.

———. "Not Seeing the Contaminated Forest for the Decontaminated Trees in Fukushima." *The Asia-Pacific Journal: Japan Focus* 19, no. 17 Legacies of Fukushima: 3.11 in Context (September 1, 2021).

———. *Nuclear Bodies: The Global Hibakusha.* New Haven: Yale University Press, 2022.

Jacobson, Brian R. "French Cinema vs the Bomb: Atomic Science and a War of Images circa 1950." *Historical Journal of Film, Radio and Television* 42, no. 2 (2022): 191–218.

Jones, Nate, ed. *Able Archer 83: The Secret History of the NATO Exercise That Almost Triggered Nuclear War.* New York: The New Press, 2016.

"Jun Yang." Accessed April 12, 2022. http://junyang.info/about/.

Kaganski, Serge. "Sur le tournage de *H Story.*" *Les Inrocks*, 2001. https://www.lesinrocks.com/2001/05/08/cinema/actualite-cinema/nobuhiro-suwa-sur-le-tournage-de-h-story-11218590/.

Kaneko, Yu, and Chiho Higashi. *Chris Marker: cinéaste nomade et engagé.* Tokyo: Mori Shosha, 2014.

Karatani, Kojin, and Sabu Kohso. "Uses of Aesthetics: After *Orientalism.*" *Boundary 2* 25, no. 2 Edward W. Said (Summer 1998): 145–60.

Kawakami, Akane. *Travellers' Visions: French Literary Encounters with Japan 1881–2004.* Liverpool: Liverpool University Press, 2005.

———. "Walking Underground: Two Francophone Flâneurs in Twenty-First-Century Tokyo." *L'Esprit Créateur* 56, no. 3 (Fall 2016): 120–33.

Kawakita, Michiaki. *Modern Currents in Japanese Art.* Translated by Charles S. Terry. Vol. 24. The Heibonsha Survey of Japanese Art. New York, Tokyo: Weatherhill/Heibonsha, 1974.

Kawamoto, Kōji. "French Views of the Japanese: Loti vs. Farrère." In *Selected Proceedings*, 259–76. Vancouver: The Institute of Asian Research, University of British Columbia, 1988.

Kear, Jon. *Sunless/Sans Soleil.* Cinetek. Wiltshire: Flicks Books, 1999.

Kennedy-Karpat, Colleen. *Rogues, Romance, and Exoticism in French Cinema of the 1930s.* Lanham, MD: Fairleigh Dickinson University Press, 2013.

Kingston, Jeff. "Contesting Fukushima." *The Asia-Pacific Journal: Japan Focus* 20, no. 12.1 (June 15, 2022).

Kinsella, John, and Drew Milne. *Nuclear Theory Degree Zero: Essays against the Nuclear Android.* New York: Routledge, 2021.

Kline, T. Jefferson. *Unraveling French Cinema: From L'Atalante to Caché.* New York: John Wiley & Sons, 2010.

Koide, Emi. "Le Japon selon Chris Marker." *Appareil* 6 (2010): 1–9.

Komatsu, Hiroshi. "The Lumière Cinématographe and the Production of the Cinema in Japan in the Earliest Period." *Film History* 8, no. 4 (December 1996): 431–38.

Kriegel-Nicholas, Isadora. "The Historical Reception of Japanese Cinema at *Cahiers du cinéma*: 1951–1961." Dissertation, Boston University, 2016.

Landrot, Marine. "Les fantômes de Hiroshima, retour sur le tournage de 'H Story,' de Nobuhiro Suwa." *Télérama*, October 17, 2001.

Lee, Edmund. "Koji Fukada on Graduating from Theatre to Become a Cannes Winner." *South China Morning Post*, April 12, 2017, sec. Culture. https://www.scmp.com/culture/film-tv/article/2086961/japanese-filmmaker-koji-fukada-cannes-winner-harmonium-his-eric.

Leonard, Garry. "Technically Human: Kubrick's Monolith and Heidegger's Propriative Event." *Film Criticism* 36, no. 1 (2012): 44–67.

Leperchey, Sarah. *Alain Resnais: une lecture topologique.* Paris: Editions L'Harmattan, 2000.

Lévi-Strauss, Claude. *L'anthropologie face aux problèmes du monde moderne.* Paris: Seuil, 2011.

———. *L'autre face de la lune: écrits sur le Japon.* Paris: Seuil, 2011.

Lippit, Akira Mizuta. *Atomic Light (Shadow Optics).* Minneapolis: University of Minnesota Press, 2005.

Lochbaum, David, Edwin Lyman, Susan Q. Stranahan, and The Union of Concerned Scientists. *Fukushima: The Story of a Nuclear Disaster.* New York: The New Press, 2015.

Lupton, Catherine. *Chris Marker: Memories of the Future.* London: Reaktion Books, 2005.

Ma, Aliza. "Film in Flux." *Criterion Collection DVD*, May 1, 2021.

Macauley, David. *Elemental Philosophy: Earth, Air, Fire, and Water as Environmental Ideas.* Albany: State University of New York Press, 2010.

MacCabe, Colin. "An Interview with Chris Marker—October 2010." *Critical Quarterly* 55, no. 3 (October 1, 2013): 84–87.

MacCabe, Colin, and Adam Bartos. *Studio: Remembering Chris Marker.* New York: OR Books, 2017.

Mainichi Daily News. "Japanese Winner of Cannes Jury Prize Directs Movies Based on Theater Experience." May 24, 2016. https://mainichi.jp/english/articles/20160524/p2a/00m/0et/019000c.

Manovich, Lev. *The Language of New Media*. Cambridge, MA: MIT Press, 2002.

Marks, Laura U. *Touch: Sensuous Theory and Multisensory Media*. Minneapolis: University of Minnesota Press, 2002.

Masco, Joseph. "The Artificial World." In *Reactivating Elements: Chemistry, Ecology, Practice*, edited by Dimitris Papadopoulos, María Puig de la Bellacasa, and Natasha Myers, 131–50. Durham: Duke University Press, 2021.

———. *The Nuclear Borderlands: The Manhattan Project in Post-Cold War New Mexico*. Princeton: Princeton University Press, 2006.

Matsuda, Matt. "East of No West: The Posthistoire of Postwar France and Japan." In *Confluences: Postwar Japan and France*, edited by Doug Slaymaker, 15–33. Ann Arbor: Center for Japanese Studies, University of Michigan, 2002.

Maurer, Anaïs. "Nukes and Nudes: Counter-Hegemonic Identities in the Nuclearized Pacific." *French Studies* 72, no. 3 (July 2018): 394–411.

Mazdon, Lucy. *Encore Hollywood: Remaking French Cinema*. London: British Film Institute, 2000.

Mellen, Joan. *Voices from the Japanese Cinema*. New York: Liveright, 1975.

Mesnildot, Stéphane du. "Génération Fukushima." *Cahiers du cinéma*, December 2019.

———. "Notes de chevet sur le Japon de Chris Marker." *Vertigo*, no. 46 (2013): 50–56.

———. "Un été avec Koumiko." *Cahiers du cinéma*, September 2012.

Milne, Drew, and John Kinsella. "Introduction: Nuclear Theory Degree Zero, with Two Cheers for Derrida." *Angelaki* 22, no. 3 (September 2017): 1–16.

Mitchell, Greg. *Atomic Cover-up: Two U.S. Soldiers, Hiroshima & Nagasaki, and the Greatest Movie Never Made*. New York: CreateSpace Independent Publishing Platform, 2012.

Miyao, Daisuke. "Japonisme and the Birth of Cinema." *Journal of Japonisme* 1, no. 1 (2016): 66–92.

———. *Japonisme and the Birth of Cinema*. Durham: Duke University Press Books, 2020.

———. *Sessue Hayakawa: Silent Cinema and Transnational Stardom*. Durham: Duke University Press, 2007.

Modern Japan and France: adoration, encounter, and interaction. "Section 1: Cuisine." Collection. National Diet Library. Accessed August 18, 2021. https://www.ndl.go.jp/france/en/column/s2_1.html.

Modern Japan and France—Adoration, Encounter and Interaction. "Section 2: Fashion." Collection. National Diet Library. Accessed August 18, 2021. https://www.ndl.go.jp/france/en/column/s2_2.html.

Modern Japan and France—Adoration, Encounter and Interaction. Collection. Accessed December 1, 2019. https://www.ndl.go.jp/france/en/index.html.

Mompo, Maite, and Chris Brazier. *Rainbow Warriors*. Oxford: New Internationalist, 2014.

Monnet, Livia, ed. *Toxic Immanence: Decolonizing Nuclear Legacies and Futures*. Montreal: McGill-Queen's University Press, 2022.

Montero, David. "Film Also Ages: Time and Images in Chris Marker's *Sans Soleil*." *Studies in French Cinema* 6, no. 2 (January 1, 2006): 107–15.

Montgomery, Michael V. *Carnivals and Commonplaces: Bakhtin's Chronotope, Cultural Studies, and Film*. New York: Peter Lang Publishing, 1994.

"Monument in Memory of the Korean Victims of the A-Bomb." Accessed November 12, 2021. http://www.pcf.city.hiroshima.jp/virtual/map-e/.

Morton, Timothy. *Hyperobjects: Philosophy and Ecology after the End of the World*. Minneapolis: University of Minnesota Press, 2013.

Musée Maillol Paris. "Foujita: peindre dans les années folles (dossier de presse)," 2018. https://www.museemaillol.com/wp-content/uploads/2021/05/DP-Foujita-janv18-FR-avec-compression.pdf.

Nancy, Jean-Luc. *After Fukushima: The Equivalence of Catastrophes*. Translated by Charlotte Mandell. New York: Fordham University Press, 2014.

Napier, Susan J. *From Impressionism to Anime: Japan as Fantasy and Fan Cult in the Mind of the West*. New York: Palgrave Macmillan, 2007.

Neupert, Richard. *A History of the French New Wave Cinema*. 2nd ed. Madison: University of Wisconsin Press, 2007.

Newman, Kim. *Apocalypse Movies: End of the World Cinema*. New York: St. Martin's Griffin, 2000.

Nichols, Bill. *Introduction to Documentary*. 2nd ed. Bloomington: Indiana University Press, 2010.

Nixon, Rob. *Slow Violence and the Environmentalism of the Poor*. Cambridge: Harvard University Press, 2013.

Nornes, Abé Mark. *Japanese Documentary Film: The Meiji Era through Hiroshima*. Minneapolis: University of Minnesota Press, 2003.

Nothomb, Amélie. *Ni d'Eve ni d'Adam*. Paris: Albin Michel, 2007.

———. *Stupeur et tremblements*. Paris: Albin Michel, 1999.

Nygren, Scott. *Time Frames: Japanese Cinema and the Unfolding of History*. Minneapolis: University of Minnesota Press, 2007.

Ōe, Kenzaburo. "Cher Claude Simon." *Le Monde*, September 28, 1995.

O'Neill, Daniel. "Rewilding Futures: Japan's Nuclear Exclusion Zone and Post 3.11 Eco-Cinema." *Journal of Japanese and Korean Cinema* 11, no. 2 (2019): 85–100.

Oshima, Nagisa. "Chronique d'un éleveur." *Cahiers du cinéma*, November 1986.

Panchasi, Roxanne. "'No Hiroshima in Africa': The Algerian War and the Question of French Nuclear Tests in the Sahara." *History of the Present* 9, no. 1 (2019): 84–112.

Pelletier, Philippe. "De la guerre totale (1941) à la guerre de Fukushima (2011)." *Outre-terre, Revue européenne de géopolitique* 35–36 (2013): 399–437.

Penney, Matthew. "Nuclear Nationalism and Fukushima." *The Asia-Pacific Journal: Japan Focus* 10, no. 11.2 (2012).

Perrine, Toni A. *Film and the Nuclear Age: Representing Cultural Anxiety*. New York: Routledge, 2018. First published 1998 by Garland Publishing Inc.

Philippe, Sebastien, and Tomas Statius. *Toxique: Enquête sur les essais nucléaires français en Polynésie*. Paris: PUF, 2021.

Phillips, Alastair. "The City: Tokyo 1958." In *The Japanese Cinema Book*, edited by Hideaki Fujiki and Alastair Phillips, 419–35. London: British Film Institute, Bloomsbury, 2020.

Pingaud, Bernard. "À propos d'*Hiroshima mon amour*." *Positif*, no. 35 (1960): 66–86.

Pinguet, Maurice. *Le texte Japon*. Edited by Michaël Ferrier. Paris: Seuil, 2009.

Poitte, Isabelle. "Chernobyl." *Télérama*, September 2, 2020. https://www.telerama.fr/chernobyl-6691485.php.

Pratt, Mary Louise. "Coda: Concept and Chronotope." In *Arts of Living on a Damaged Planet*, edited by Anna Tsing, Heather Swanson, Elaine Gan, and Nils Bubandt, 169–74. Minneapolis, London: University of Minnesota Press, 2017.

———. *Imperial Eyes: Travel Writing and Transculturation*. 2nd rev. ed. New York: Routledge, 2008.

Prédal, René. *Jean-Claude Carrière, Scénariste: L'art de raconter des histoires*. Paris: Éditions du Cerf, 1994.

PRIS: Power Reactor Information System (website). Accessed April 28, 2022. https://pris.iaea.org/PRIS/home.aspx.

"Proposal for a Diacritics Colloquium on Nuclear Criticism." *Diacritics* 14, no. 2, Nuclear Criticism (Summer 1984): 2–3.

Pugsley, Peter C., and Ben McCann. *The Cinematic Influence: Interaction and Exchange between the Cinemas of France and Japan*. London: Bloomsbury Academic, 2023.

Puiseux, Hélène. *L'apocalypse nucléaire et son cinéma*. Paris: Les Éditions du Cerf, 1987.

Quentin, Corinne, and Cécile Sakai, eds. *L'archipel des séismes: écrits du Japon après le 11 mars 2011*. Arles: Éditions Philippe Picquier, 2012.

Rafoni, Béatrice. "Le néo-japonisme en France: de l'influence de la culture médiatique japonaise." *Compar(a)ison* 2 (2002): 113–23.

Rancière, Jacques. "Re-Visions: Remarks on the Love of Cinema: An Interview by Oliver Davis." *Journal of Visual Culture* 10, no. 3 (December 1, 2011): 294–304.

Ravar, Raymond. *Tu n'as rien vu à Hiroshima!* Bruxelles: Institut de Sociologie, 1962.

Reed, Christopher. *Bachelor Japanists: Japanese Aesthetics and Western Masculinities.* New York: Columbia University Press, 2016.

Régamey, Félix. *Le Japon pratique.* Paris: J. Hetzel et Cie, 1891.

Renov, Michael. "Toward a Poetics of Documentary." In *Theorizing Documentary*, edited by Michael Renov, 12–36. London: Routledge, 1993.

Resnais, Alain. "Conversation avec Alain Resnais." Interview by Pierre Wildenstein. *Téléciné* 1–6, April 1960.

———. "Histoire sans images: Hiroshima mon amour." Interview by Michel Polac. INA, Argos Films, Arte Video, 2004, DVD, 1966.

———. "Un entretien avec Alain Resnais." Interview by Michel Delahaye. *Cinéma* n. 38 (July 1959): 4–14.

Riambau, Esteve. "Forbidden Loves: *Merry Christmas, Mr. Lawrence* and *Max Mon Amour*." In *Nagisa Oshima*, 266–77. Festival Internacional de Cine de Donostia-San Sebastían S. A. Ministerio de Educacíon, Cultura y Deporte/I.C.A.A./Filmoteca Española, 2013.

Richie, Donald. *Japanese Cinema: An Introduction.* New York, Oxford: Oxford University Press, 1990.

———. "'Mono No Aware': Hiroshima in Film." In *Hibakusha Cinema: Hiroshima, Nagasaki and the Nuclear Image in Japanese Film*, 20–37. London: Kegan Paul International, 1996.

Richie, Donald, and Paul Schrader. *A Hundred Years of Japanese Film: A Concise History, with a Selective Guide to DVDs and Videos.* Revised edition. New York: Kodansha USA, 2012.

Ropars-Wuilleumier, Marie-Claire. "How History Begets Meaning: Alain Resnais' *Hiroshima mon amour* (1959)." In *French Film: Texts and Contexts*, edited by Susan Hayward and Ginette Vincendeau, 173–85. London: Routledge, 1990.

Ropeik, David. "How the Unlucky Lucky Dragon Birthed an Era of Nuclear Fear." *Bulletin of the Atomic Scientists* (blog), February 28, 2018. https://thebulletin.org/2018/02/how-the-unlucky-lucky-dragon-birthed-an-era-of-nuclear-fear/.

Roud, Richard. "The Left Bank." *Monthly Film Bulletin* 32, no. 1 (Winter 1963): 24–27.

Rouy, Philippe, ed. "Fukushima (3 Films) Textes et Entretiens," n.d.

———. Interview with Philippe Rouy: Blindness in images, blindness of society off-camera. Interview by Élise Domenach. Print: Fukushima en cinéma. Voix du cinéma japonais. Tokyo: University of Tokyo Center for Philosophy, 2015.

Rucht, Dieter. "The Anti-Nuclear Power Movement and the State in France." In *States and Anti-Nuclear Movements*, edited by Helena Flam, 129–62. Edinburgh: Edinburgh University Press, 1994.

Ruiko, Muto, and Norma Field. "This Will Still Be True Tomorrow: 'Fukushima Ain't Got the Time for Olympic Games': Two Texts on Nuclear Disaster and Pandemic." *The Asia-Pacific Journal: Japan Focus* 18, no. 13 (June 25, 2020): 20.

Said, Edward W. *Orientalism*, 25th anniversary ed. (New York: Vintage Books, 2003), xvii. First published 1978 by Pantheon Books.

Sanger, David E., William J. Broad, and Choe Sang-Hun. "Biden Is Facing an Uneasy Truth: North Korea Isn't Giving Up Its Nuclear Arsenal." *The New York Times*, May 20, 2021, sec. U.S. https://www.nytimes.com/2021/05/20/us/politics/biden-north-korea-nuclear-weapons.html.

Schwab, Gabriele. *Radioactive Ghosts*. Minneapolis: University of Minnesota Press, 2020.

Seki, Mirei. "La réception de *Hiroshima mon amour* au Japon." In *Orient(s) de Marguerite Duras*, edited by Florence de Chalonge, Akiko Ueda, and Yann Mével, 223–35. Amsterdam: Rodopi, 2014.

Shapiro, Jerome F. *Atomic Bomb Cinema: The Apocalyptic Imagination on Film*. New York: Routledge, 2002.

Sheldrick, Aaron, and Yuka Obayashi. "Japan to Release Fukushima Water into Sea after Treatment." *Reuters*, April 12, 2021, sec. Asia Pacific. https://www.reuters.com/world/asia-pacific/japan-says-release-contaminated-fukushima-water-into-sea-2021-04-12/.

Shibata, Yuko. "Postcolonial *Hiroshima, mon amour*: Franco-Japanese Collaboration in the American Shadow." In *The Trans-Pacific Imagination: Rethinking Boundary, Culture and Society*, 215–51. Singapore: World Scientific Publishing Company, 2012.

———. *Producing Hiroshima and Nagasaki: Literature, Film, and Transnational Politics*. Honolulu: University of Hawai'i Press, 2018.

Sieffert, René, ed. *Le Japon et la France: Images d'une découverte*. Paris: Publications Orientalistes de France, 1974.

Silberman, Serge. "Vivre le film: entretien avec Serge Silberman." *Cahiers du cinéma*, November 1986.

Simon, Claude. "Cher Kenzaburo Ōe." *Le Monde*, September 21, 1995.

Slaymaker, Doug. "Confluences: An Introduction." In *Confluences: Postwar Japan and France*, edited by Doug Slaymaker. Ann Arbor: Center for Japanese Studies, University of Michigan, 2002.

Smith, Iain Robert, and Constantine Verevis. "Introduction: Transnational Film Remakes." In *Transnational Film Remakes*, edited by Constantine Verevis and Iain Robert Smith, 1–18. Edinburgh: Edinburgh University Press, 2017.

Sobchack, Vivian. "Lounge Time: Postwar Crisis and the Chronotope of Film Noir." In *Refiguring American Film Genres: History and Theory*, edited by Nick Browne, 129–70. Berkeley: University of California Press, 1998.

———. *The Address of the Eye: A Phenomenology of Film Experience*. Princeton: Princeton University Press, 1991.

Solomon, Matthew. "Up-to-Date Magic: Theatrical Conjuring and the Trick Film." *Theatre Journal* 58, no. 4 (2006): 595–615.

Stam, Robert. *Film Theory: An Introduction*. Oxford: Blackwell Publishers, 2000.

Statistics Bureau of Japan. "Current Population Estimates as of October 1, 2011." Accessed May 19, 2021. http://www.stat.go.jp/english/data/jinsui/2011np/.

Szarka, Joseph. "France, the Nuclear Revival and the Post-Fukushima Landscape." In *The Fukushima Effect: A New Geopolitical Terrain*, edited by Richard Hindmarsh and Rebecca Priestley, 203–22. New York: Routledge, 2015.

Tacchella, Jean-Charles. *Jean-Charles Tacchella, mémoires*. Biarritz: SEGUIER, 2017.

Takashina, Shūji, J. Thomas Rimer, Gerald D. Bolas, Washington University Saint Louis, Japan House Gallery, and Frederick S. Wight Art Gallery. *Paris in Japan: The Japanese Encounter with European Painting*. Tokyo, St. Louis: Japan Foundation, Washington University, 1987.

"TEPCO: Nuclear Power Station | Fukuichi Live Camera (Images of Unit 4 Side)." Accessed August 31, 2020. https://www.tepco.co.jp/en/nu/f1-np/camera/index-e.html.

Tesson, Charles. "Le secret derrière la cage." *Cahiers du cinéma*, June 1986.

———. "Rencontre/Nobuhiro Suwa." *Cahiers du cinéma* no. 561, 2001.

Tezuka, Yoshiharu. "A Constellation of Gazes: Europe and the Japanese Film Industry." In *The Japanese Cinema Book*, edited by Hideaki Fujiki and Alastair Phillips, 541–55. London: British Film Institute, Bloomsbury, 2020.

———. *Japanese Cinema Goes Global: Filmworkers' Journeys*. Hong Kong: Hong Kong University Press, 2012.

The Observatory of Economic Complexity. "Products That France Exports to Japan (2010)." Accessed May 5, 2017. http://atlas.media.mit.edu/en/visualize/tree_map/hs92/export/fra/jpn/show/2010/.

The Observatory of Economic Complexity. "Products That Japan Exports to France (2010)." Accessed May 5, 2017. http://atlas.media.mit.edu/en/visualize/tree_map/hs92/export/jpn/fra/show/2010/.

Topçu, Sezin. "Atome, gloire et désenchantement: Résister à la France atomique avant 1968." In *Une autre histoire des "Trente Glorieuses": modernisation, contestations et pollutions dans la France d'après-guerre*, 189–209. Paris: La Découverte, 2013.

———. "Les physiciens dans le mouvement antinucléaire : entre science, expertise et politique." *Cahiers d'histoire. Revue d'histoire critique*, no. 102 (October 1, 2007): 89–108.

"TOWERPEDIA | TokyoTower." Accessed July 29, 2021. https://www.tokyo-tower.co.jp/en/towerpedia/.

Tranchant, Marie-Noëlle. "Tokyo Fiancée : à la découverte du Japon." *Le Figaro*, March 3, 2015, sec. Cinéma.

Truffaut, François. "Le cinéma français crève sous les fausses légendes." *Arts, Spectacles*, May 15, 1957.

Turim, Maureen Cheryn. *The Films of Oshima Nagisa: Images of a Japanese Iconoclast*. Berkeley: University of California Press, 1998.

Tweedie, James. *The Age of New Waves: Art Cinema and the Staging of Globalization*. New York: Oxford University Press, 2013.

Van Gogh Museum. "Flowering Plum Orchard (after Hiroshige) Vincent van Gogh, 1887." Accessed April 27, 2022. https://www.vangoghmuseum.nl/en/collection/s0115V1962.

Vergun, David. "U.S. Facing Increasing Nuclear, Space-Based Threats, Leaders Say." U.S. DEPARTMENT OF DEFENSE, April 20, 2021. https://www.defense.gov/Explore/News/Article/Article/2579031/us-facing-increasing-nuclear-space-based-threats-leaders-say/.

"Villa Kujoyama | Philippe Rouy." Accessed December 31, 2022. http://www.villakujoyama.jp/resident/philippe-rouy-fr/.

Volkmar, Anna. *Art and Nuclear Power: The Role of Culture in the Environmental Debate*. Lanham, MD: Lexington Books, 2022.

Wallace, Molly. *Risk Criticism: Precautionary Reading in an Age of Environmental Uncertainty*. Ann Arbor: University of Michigan Press, 2016.

Weart, Spencer R. *Nuclear Fear: A History of Images*. Cambridge: Harvard University Press, 1988.

Weisberg, Gabriel P. "Reflecting on Japonisme: The State of the Discipline in the Visual Arts." *Journal of Japonisme* 1, no. 1 (2016): 3–16.

———. "Rethinking Japonisme: The Popularization of a Taste." In *The Orient Expressed: Japan's Influence on Western Art 1854–1918*, 17–73. Jackson, MS: Mississippi Museum of Art, 2011.

Weisberg, Gabriel P., Phillip Dennis Cate, Gerald Needham, Martin Eidelberg, and William R. Johnston. *Japonisme: Japanese Influence on French Art, 1854–1910*. Cleveland: The Cleveland Museum of Art, The Rutgers University Art Gallery, The Walters Art Gallery, 1975.

Weisberg, Gabriel P., and Yvonne M. L. Weisberg. *Japonisme: An Annotated Bibliography*. New Brunswick, New York, London: International Center for Japonisme, Jane Voorhees Zimmerli Art Museum, Rutgers–The State University of New Jersey; Garland Publishing, 1990.

Werly, Richard. "Un thème qui tétanise les cinéastes japonais: l'atomisation de Hiroshima et Nagasaki reste taboue." *Libération*, October 17, 2001.

Wichmann, Siegfried. *Japonisme: The Japanese Influence on Western Art since 1858*. London: Thames and Hudson, 1981.

Wilson, Emma. *Alain Resnais*. Manchester: Manchester University Press, 2006.

Woods Hole Oceanographic Institution. "Fukushima Site Still Leaking after Five Years, Research Shows," March 7, 2016. http://www.whoi.edu/news-release/fukushima-site-still-leaking.

Wu, Chinghsin. "Institutionalizing Impressionism: Kuroda Seiki and Plein-Air Painting in Japan." In *Mapping Impressionist Painting in Transnational Contexts*, 133–44. New York: Routledge, 2021.

Yamagata International Documentary Film Festival. *Memories of the Future. Chris Marker's Travels and Trials*. Yamagata, 2013.

Yang, Jun. "Paris Syndrome." Jun Yang. Accessed April 6, 2022. http://junyang.info/project/paris-syndrome/.

———. "The Age of Guilt and Forgiveness." Accessed January 14, 2022. http://junyang.info/project/the-age-of/.

Yohann. "Interview de Jill Coulon pour son film 'Tu seras sumô.'" Dosukoi, le site français du sumo. Accessed October 5, 2013. http://www.dosukoi.fr/interview-de-jill-coulon-pour-son-film-tu-seras-sumo/.

Yoneyama, Lisa. *Hiroshima Traces: Time, Space, and the Dialectics of Memory*. Berkeley: University of California Press, 1999.

Zimmermann, Laurent, ed. *D'après le Japon*. Nantes: Editions Cécile Defaut, 2012.

Zwigenberg, Ran. "'The Coming of a Second Sun': The 1956 Atoms for Peace Exhibit in Hiroshima and Japan's Embrace of Nuclear Power." *The Asia-Pacific Journal: Japan Focus* 10, no. 6 (February 2, 2012).

Index

conflict: comparison and, 184–85,
191; Eisenstein and, 181–182;
formal, 180; graphic, 181–82; as
method, 180, 181
containment: 12, 160, 161, 199,
200
contamination. *See under*
environment
continuity: disruption of, 59;
formal, 70, 79; narrative, 29, 74;
subterranean, 79; temporal, 103,
187
Cooper, Sarah, 224n11
coproductions: collaboration and,
81, 84, 93, 117, 140–41, 143, 145,
150, 162; as financial strategy,
33–34; *Hiroshima mon amour* as,
3, 36, 56, 58–59; *H Story* as, 91;
Marker and, 118; transnational,
Franco-Japanese, 11, 15–16, 18,
34, 47, 49, 56, 60–67, 80, 84,
110–11, 171, 197, 199
Cornell University, 5
Coubertin, Pierre de, *124*, 124–25
Coulon, Jill, 49, 215n131
Courdy, Keiko, 18, 49, 50, 139–40,
141–52, 164, 198; Japan and, 143,
144, 149–51
Coutard, Raoul, 84
Cowie, Peter, 65
Croteau, Melissa, 68
crowdfunding, 18, 143, 150, 152
crystal (Deleuze), 83, 90–91, 93, 94,
105, 221n7
crystal-image (Deleuze), 83, 91,
92–93, 102–4
Cuban Missile Crisis, 115, 119
Cubitt, Sean, 1–2
cultural exchange, 3; Franco-
Japanese, cinematic, 14–15, 17,
28, 45–52, 58, 59, 82, 84, 117,
137, 152, 179, 182, 197; lateral,

reciprocal, 11, 37, 52, 53, 82, 165,
197; music and, 185; tradition of,
174
cultural heritage, 27
Curie, Marie, 11, 33
Curie, Pierre, 33

Daiei Studios, 34, 36, 56
Dale, Joshua Paul, 52
Dalle, Béatrice, 91, *97*, 98, *101*, 110
Darke, Chris, 115, 119, 121
Darrieux, Danielle, 60
databases, 142, 146, 149
Dauman, Anatole, 36, 115
The Days, 199
Dead Sea, 114
Deamer, David, 123
Delâtre, Auguste, 24
Deleuze, Gilles, 14, 74, 83, 90–94,
98, 168, 182, 191
Delon, Alain, 62
Democratic Socialist Party, 44
Deneuve, Catherine, 47
Denis, Claire, 47, 93
Le dépays, (1982), 38
Derrida, Jacques, 6
Deschamps, Jacques, 48
*Description of a Struggle (Description
d'un combat)* (1960), 114
Desoye, Madame, 207n12
Desser, David, 37
Deswarte, Bénie, 118
Diacritics, 6
digital age, 94; collaboration in, 17;
decay in, 150, 165; endurance in,
18; filmmaking in, 140, 142–44,
146–50, 159, 162, 165; space
and time in, 159, 161; visions of
Japan in, 148, 159, 165
digital media, 15, 142, 149, 164,
165
dissolves, 61, 70, 90, 120, 171

mise en abyme, 93–95, 103
Mishima, Michael, 168, *172*
mission civilisatrice, 35, 80
Mission pacifique (1989), 117, 205n39
Mitterand, François, 42, 137
mixed oxide fuel (MOX), 186
Miyako, 139, 226n1
Miyao, Daisuke, 28, 30, 63
Mizoguchi, Kenji, 34, 37, 85
Mizubayashi, Akira, 46
modernity, 37, 53, 80, 90
Le Monde, 43
Monet, Claude, 25, 27
mono no aware, 45, 63
monsters, 2, 11, 40
montage, 92, 116, 122, 161, 163, 181–83
Montaigne, Michel de, 30
Montero, David, 126
Montesquieu, 23
Monument in Memory of the Korean Victims of the A-bomb, 107–8
mortality, 156, 179, 190–91
Morton, Timothy, 13, 159, 161
motherhood, 187–91, 198
"Mount Fuji in Red," 10
mu, 38, 68
multisensory perception, 14, 17, 114, 116–17, 121, 123, 127–32, 136–37, 157, 177, 200
Muraoka, Koumiko, 49, *123*
Musée de l'homme, 69
Musée Guimet, 25
mushroom clouds: alternatives to, avoidance of, 67, 72–73, 86, 143; Hollywood and, 2; as iconic, overused image, 31, 56, 143, 170; reproduction of, 10, 114; root system and 6; shadow of, 132–36; as sign of terror, 71–73

Nagasaki, 23, 25–26, 60, 63, 67. *See also* atomic bombings; *Typhoon over Nagasaki*
Nagata, Masaichi, 34, 36–37
Nakagawa, Ayumi, 198
Nakasone, Yasuhiro, 39
Nancy, Jean-Luc, 4, 167–68, 228n4
Napier, Susan, J., 206n2
nappes de passé (layers of past), 74. See also *points de présent*
narrative: breakdown, destruction of, 69, 161; instability of, 93; linear, 83, 86, 93, 149; refusal of conclusion, 16, 66, 86, 91, 94, 107
national cinemas, 3, 30, 31
National Diet Library (Japan), 62
national identity, 27, 37, 50, 174
nationalism, 30, 38–41, 44
NATO, 221n20
New START Treaty, 8
The New Yorker, 32
Nichols, Bill, 70
Night and Fog (*Nuit et brouillard*) (1955), 56, 69, 85, 164
Night and Fog in Japan (*Nihon no yoru to kiri*) (1960), 85, 221n17
Nijūyo jikan no jōji. See *Hiroshima mon amour*: title of
Nishimura, Yuichiro, 194
Nixon, Rob, 7, 15
"No Apocalypse, Not Now" (Derrida), 6
Nogent-sur-Seine Nuclear Power Plant, 198
North Korea, 8
Nos Voisins Lointains 3.11, 50, 165
Nothomb, Amélie, 1, 45
nouveau roman, 62
nouvelle vague, 16, 35, 37, 62, 93. *See also* French New Wave

Milton Keynes UK
Ingram Content Group UK Ltd.
UKHW030135021124
450599UK00002B/8